JUNIOR
LISTENING EXPERT

A Theme-Based Lis... ...ung EFL Learners

Level **2**

JUNIOR
LISTENING EXPERT

Level 2

Series Editor	Dong-sook Kim
Project Editors	Yu-jin Lee, Hyun-joo Lee, Ji-hee Lee
Contributing Writers	Patrick Ferraro, Rebecca Cant, Susan Kim
Illustrators	Kyung-ho Jung, Eun-jung Shin
Design	Hoon-jung Ahn, Ji-young Ki, Hye-jung Yoon, Min-shin Ju
Editorial Designer	Jong-hee Kim
Sale	Ki-young Han, Kyung-koo Lee, In-gyu Park, Cheol-gyo Jeong, Nam-jun Kim, Woo-hyun Lee
Marketers	Hye-sun Park, Kyung-jin Nam, Ji-won Lee, Yeo-jin Kim
ISBN	979-11-253-4045-4
Photo Credits	www.fotolia.com
	www.dreamstime.com
	www.istockphoto.com

INTRODUCTION

Junior Listening Expert is a four-level listening series for EFL learners, particularly older elementary school students and junior high school students. Systematically designed to improve listening skills, its audio material is offered in a variety of formats, covering a wide-range of topics.

Features

Theme-Based Units

Every level contains twelve units, each covering a lively topic such as food, lifestyle, sports, IT, or social issues. A variety of listening formats expose students not only to everyday dialogues, but also to more advanced informative material.

Systematic Design

Each unit is composed of five closely related sections that allow students to develop their listening skills step-by-step. As students pass through each of the five sections, they have the opportunity to evaluate their progress and build confidence in their listening abilities.

A Variety of Question Types

A variety of question types are provided, including identifying the main idea, finding specific details, and making inferences. These serve to familiarize students with the standard types of listening test formats.

A Focus on Critical Thinking

Students are not only exposed to social issues through the listening material, but are also encouraged to think about these issues and form their own opinions.

Format

Getting Ready

This section utilizes a quiz to introduce the key vocabulary words and expressions that will appear in the unit. It is designed to facilitate easier understanding for students preparing to tackle challenging topics in English.

Listening Start

In this section, students have the chance to check their listening comprehension and master key expressions by answering questions and taking dictation. This prepares them for the Listening Practice and Listening Challenge sections.

Listening Practice

Students are given the opportunity to practice a variety of listening question types in this section. It enables them to develop the different listening skills required for each question type.

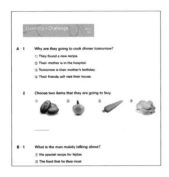

Listening Challenge

This section presents students with two long listening passages and a pair of checkup questions for each passage. This section challenges students to understand a higher level of English and upgrade their listening skills.

Critical Thinking

This section encourages students to think about a social issue related to the unit's topic. After listening to different opinions about an issue, students develop their own opinion, which they then express in a speaking activity.

Vocabulary List

This section provides easy access to key vocabulary. It contains the new vocabulary words from each unit.

Dictation

This section focuses on helping students improve the accuracy of their listening skills by requiring them to take dictation.

Table of **Contents**

01
Food

Getting ★ Ready

A

Choose the odd one out in each group.

1
ⓐ oily
ⓑ order
ⓒ spicy
ⓓ sour

2
ⓐ fried
ⓑ boiled
ⓒ grilled
ⓓ crowded

3
ⓐ nut
ⓑ onion
ⓒ allergic
ⓓ tuna

B

Match each word with the correct definition.

1 any food item on top of another food   •   • ⓐ recipe
2 something that tells you how to prepare a meal   •   • ⓑ wrap
3 to cover something with paper, cloth, or other material •   • ⓒ topping

C

Choose the best sentence for each blank.

ⓐ What would you like to have?   ⓑ Have you ever tried "fajitas" before?   ⓒ It looks delicious.   ⓓ Let's find a recipe on the Internet.   ⓔ The taste of the soup is different from region to region.   ⓕ I haven't decided yet.

---

1 W: Here's your dinner. What do you think?
   M: _____
2 W: _____
   M: I'd like a ham sandwich.
3 W: _____
   M: No, it is my first time to have them.

1 What will they have for dinner?

 ①  ②  ③  ④

+ Listen again and fill in the blanks.

M: Mom, I'm hungry.

W: I'm sorry. I haven't started dinner yet. You'll have to _____ _____ _____.

M: Okay. What are you going to cook?

W: Hmm... _____ _____ _____ _____ and vegetable soup?

M: Again? We had fried rice yesterday.

W: Then, _____ _____ _____ _____ to have for dinner?

M: I'd like to have chicken and potatoes.

W: Okay. It will _____ _____ soon.

M: Thank you, Mom.

9

2 Which is the man's favorite dish at each restaurant?

(1) Real India: _____

(2) Hello China: _____

@ Tandoori chicken	ⓑ beef curry
ⓒ fried pork	ⓓ fried noodles

+ Listen again and fill in the blanks.

M: In my town, there are two _____ _____, Real India and Hello China. Real India has many kinds of curry on the menu, _____ _____ _____ Tandoori chicken. I like beef curry the most. It is very spicy and a little bit sweet. Hello China _____ _____ _____ its fried pork. It is quite oily, but the sweet and sour sauce on it is really delicious. _____ _____ _____ there is fried noodles.

1   Why did the man NOT eat a chocolate?

      ① He is on a diet.

      ② He shouldn't eat nuts.

      ③ He doesn't like chocolate.

      ④ He ate too much chocolate earlier.

2   Choose the wrong information.

> **MEMO**
> ① What to buy: mangoes
> ② How many: five
> ③ Color: yellow or orange
> ④ How they should feel: soft

3   What will they probably do next?

      ① Buy a birthday gift

      ② Buy a cooking book

      ③ Go shopping at the supermarket

      ④ Find information on the Internet

4   Choose the food that the woman is talking about.

①  ②  ③  ④

5 Choose the correct reason why each person dislikes a certain food.

(1) Janice dislikes fish because _____.

(2) Alex dislikes fried chicken because _____.

ⓐ it smells bad	ⓑ it tastes too salty
ⓒ it is raw, not cooked	ⓓ it makes him/her feel sick

6 Why was the woman angry about the restaurant?

① It was too crowded.

② The service was poor.

③ The food was terrible.

④ It was too expensive.

7 Check [✓] the menu items that the man will order.

Sandwich & Burger		Side Menu		Drinks	
Ham sandwich	☐	Potato chips	☐	Orange juice	☐
Tuna sandwich	☐	Corn salad	☐	Coke	☐
Cheeseburger	☐	Chicken salad	☐	Iced tea	☐

8 Number the pictures in the correct order.

_____ → _____ → _____ → _____

A - 1   Why are they going to cook dinner tomorrow?

① They found a new recipe.

② Their mother is in the hospital.

③ Tomorrow is their mother's birthday.

④ Their friends will visit their house.

2   Choose two items that they are going to buy.

①    ②   ③    ④

B - 1   What is the man mainly talking about?

① His special recipe for fajitas

② The food that he likes most

③ Various kinds of Mexican food

④ His favorite Mexican restaurant

2   Where did the man first try fajitas?

① at a school party

② in a cooking class

③ at his friend's house

④ at a Mexican restaurant

Junk Food

1 What are they mainly talking about?

① Banning junk food in schools

② Making students' diets healthier

③ Banning junk food advertisements on TV

④ Teaching students about the dangers of junk food

2 Write T for true or F for false.

(1) The girl thinks students should know how harmful junk food is. _____

(2) The boy thinks students can buy junk food easily outside school. _____

(3) The boy thinks eating some junk food is not too bad for our health. _____

13

What do you think?

1

Check [✓] if you have the same opinion. You can add your own opinion in the blank.

☐ Schools need to control the food that students eat.

☐ Schools should teach students that junk food is unhealthy.

☐ Students are not stupid. They can decide what to eat.

_____

2

Talk about the following questions with your partner.

· What kinds of junk food can you buy at your school?

· How often do you eat junk food?

Getting ★ Ready

A

Choose the correct word for each definition.

ⓐ facility 　ⓑ fine 　ⓒ provide 　ⓓ necessary

ⓔ graduate 　ⓕ income 　ⓖ include 　ⓗ presentation

1 to have as a part: _____

2 to give something to somebody: _____

3 the money that is earned from work: _____

4 a talk given to a group of people on a certain subject: _____

5 an amount of money that must be paid for breaking a rule: _____

B

Choose the best sentence for each blank.

ⓐ Can I check out this book? 　ⓑ I did a little bit better than on the midterm exam.

ⓒ Can I see your student ID? 　ⓓ When are we going on the field trip? 　ⓔ I was

saving the seat for my friend. 　ⓕ This presentation is worth 25 points.

1 W: _____

　M: No. You haven't returned one book.

2 W: _____

　M: It's on the 4th of June.

3 W: How did you do on the math test?

　M: _____

1 Choose the thing that the boy does NOT like about each teacher.

(1) Ms. Simpson: _____

(2) Ms. Fox: _____

ⓐ personality	ⓑ appearance
ⓒ fashion style	ⓓ teaching style

+ Listen again and fill in the blanks.

M: _____ _____ _____ _____, I like Ms. Simpson and Ms. Fox the most. Ms. Simpson is very kind to us. She helps us when _____ _____ _____. But her classes are very boring and make me sleepy. _____ _____ _____ _____, Ms. Fox teaches us in a very interesting way. She often tells us funny stories about the subject. But her clothes and hairstyle are _____ _____ _____ _____.

2 Which is NOT true about the boy's exam schedule?

	Monday	Tuesday	Wednesday
1 p.m.		Music	
2 p.m.	① Japanese		English
3 p.m.	② History	③ Math	
4 p.m.			④ Science

+ Listen again and fill in the blanks.

M: I lost my _____ _____. Is the Japanese test at 1 p.m. on Monday?

W: No, it isn't. It's at 2 p.m.

M: Really? I have a history exam _____ _____ _____.

W: Right after the Japanese exam? That's too bad!

M: Also, do you know _____ _____ _____ _____ _____? Isn't it at 4 p.m. on Tuesday?

W: No, it's on Wednesday at 4 p.m. _____ _____ at 4 p.m., we have a math exam.

15

1   Match each person with the library manners they're talking about.

(1) Alex   •   • ⓐ Don't eat anything.

(2) Megan •   • ⓑ Don't make phone calls.

(3) Colin   •   • ⓒ Don't keep seats for your friends.

2   What will the girl probably do next?

① Pay the fine

② Do her homework

③ Borrow *The Little Prince*

④ Go home to get *The Little Prince*

3   What is the relationship between the speakers?

① son – mother

② parent – teacher

③ student – teacher

④ boyfriend – girlfriend

4   Choose the wrong information.

<Today's homework – Group presentation>

* By next Thursday

① Five members in a group

② About any festival in the world

③ For 20 minutes

④ Worth 20 points

5 What will be the boy's report title?

① The Life of Mark Twain

② My Favorite Author — Hemingway

③ After Reading *The Old Man and the Sea*

④ Who is Emily Brontë?

6 Choose the wrong information.

> **Notice**
>
> ① Gym: Not available from July 6th to July 19th
>
> ② Language lab: Not available during the whole vacation
>
> ③ Computer lab: Available from July 20th
>
> ④ Library: Available during the whole vacation

7 Which is the girl's picture?

①  ②  ③  ④

8 What is the boy's advice about?

① How to get good grades

② How to make a study plan

③ How to decide on your major

④ How to enter a good university

A - 1 Where are they going for their field trip?

①  ②  ③  ④

2 Which will the boy NOT bring on his field trip?

① a lunch box

② a cap

③ a drink

④ a pen and paper

B - 1 Why did the girl get a bad grade in math?

① She slept during the exam.

② She didn't study one chapter.

③ She forgot to answer some questions.

④ She didn't read the questions carefully.

2 What grade did the boy get this time?

① A

② B⁺

③ C⁺

④ C

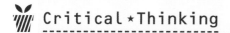

University

1 What are they mainly talking about?

① How people get good jobs

② What people learn at university

③ Why people need to go to university

④ Why people need to enter a good university

2 Choose the woman's two opinions about university life.

① It helps people prepare for a future job.

② It gives people the chance to earn more money.

③ It is a waste of money and time.

④ It is more important than experience in the real world.

What do you think?

1

Check [✓] if you have the same opinion. You can add your own opinion in the blank.

☐ Studying at university is not useful in the real world.

☐ While studying at university, I can prepare for my future job.

☐ I think I can get a good job just after graduating from high school.

_____

2

Talk about the following questions with your partner.

• Do you want to enter university? Why or why not?

• If you don't go to university, how can you prepare for your future job?

03

Hobbies

A

Match each word with the correct definition.

1	a written text of a movie or play	•		• ⓐ	save
2	a person in a book or a movie	•		• ⓑ	thrill
3	a feeling of great excitement	•		• ⓒ	script
4	to keep away from something	•		• ⓓ	avoid
5	to keep information on a computer	•		• ⓔ	character

B

Choose the best sentence for each blank.

ⓐ I'm so excited about seeing you act.   ⓑ Why don't you learn to play the trumpet?
ⓒ Do you want to join our dance club?   ⓓ I cheer for our soccer team.   ⓔ What do
you do in your free time?   ⓕ How often do the club members get together?

---

1 M: _____
   W: I like to go mountain biking.

2 M: _____
   W: Once a week.

3 M: What do you do in your club?
   W: _____

1   What are they going to do this weekend?

①   Take some pictures   ②   Drink coffee and read books

③   Go shopping for a camera   ④   Buy some new accessories

+ Listen again
and fill
in the blanks.

M: Catherine, what are you doing this weekend?

W: I don't _____ _____ _____ yet.

M: Then, could you be my model?

W: Model? What are you talking about?

M: Well, you know I like taking pictures. I want to _____
_____ _____ you this time.

W: I see. So where do you want to take my picture?

M: _____ _____ shopping malls, bookstores and coffee
shops downtown.

W: _____ _____ _____. Should I bring anything?

M: Just bring some accessories, like hats or sunglasses.

21

2   Which character will the girl be tomorrow?

①      ②      ③      ④

+ Listen again
and fill
in the blanks.

W: Our costume play club _____ _____ _____ meet
tomorrow. At every meeting, our club members dress up like
characters from movies. Last month, I was Princess Fiona. I
_____ _____ _____ _____ and wore a long
dress. Tomorrow, I'll be Pippi Longstocking. I'll wear a _____
_____ and long socks. Also, my hair will be red. My friend
Sarah will be Hermione. She'll be wearing a coat and a white shirt
_____ _____ _____.

1 Choose the wrong information.

> Dance Club Weekly Practice
>
> • When?   ① Wednesdays at 7 p.m.
> • Where?   ② the school gym
> • What to wear? ③ casual sports clothes and ④ running shoes

2 What is the woman's hobby?

① Playing computer games

② Travelling around the world

③ Reading books about Cambodia

④ Searching for travel information

3 Why is the woman against the man buying a trumpet?

① The price of the trumpet is too high.

② It is hard to learn to play the trumpet.

③ The trumpet will be too loud.

④ The man will lose interest in playing the trumpet soon.

4 Choose the teddy bear the man will make.

①    ②    ③    ④

5   Write T for true or F for false.

(1) He has sunburn on his arms.   _____

(2) He didn't wear sunblock when he played tennis.   _____

(3) He won't play tennis around midday.   _____

6   Choose the person who can NOT join the club.

① I'm free every Thursday evening.

Steve

② I love soccer, but I can't dance well.

Mary

③ I'm in the 9th grade.

Ryan

7   Choose the correct club for each person.

(1) Kevin: _____   (2) Michele: _____   (3) Laura: _____

ⓐ school orchestra	ⓑ cycling club	ⓒ baseball club
ⓓ play club	ⓔ pop music club	ⓕ travel club

8   Which is NOT mentioned about a lithops plant?

① Where it comes from

② What it looks like

③ How to grow it

④ How long it lives

A - 1   How does the woman feel now?

① happy

② angry

③ nervous

④ disappointed

2   What will the woman probably do next?

① Take a seat

② Put on makeup

③ Study her script

④ Change her clothes

B - 1   What are they doing?

① Climbing a mountain

② Watching sports on TV

③ Studying English words

④ Solving a crossword puzzle

2   Which picture shows Yamakasi?

①

②

③

④

 Critical ★ Thinking

Extreme Sports

1   According to the man, what are two good points of extreme sports?

   ① They are thrilling.

   ② They are easy to learn.

   ③ They make your body stronger.

   ④ They offer a feeling of success.

2   Why is the woman against extreme sports?

   ① They are too dangerous.

   ② It takes a long time to learn them.

   ③ They require expensive clothing.

   ④ It's difficult to find a place to do them.

What do you think?

1

Check [✓] if you have the same opinion. You can add your own opinion in the blank.

   ☐   It's thrilling to try something dangerous.

   ☐   I don't want to get hurt by trying extreme sports.

   ☐   I want to try sports that people don't usually do.

   _____

2

Talk about the following questions with your partner.

   • Have you seen anyone doing extreme sports?

   • Are there any extreme sports that you want to try?

04 Animals

Getting ★ Ready

A

Match each word with the correct definition.

1 to give food to an animal • • ⓐ wild
2 a type of small animal with six legs • • ⓑ insect
3 an item that helps you to do something • • ⓒ raise
4 living in nature • • ⓓ feed
5 to take care of an animal while it grows • • ⓔ tool

B

Choose the best sentence for each blank.

ⓐ Have you had a pet before?　ⓑ You should take care of dogs and feed them.
ⓒ Do animals catch colds?　ⓓ I have a cat named Happy.　ⓔ I lost my dog while
walking him.　ⓕ She barks loudly when people visit.

1 M: Do you have a pet?
　 W: Yes. _____
2 M: _____
　 W: Yes, I had a rabbit for two years.
3 M: What is your dog's problem?
　 W: _____

1   Which animal is the man's pet?

①   ②    ③   ④

+ Listen again
and fill
in the blanks.

W: _____ _____ this picture. Isn't my cat cute?

M: Yes, she is. She's a nice _____ _____ _____.

W: Do you have a pet, too?

M: I have a pet named Piggy.

W: Are you _____ _____ _____?

M: No. Piggy is a giant spider.

W: Then why do you _____ _____ _____? That's strange.

M: I call it that because he eats too much.

W: Wow. How can you raise a spider?

M: You don't know _____ _____ _____ _____.

2   Where is this conversation taking place?

① in a drugstore   ② in a pet shop

③ in a pet clinic   ④ in an animal café

+ Listen again
and fill
in the blanks.

W: My pet seems sick.

M: What's wrong with her?

W: She _____ _____ _____ _____ and she doesn't eat anything.

M: Let me see. It looks like she caught a cold.

W: Do puppies catch colds?

M: Yes, they do. Did you _____ _____ _____ after washing her?

W: Maybe I didn't dry her enough last Tuesday.

M: That could be the reason. I'll give you _____ _____ for her.

W: Okay. Thank you.

1 Which animal is the man talking about?

①    ②    ③    ④

2 What are they talking about?

① a zoo

② a magazine

③ a newspaper

④ a TV documentary

3 Write the day that each person will visit the zoo.

(1) I'll see pink dolphins dance!

Katie _____

(2) I'd like to see a snake!

Jessica _____

(3) I can't wait to watch the magic show!

Ian _____

4 Why does the woman's mom NOT want to have a cat?

① She hates cats.

② She prefers dogs.

③ She is tired of raising cats.

④ She doesn't want to see the cat die.

5   What is the man's job?

 ① a zookeeper

 ② a dog trainer

 ③ an animal doctor

 ④ a pet shop owner

6   Choose the wrong information.

> **Are you looking for a fun part-time job?**
>
> • What you'll do: ① Walk and feed pets
>
> • You must: ② Be over 18 years old
>
>   ③ Have a cellphone
>
> • How to apply: ④ By phone

7   Choose the picture of Bo.

 ①  ②  ③  ④

8   Write T for true or F for false about crows.

 (1) They are the smartest birds. _____

 (2) They can use tools when they hunt. _____

 (3) They take care of their babies for life. _____

A - 1   What is the relationship between the speakers?

① teacher – student

② zookeeper – visitor

③ animal doctor – customer

④ pet shop owner – customer

2   Who is treating the rabbit well?

①    ②    ③    ④

B - 1   What are they talking about?

① How to keep a pet healthy

② How to take a pet on an airplane

③ What kind of cage is good for a pet

④ Why a sick pet can't get on an airplane

2   What will the man probably do next?

① Get on a plane

② Call the airline

③ Visit a pet clinic

④ Pay for plane tickets

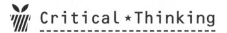 Critical ★ Thinking

Pets

1 Which is NOT true?

① Joe has owned Rex for three years.

② Rex wears clothes and accessories.

③ Joe and Rex often go to dog cafés.

④ Joe is planning to give Rex a present.

2 Choose each person's opinion.

(1) Joe: _____   (2) Sally: _____

ⓐ Pets don't need any clothes or accessories.

ⓑ People shouldn't spend a lot of money on their pets.

ⓒ Buying things for pets is just like spending money on family members.

What do you think?

1

Check [✓] if you have the same opinion. You can add your own opinion in the blank.

☐ I don't understand why some people buy clothes and accessories for their pets.

☐ I would rather spend money on poor people instead of pets.

☐ Pets are more than just animals. They are like our friends or family members.

_____

2

Talk about the following questions with your partner.

• Have you ever raised a pet?

• How much care do you think is enough for a pet?

Daily Life

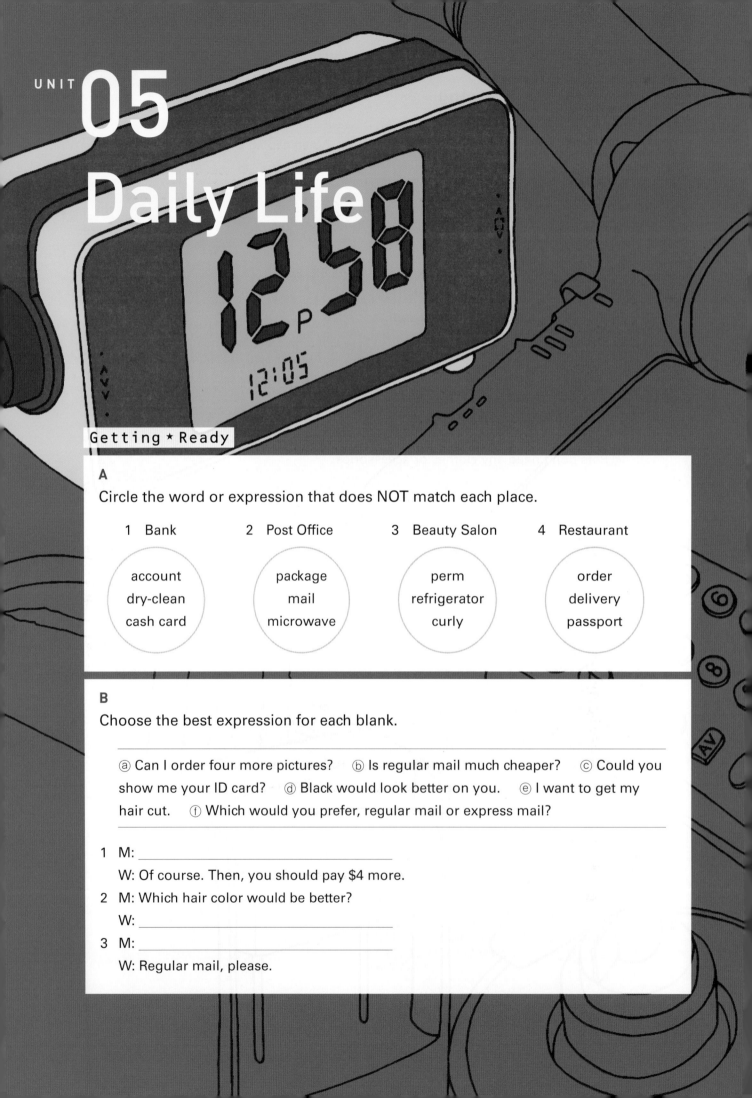

Getting ★ Ready

A

Circle the word or expression that does NOT match each place.

1 Bank

- account
- dry-clean
- cash card

2 Post Office

- package
- mail
- microwave

3 Beauty Salon

- perm
- refrigerator
- curly

4 Restaurant

- order
- delivery
- passport

B

Choose the best expression for each blank.

ⓐ Can I order four more pictures?   ⓑ Is regular mail much cheaper?   ⓒ Could you show me your ID card?   ⓓ Black would look better on you.   ⓔ I want to get my hair cut.   ⓕ Which would you prefer, regular mail or express mail?

1 M: _____
   W: Of course. Then, you should pay $4 more.

2 M: Which hair color would be better?
   W: _____

3 M: _____
   W: Regular mail, please.

1　Why did the man feel sorry?

① He came too late.　　　② The pizza was cold.

③ He forgot one cola.　　④ He brought the wrong pizza.

+ Listen again
and fill
in the blanks.

(*Doorbell rings.*)

W: _____ _____ _____ ?

M: Pizza Hot delivery.

W: Wow. That was quick. _____ _____ _____ _____ ?

M: It's $20.

W: Okay, but did you only bring one cola?

M: _____ _____ _____ a large pizza and a cola?

W: Actually, I ordered two colas.

M: Oh, I'm terribly sorry. I'll come back with it soon.

W: No, _____ _____ about it. I'll just take the one cola.

M: Then the price is just $17. Again, I'm sorry about that.

2　Choose the two kinds of flowers they are going to plant.

① 　② 　③ 　④

+ Listen again
and fill
in the blanks.

W: Honey, we should _____ _____ _____ in the garden.

M: Flowers?

W: It's going to be spring soon. _____ _____ the white
    tulips, all the flowers in the garden are dead.

M: _____ _____ _____ flowers do you want?

W: I was thinking of pink daisies.

M: Wouldn't red ones be better?

W: Oh, _____ _____. They'd be more colorful.

M: And how about some yellow roses? You know I love yellow flowers.

W: Good idea. Our garden will _____ _____ with those flowers.

1 How much money is the man going to pay?

① $8

② $10

③ $12

④ $14

2 What is the man talking about?

① Ways to clean your kitchen

② Tips for washing dishes well

③ The difficulties of washing oily dishes

④ Ways to save water while washing dishes

3 What is the problem with the woman's shirt?

① It is still dirty.

② It became smaller.

③ It changed color.

④ It changed shape.

4 Choose the cake that the woman ordered.

①  ②   ③   ④

5   Why did the man go to the bank?

    ① To open an account

    ② To get a cash card

    ③ To get a credit card

    ④ To put money in his account

6   Choose the hairstyle that the woman wants.

    ①  ②  ③   ④

7   Choose what the girl does NOT do after school.

    ① Doing homework

    ② Setting the table

    ③ Playing badminton

    ④ Watching television

8   Choose the wrong information.

> **Post Office Receipt**
>
> • **To where:** U.S.
> • **Contents:** ① books and clothes
> • **Weight:** ② 850 g
> • **Type of service:** ③ regular mail
> • **Price:** ④ $100

A - 1 Why did the boy decide to go to the market?

① He wanted to eat some fruit.

② He wanted to help his mother.

③ His mom offered to make spaghetti for him.

④ His mom offered to buy him a comic book.

2 Choose the two kinds of fruit that the boy will buy.

① ② ③ ④

B - 1 What is the woman doing?

① She's ordering more food.

② She's asking for the menu.

③ She's canceling her order.

④ She's making a reservation.

2 Choose the wrong information.

Delivery Order # 48

• **Address:** ① 135 New York Street

• **Phone number:** ② 3142-0357

• **Order:** ③ 1 fried rice, 1 seafood noodle, 2 egg rolls

④ Don't forget chopsticks!

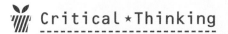 Critical ★ Thinking

Housework

1 What are they mainly talking about?

① Sharing housework

② Various kinds of housework

③ The difficulties of doing housework

④ A mother's role in a family

2 Choose the two kinds of housework that the girl does.

① Cooking

② Setting the table

③ Washing dishes

④ Cleaning the bathroom

What do you think?

1

Check [✓] if you have the same opinion. You can add your own opinion in the blank.

☐ I don't think all the housework is a mother's job.

☐ Students don't need to help do the housework. They should focus on studying.

☐ Everyone in the family should help with the housework.

_____

2

Talk about the following questions with your partner.

• How often do you help with the housework?

• What would be the best way to share the housework?

06 Entertainment

A

Choose the correct word for each definition.

ⓐ select	ⓑ satisfied	ⓒ audition	ⓓ available
ⓔ showmanship	ⓕ audience	ⓖ performance	ⓗ cancel

1 happy because you have achieved what you wanted: _____

2 able to be gotten or used: _____

3 the act of being in a play or a musical: _____

4 to choose someone or something carefully: _____

5 the group of people who are watching a show: _____

B

Choose the best sentence for each blank.

ⓐ It looked like a real classroom.   ⓑ Do you want to cancel the reservation?
ⓒ The tickets are sold out.   ⓓ I played the part of Juliet.   ⓔ Only C section seats
are available.   ⓕ At which theater is the play showing?

1 W: _____

M: The Gallery Theater.

2 W: I want to make a reservation for *Hamlet*.

M: I'm sorry. _____

3 W: Can I get a seat in section A?

M: I'm sorry. _____

1   What musical are they going to see?

①　*Mamma Mia!*   ②　*The Lion King*

③　*Cats*   ④　*Notre Dame de Paris*

+ Listen again
and fill
in the blanks.

M: Laura, how about _____ _____ _____ _____ this weekend?

W: That's a wonderful idea. I still _____ _____ *The Lion King* at Eastside Theater.

M: Yes, it was great. Now that theater is showing *Cats*.

W: Right. I _____ _____ _____ about it.

M: Also, *Notre Dame de Paris* is playing at Gallery Theater. Which one do you want to see?

W: Well, *Cats* _____ _____ _____ than *Notre Dame de Paris*.

M: Good. Let's see that, then.

2   How does the man feel now?

①　relieved   ②　excited

③　satisfied   ④　disappointed

+ Listen again
and fill
in the blanks.

W: Michael, how was the ice ballet? You were _____ _____ about it.

M: Well, the show was beautiful.

W: But you don't _____ _____.

M: I went there to see my favorite skater, Rachel Wake.

W: Yes, you're a big fan of hers.

M: But she didn't skate in the show yesterday. Helen Bloom _____ _____ _____ instead.

W: Helen Bloom is also famous.

M: Yes, but Rachel is _____ _____. I really wanted to see her.

W: I'm sorry to hear that.

1 Why did the woman call Eden Theater?

① To make a reservation

② To cancel her reservation

③ To change her reservation

④ To get a seat in another section

2 Which best describes the situation?

3 Which is true about drawing shows?

① They are held in an art gallery.

② They show how a picture is drawn.

③ They show paintings by famous artists.

④ The audience can draw a picture together.

4 Check [✓] how the man felt about the play.

	Good	Bad
(1) Story	☐	☐
(2) Stage sets	☐	☐
(3) Acting	☐	☐
(4) Audience's manners	☐	☐

5 When will they watch the play?

① May 14th at 4 p.m.

② May 14th at 8 p.m.

③ May 15th at 4 p.m.

④ May 15th at 7 p.m.

6 Choose the wrong information.

Toronto Grand Theater

① Hamlet

* Saturday ② May 5th

* ③ 7 p.m. show

* ④ 2 adults

7 What is the woman mainly talking about?

① How a musical is made

② How to become a musical actor

③ The qualities that musical actors need

④ The difficulties that musical actors have

8 What did the man like most about the dance performance?

① the male dancers

② the stage sets

③ the ballerina

④ the music

A - 1   What day will they see the musical *Rent*?

     ① Thursday

     ② Friday

     ③ Saturday

     ④ Sunday

2   What will they probably do next?

     ① Go to rent a DVD

     ② Go to the woman's house

     ③ Meet Daniel Parker at the theater

     ④ Buy musical tickets on the Internet

B - 1   What is the title of the news?

     ① The First Ever Online Orchestra

     ② The First Ever International Orchestra

     ③ The History of the New York Orchestra

     ④ The Biggest Ever Audition for an Orchestra

2   Check [✓] T for true or F for false about the orchestra.

	T	F
(1) About 4,000 people took part in the video audition.	☐	☐
(2) Its members practiced together in New York for months.	☐	☐
(3) Its performance was a great success.	☐	☐

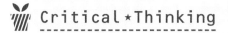

Critical ★ Thinking

TV Stars in a Musical

1 Which is NOT true about Ricky Smith?

   ① He played the main role in the musical.

   ② He was in a TV series.

   ③ He has appeared in musicals before.

   ④ He is popular with teenagers.

2 Choose two reasons why Jeremy was NOT satisfied with the musical.

   ① The main actor didn't sing well.

   ② He couldn't see the actors close up.

   ③ It was too noisy during the performance.

   ④ The tickets were very expensive.

What do you think?

1

Check [✓] if you have the same opinion about TV stars being in musicals. You can add your own opinion in the blank.

   ☐ If a TV star appears in a musical, the ticket prices will go up. That's not good.

   ☐ More people will want to see a musical if a TV star appears in it.

   ☐ Some TV stars don't sing or dance well enough to be in a musical.

_____

2

Talk about the following questions with your partner.

   • Do you know of any TV stars who have appeared in a musical?

   • Have you ever seen a musical because your favorite star was in it?

Health

A

Choose the correct word or expression for each picture.

| ⓐ cough | ⓑ stomachache | ⓒ fever | ⓓ headache | ⓔ runny nose |

1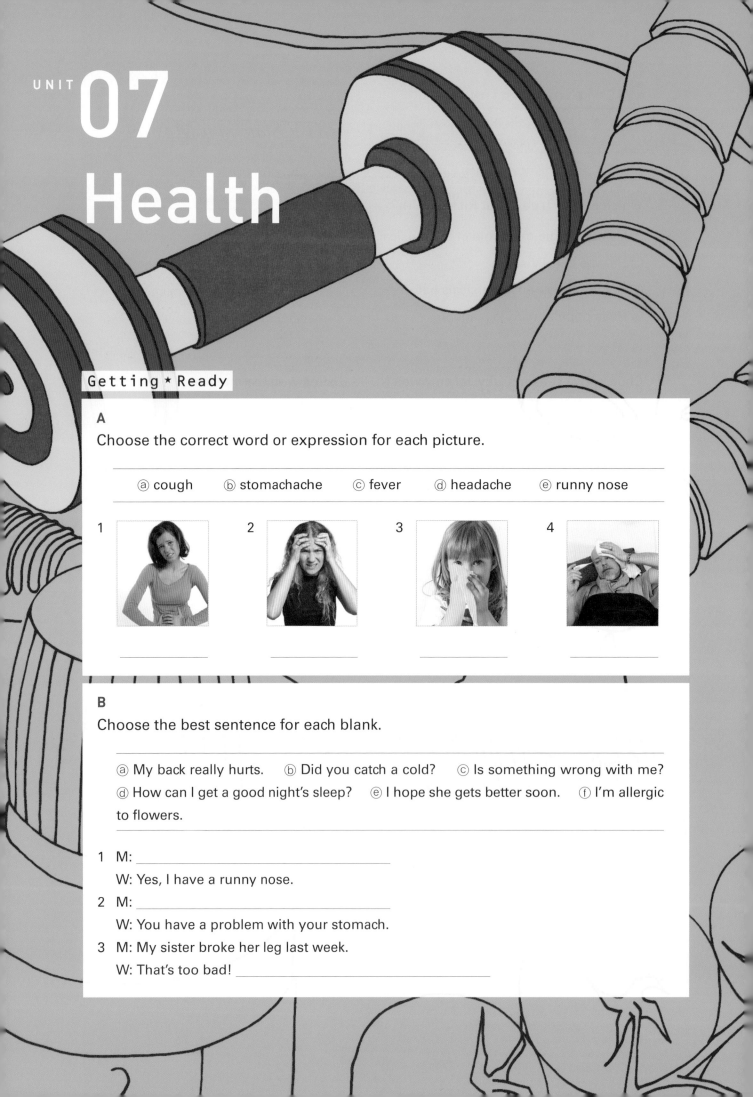

2

3

4

_____   _____   _____   _____

B

Choose the best sentence for each blank.

ⓐ My back really hurts.   ⓑ Did you catch a cold?   ⓒ Is something wrong with me?
ⓓ How can I get a good night's sleep?   ⓔ I hope she gets better soon.   ⓕ I'm allergic to flowers.

1 M: _____
  W: Yes, I have a runny nose.

2 M: _____
  W: You have a problem with your stomach.

3 M: My sister broke her leg last week.
  W: That's too bad! _____

1   When is the man going to visit the hospital?

① 3 p.m.   ② 4 p.m.   ③ 5 p.m.   ④ 6 p.m.

+ Listen again
and fill
in the blanks.

(*Telephone rings.*)

W: City Hospital. How may I help you?

M: My back really hurts. I want to _____ _____ _____ for today.

W: Okay. What time can you come in?

M: How about 4 p.m.?

W: Our 4 p.m. appointments are full. Could you _____ _____ at 5 p.m. instead?

M: Well, I guess I can _____ _____.

W: Great. Could you tell me your name?

M: My name is Jake Brown.

W: Okay. We'll _____ _____ _____.

2   Choose the son's two problems.

①    ②    ③   ④

+ Listen again
and fill
in the blanks.

M: _____ _____ _____?

W: Doctor, my son has a fever, and it won't go away.

M: Does he cough?

W: Yes, a lot. He _____ _____.

M: Let me look at him. Does he have a runny nose?

W: No. _____ _____ _____ _____?

M: Don't worry too much. He just has a cold.

W: What should I do?

M: I'll give you _____ _____ _____ for him. It should be taken twice a day.

W: Okay. Thanks.

1 Choose the wrong information on the chart.

Medical Information

Name: Ben Smith

Age: ① 27

Blood Type	② AB
Diseases	③ None
Allergies	④ Fish

2 What will the woman probably do next?

① Go home

② Have breakfast

③ Take the test again

④ Make an appointment

3 Where is this conversation taking place?

①  ②  ③  ④

4 How does the woman feel now?

① bored   ② worried   ③ angry   ④ happy

5   Choose two pieces of advice that the woman will follow.

      ① Drink warm milk.

      ② Exercise in the evening.

      ③ Try not to worry about things.

      ④ Don't eat too much before sleeping.

6   Choose the correct picture for each person.

      (1) Tom: _____   (2) Brad: _____   (3) Ron: _____

      ⓐ    ⓑ    ⓒ

7   What is the woman's problem?

      ① She caught a cold.

      ② She has an allergy.

      ③ She has an eye problem.

      ④ She has a sore throat.

8   What is the man mainly talking about?

      ① How to take pills correctly

      ② How pills work in our bodies

      ③ The dangers of taking a lot of pills

      ④ Why we should take pills after meals

A - 1   Which is NOT the man's problem?

① His stomach hurts.

② He has a fever.

③ He has a headache.

④ His hands and feet are cold.

2   According to the doctor, why does the man feel sick?

① He has a cold.

② He drank some old milk.

③ He has a lot of stress.

④ He ate breakfast too fast.

B - 1   What kind of talk is this?

① news story

② announcement

③ advertisement

④ documentary

2   Check [✓] T for true or F for false.

	T	F
(1) This clinic closes at 9:00 p.m. during the week.	☐	☐
(2) You can get free checkups after your first visit.	☐	☐
(3) The clinic is located in the W Department Store.	☐	☐

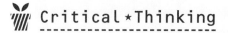

Critical ★ Thinking

Teen Smoking

1 What are they mainly talking about?

① Why smoking is wrong for students

② Why students start smoking in school

③ What schools should do to stop students from smoking

④ Whether schools should teach students about the dangers of smoking

2 Choose Mr. Robin and Ms. Claire's opinions.

(1) Mr. Robin: _____   (2) Ms. Claire: _____

ⓐ Students who smoke should be punished.

ⓑ It's too much to make students who smoke leave school.

ⓒ Schools should teach students about the dangers of smoking.

What do you think?

1

Check [✓] if you have the same opinion. You can add your own opinion in the blank.

☐ Strong punishment will cause students to stop smoking.

☐ Schools need to educate students about how bad smoking is.

☐ Parents should educate their children, not schools.

2

Talk about the following questions with your partner.

• What do you think of teenagers smoking?

• Do you have any ideas how to stop teenagers from smoking?

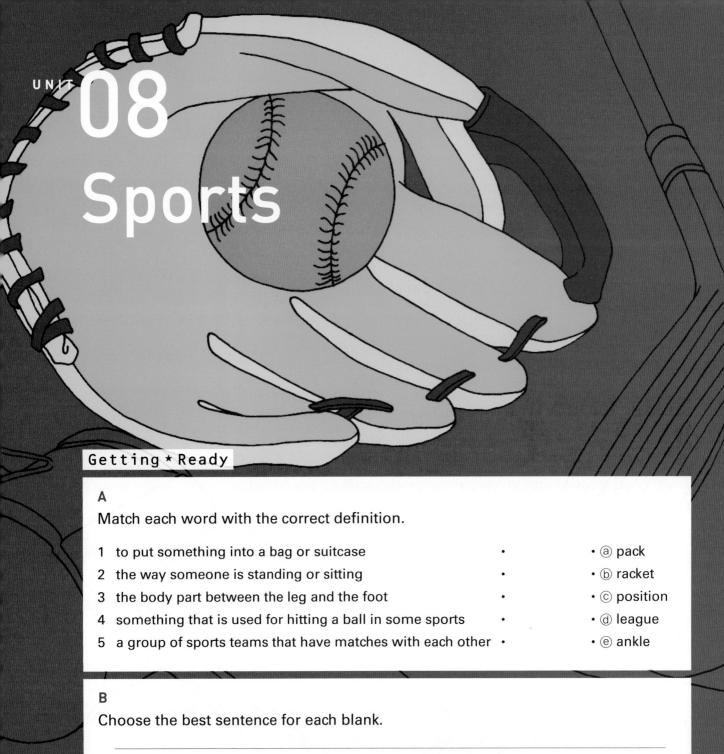

Sports

Getting ★ Ready

A

Match each word with the correct definition.

1 to put something into a bag or suitcase   •
2 the way someone is standing or sitting   •
3 the body part between the leg and the foot   •
4 something that is used for hitting a ball in some sports   •
5 a group of sports teams that have matches with each other   •

• ⓐ pack
• ⓑ racket
• ⓒ position
• ⓓ league
• ⓔ ankle

B

Choose the best sentence for each blank.

ⓐ The game lasted for an hour.   ⓑ Which sport are you going to play?   ⓒ My team lost by one point.   ⓓ How long should I stay like this?   ⓔ My scores have been getting worse.   ⓕ Do you know how to play tennis?

1 W: _____

   M: I'm going to run in a relay race.

2 W: How did the game end?

   M: _____

3 W: _____

   M: Yes. I'm taking lessons these days.

1 How does the woman feel now?

① bored

② excited

③ nervous

④ disappointed

+ Listen again
and fill
in the blanks.

W: Yesterday, I went to _____ _____ _____ _____ between the New York Yankees and the Boston Red Sox. It was my first time to go to a stadium. I couldn't believe that I could see the players _____ _____ _____! The game lasted for about four hours. It was quite long, but I _____ _____ for a minute. I will never forget that amazing game.

2 Which is NOT needed for the boy?

①  ②  ③   ④

+ Listen again
and fill
in the blanks.

M: Mom, did I tell you that tomorrow is _____ _____?

W: No, you didn't. Which sports are you going to play?

M: I'm going to run in a relay race and _____ _____.

W: Oh, you should take your running shoes, then.

M: Of course.

W: What about your uniform?

M: _____ _____ _____ already.

W: Good. And don't forget to wear sunblock on your face.

M: I don't need it. I'm going to _____ _____ _____.

1   What will the girl probably do next?

① Look for a tennis court

② Take a tennis lesson

③ Go to find her tennis racket

④ Make a reservation for a tennis court

2   What program are they going to watch?

①    ②    ③    ④

3   Which is NOT mentioned as a good point of in-line skating?

① It is an outdoor sport.

② People of all ages can enjoy it.

③ It is possible to practice in the neighborhood.

④ The number of people doesn't matter.

4   What is the relationship between the speakers?

① coach – player

② player – player

③ doctor – player

④ news reporter – player

5   What kind of sports event are they watching?

    ① a golf match

    ② a hockey game

    ③ a bowling tournament

    ④ a basketball game

6   What is the man mainly talking about?

    ① Tips for running a marathon

    ② The best exercise for teenagers

    ③ How to become a marathon runner

    ④ The importance of warm-up exercise

7   Choose the position that the woman is explaining.

    ①   ②   ③   ④

8   Why does the man feel bad?

    ① His team lost the game.

    ② He got hurt during the game.

    ③ He failed to become the MVP.

    ④ Few people came to watch the game.

A - 1   What is the advertisement for?

① A junior football camp

② Chelsea FC's fan club

③ A football club in school

④ A football league in England

2   Choose the wrong information.

> ### Don't Miss Your Chance!
>
> ① Where? In London
> ② When? February 13th to 30th
> ③ Who can join? 10 to 13 year-old children
>
> *④ Sign up for it before December 15th*

B - 1   What is the relationship between the speakers?

① fan – player

② coach – player

③ reporter – player

④ reporter – coach

2   Choose the result of the game.

① 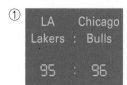   ② 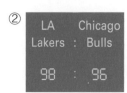   ③ 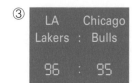   ④

LA Chicago
Lakers : Bulls

99 : 95

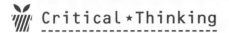 Critical ★ Thinking

Sports Stars on TV

1 Check [✓] if each person is for or against sports players being on TV shows.

	For	Against
(1) Jack	☐	☐
(2) Lisa	☐	☐
(3) Chad	☐	☐

2 Match each person with their opinion.

(1) Jack ・   ・ ⓐ Players appear on TV because of their popularity.

(2) Lisa ・   ・ ⓑ Players should focus on practicing only.

(3) Chad ・   ・ ⓒ Players can make money for training by appearing on TV.

What do you think?

1

Check [✓] if you have the same opinion. You can add your own opinion in the blank.

☐ It should be the players' decision whether they'll appear on TV or not.

☐ If players earn a lot of money, they can get better training and sportswear.

☐ When unpopular players see sports stars on TV shows, they probably feel upset.

_____

2

Talk about the following questions with your partner.

・ Are there any sports players who often appear on TV in your country?

・ How do you feel when you see sports players on TV shows?

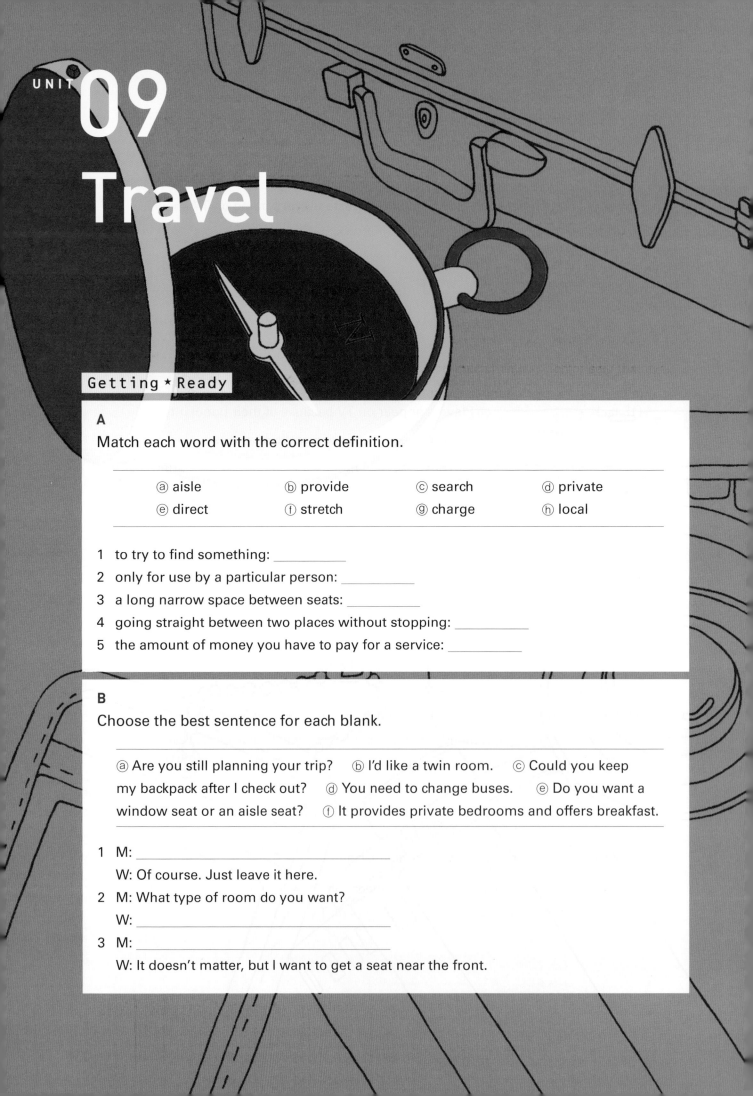

Travel

A

Match each word with the correct definition.

ⓐ aisle	ⓑ provide	ⓒ search	ⓓ private
ⓔ direct	ⓕ stretch	ⓖ charge	ⓗ local

1 to try to find something: _____
2 only for use by a particular person: _____
3 a long narrow space between seats: _____
4 going straight between two places without stopping: _____
5 the amount of money you have to pay for a service: _____

B

Choose the best sentence for each blank.

ⓐ Are you still planning your trip?　ⓑ I'd like a twin room.　ⓒ Could you keep my backpack after I check out?　ⓓ You need to change buses.　ⓔ Do you want a window seat or an aisle seat?　ⓕ It provides private bedrooms and offers breakfast.

1 M: _____
　W: Of course. Just leave it here.
2 M: What type of room do you want?
　W: _____
3 M: _____
　W: It doesn't matter, but I want to get a seat near the front.

1 When is the woman's flight?

① September 6th, 10 a.m.   ② September 6th, 1 p.m.

③ September 8th, 10 a.m.   ④ September 8th, 1 p.m.

+ Listen again and fill in the blanks.

(*Telephone rings.*)

M: USA Airlines. How may I help you?

W: I _____ _____ _____ _____ yesterday, but I want to change the date.

M: Okay. What is your name?

W: Kelly Grant. It was for a flight to Toronto on September 6th, 10 a.m.

M: Okay. _____ _____ do you want to change it to?

W: The same time on September 8th.

M: I'm sorry. That flight is _____ _____.

W: Really? What time is the next flight after that?

M: 1 p.m.

W: _____ _____ _____ _____.

M: Okay.

2 What is the man mainly talking about?

① The best seat on an airplane

② The flight services you can get

③ Exercises you can do on an airplane

④ How to stay comfortable on an airplane

+ Listen again and fill in the blanks.

M: Do you have any plans to _____ _____ _____? Then let me give you some tips. First, the air inside a plane is dry, so drink _____ _____ _____ or juice. But don't drink too much alcohol, coffee, or tea. Caffeine will _____ _____ _____ during the flight. Also, you may be in an uncomfortable position for a long time. So, it's good to stretch your body and _____ _____ _____ _____ often.

1   Where will the woman stay in London?

① at a hotel

② at a B&B

③ at her friend's house

④ at a youth hostel

2   What time will the man check out?

① 11 a.m.

② 1 p.m.

③ 4 p.m.

④ 11 p.m.

3   How will the man get to the British Museum?

①    ②    ③    ④

4   Choose the wrong information.

Hilltop Hotel Reservation # 5	
Name	Steve Arnold
Check-in date	① July 15th
Check-out date	② July 17th
Room type	③ Twin room
Total rate	④ $180

5   What is the man's problem?

     ① He doesn't know his flight number.

     ② He picked up the wrong bag.

     ③ He lost his baggage tag.

     ④ His bag was sent to the wrong airport.

6   Write T for true or F for false about the online check-in service.

     (1) It has been offered for a month.   _____

     (2) It will make check-in faster at the airport.   _____

     (3) It is available two hours before the flight.   _____

7   Which is NOT the woman's advice?

     ① Leave some empty space when packing.

     ② Pack some old clothes.

     ③ Put things you use often on the top.

     ④ Bring plastic bags for wet or dirty clothes.

8   Choose the man's seat.

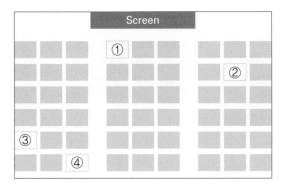

A - 1   What will the woman probably do next?

① Read a travel guidebook

② Make a flight reservation

③ Cancel her flight ticket

④ Search for information on the Internet

2   Which is NOT true about Lion Airlines?

① It has flights all over the world.

② It is famous for low prices.

③ Buying a ticket early saves money.

④ It doesn't offer drinks or meal service.

B - 1   Which country are they going to visit?

① Turkey

② Greece

③ Austria

④ Australia

2   Choose the activity that they are going to do.

①    ②    ③    ④

 Critical★Thinking

Package Tours

1 Check [✓] if each person is for or against package tours.

	For	Against
(1) May	☐	☐
(2) Chris	☐	☐
(3) Tina	☐	☐

2 Choose each person's opinion.

(1) May: _____   (2) Chris: _____   (3) Tina: _____

ⓐ I'd like to visit only the places I'm interested in.

ⓑ I can save time planning a trip by taking a package tour.

ⓒ If I take a package tour, I can travel around without wasting time.

ⓓ It's hard to mix with local people and learn their culture during a package tour.

What do you think?

1

Check [✓] if you have the same opinion. You can add your own opinion in the blank.

☐ I think planning my own trip would be more exciting.

☐ I could travel around more easily with a tour guide.

☐ I wouldn't like to follow the set schedule of a tour.

_____

2

Talk about the following questions with your partner.

• Have you ever been on a package tour?

• What type of trip would you like to go on during your next vacation?

10
IT

Getting ★ Ready

A

Match each word with the correct definition.

1 a small computer that can easily be carried •   • ⓐ spam

2 unwanted email sent to many people at once •   • ⓑ laptop

3 the manners that you should keep on the Internet •   • ⓒ netiquette

B

Choose the best word for each blank.

1 _____ the Internet

2 _____ into messenger

3 _____ text messages

ⓐ log	ⓑ rank
ⓒ surf	ⓓ exchange

C

Choose the best sentence for each blank.

ⓐ Why don't you contact her by email?   ⓑ I can't hear the other person.   ⓒ How much time do you spend on the Internet each day?   ⓓ When did you send the email?   ⓔ Do you have enough storage space in your mailbox?   ⓕ The days of paper books are coming to an end.

---

1 M: _____

   W: Around two hours a day.

2 M: Does your cellphone have a problem?

   W: Yes. _____

3 M: _____

   W: Maybe I should do that.

SAMSUNG

1 What will the boy probably do next?

① Call Paul

② Surf the Internet

③ Visit a service center

④ Work on his homework

+ Listen again
and fill
in the blanks.

M: Are you busy right now?

W: No, I'm _____ _____ _____. Why?

M: I'm in big trouble. I don't know what to do.

W: _____ _____?

M: I was doing my Chinese homework when my computer _____
_____ again.

W: I don't know much about computers. Do you need to do homework
all over again?

M: I think so. I _____ _____ _____.

W: Why don't you ask Paul about it? He knows a lot about computers.

M: Good idea. I'll call him _____ _____.

2 What is the girl talking about?

① ② ③ ④

+ Listen again
and fill
in the blanks.

W: Last year, my dad _____ _____ _____ _____
on my 12th birthday. Because of its small size, it's easy to carry
around. It's very useful when studying English. I can _____
_____ _____ from computers and listen to them over
and over. Plus, I can download my favorite songs whenever I want
to. Sometimes, I _____ _____ with it. It helps me review
my classes later on.

1   What are they doing?

①    ②    ③    ④

2   Check [✓] how the man feels about *Aliens*.

	Good	Bad
(1) Characters		
(2) Story		
(3) Sound		

3   Why did the man NOT get the photos?

① It was sent to the wrong address.

② The woman sent the wrong file.

③ It came to his spam mailbox.

④ His mailbox didn't have enough storage space.

4   What are they mainly talking about?

① Keeping online manners

② Making new friends online

③ Teaching netiquette to teenagers

④ Playing online games for a long time

5 Choose the video that the woman watched.

①  ②  ③  ④

6 Which is NOT mentioned as a good point of e-books?

① various reading devices

② cheap price

③ various letter sizes

④ a search program

7 How is the man going to contact Jennifer?

① by blog

② by phone

③ by email

④ through messenger

8 What are they talking about?

①  ②  ③  ④

A - 1 Choose the two problems with the woman's phone.

① She can't hear the other speaker.

② Other people can't hear her.

③ There's a lot of noise during her calls.

④ The screen is broken.

2 When is the woman going to pick up her phone?

① Monday   ② Tuesday

③ Wednesday   ④ Thursday

B - 1 Choose the right country for each blank.

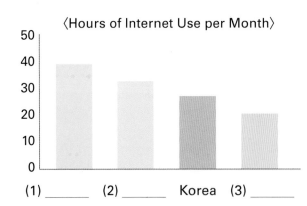

⟨Hours of Internet Use per Month⟩

ⓐ USA

ⓑ Canada

ⓒ Japan

ⓓ Israel

(1) _____   (2) _____   Korea   (3) _____

2 Which website do people visit the most?

① Yahoo   ② Google

③ Microsoft   ④ Wikipedia

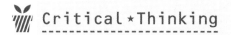

Critical ★ Thinking

Cellphones

1   Check [✓] if each person is for or against students using cellphones.

	For	Against
(1) Mike	☐	☐
(2) Judy	☐	☐
(3) Alex	☐	☐

2   Choose each person's opinion.

(1) Mike: _____   (2) Judy: _____   (3) Alex: _____

ⓐ Cellphones are not good for our health.

ⓑ Cellphones are useful for studying.

ⓒ Students can't focus on studying because of cellphones.

ⓓ Text messaging is how students connect with their friends.

What do you think?

1

Check [✓] if you have the same opinion. You can add your own opinion in the blank.

☐ We can do many useful things with cellphones.

☐ Text messaging makes it hard to focus on studying in class.

☐ It's hard to contact friends without a cellphone nowadays.

_____

2

Talk about the following questions with your partner.

· About how much time do you spend using your cellphone each day?

· What is good or bad about using cellphones?

UNIT 11 Superstitions

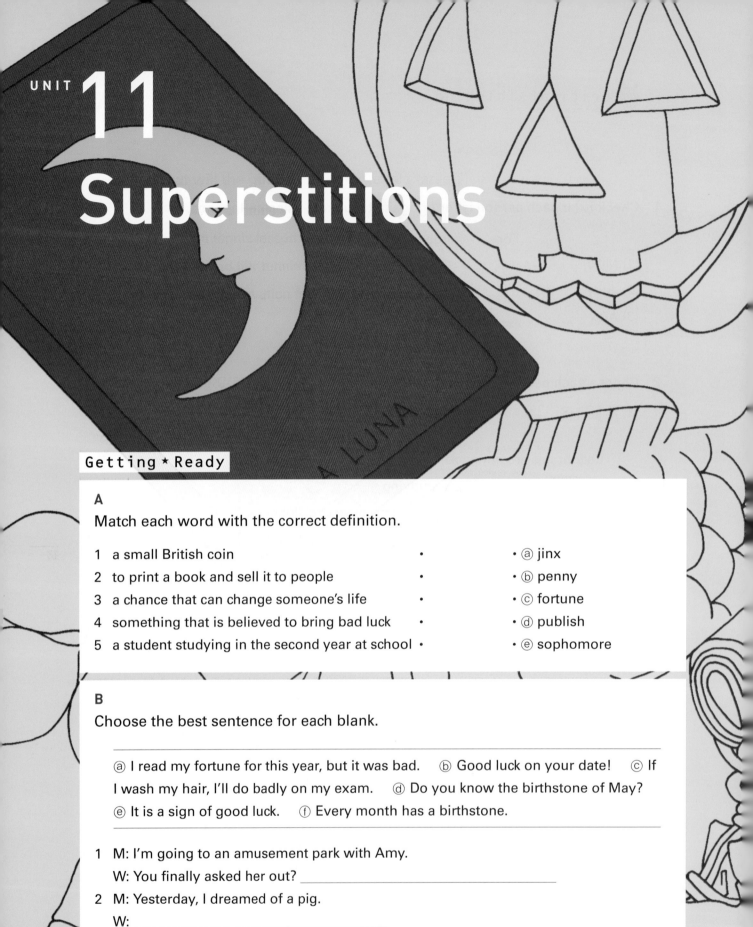

Getting ★ Ready

A

Match each word with the correct definition.

1 a small British coin •
2 to print a book and sell it to people •
3 a chance that can change someone's life •
4 something that is believed to bring bad luck •
5 a student studying in the second year at school •

• ⓐ jinx
• ⓑ penny
• ⓒ fortune
• ⓓ publish
• ⓔ sophomore

B

Choose the best sentence for each blank.

ⓐ I read my fortune for this year, but it was bad.   ⓑ Good luck on your date!   ⓒ If I wash my hair, I'll do badly on my exam.   ⓓ Do you know the birthstone of May?   ⓔ It is a sign of good luck.   ⓕ Every month has a birthstone.

1 M: I'm going to an amusement park with Amy.
   W: You finally asked her out? _____
2 M: Yesterday, I dreamed of a pig.
   W: _____
3 M: You look worried. What's up?
   W: _____

1   What is the man mainly talking about?

① Countries in which red means good luck

② Chinese people's love for the color red

③ The various meanings of red around the world

④ The Chinese way of celebrating the New Year

+ Listen again
and fill
in the blanks.

M: In China, people think of red _____ _____ _____
_____. They think that red brings money and keeps ghosts
away. So, on someone's wedding day, Chinese people _____
_____ _____ _____ in red and the bride wears a
red dress. On New Year's Day, many items in stores are _____
_____ _____ and people celebrate with red fireworks.
Also, many servers in Chinese restaurants _____ _____
_____.

2   Who will have good luck?

① This morning,
a black cat walked in
front of me.

Kate

② I saw a spider
on my desk
in the evening.

Dave

③ I picked up
a penny on the
street today.

Mark

+ Listen again
and fill
in the blanks.

W1: In the US, if _____ _____ _____ walks in front of
you, it's bad luck.

M: In England, if you _____ _____ _____ on the
ground, you'll have good luck all day.

W2: In Japan, if you _____ _____ _____ in the
morning, it's a sign of good luck. But if you see one in the evening,
it's _____ _____ _____.

1 Where is this conversation taking place?

① in a library

② at a beauty shop

③ in a classroom

④ in a teacher's room

2 Which did NOT happen to the girl?

① She had a fight with a taxi driver.

② She arrived late at school.

③ She did badly on her test.

④ She lost her cellphone.

3 How will the woman solve her problem?

① By making her own dress

② By borrowing a wedding dress

③ By finding another wedding dress shop

④ By asking her friend to make a dress

4 Which is the man's birthstone?

①   ②   ③   ④

5   What will the man probably do next?

6   What do some British people do to have good luck?

① Say "white rabbits" two times every morning

② Put some bills in the pocket of new pants

③ Open an umbrella in their house

④ Keep a bird in their house

7   Which is the boy going to buy for his girlfriend?

① a necklace

② a ring

③ a doll

④ a keychain

8   Which best describes the girl's opinion?

① Everything in life is luck.

② We make our own fortune.

③ Bad luck never comes alone.

④ Bad luck often brings good luck.

A - 1   Which is the woman's ring?

①    ②    ③    ④

2   Why is the ring important to the woman?

① Her boyfriend gave it to her.

② She thinks it brings victory.

③ She paid a lot of money for it.

④ She thinks it prevents her from getting hurt.

_____

B - 1   What is the relationship between the speakers?

① mother – son

② doctor – patient

③ counselor – customer

④ fortune teller – customer

2   According to the woman, write T for true or F for false.

(1) The man will get a job at a big company this year.   _____

(2) There will be some problems with the man's stomach.   _____

(3) The man will get married to his girlfriend.   _____

 Critical ★ Thinking

Jinxes

1 What is the woman's job?

① a dancer

② an author

③ an actress

④ a singer

2 Who had the sophomore jinx?

①

Eva

> I got a better grade in my second year than my first year at school.

②

Dan

> My first movie was a big hit, but my second movie failed.

③

Emma

> My first and second books both failed.

What do you think?

1

Check [✓] if you have the same opinion. You can add your own opinion in the blank.

☐ There is no such thing as a jinx.

☐ Jinxes happen to only a few unlucky people.

☐ Jinxes happen when someone doesn't make enough effort.

_____

2

Talk about the following questions with your partner.

• Have you ever experienced a jinx?

• What do you think is the reason for a jinx?

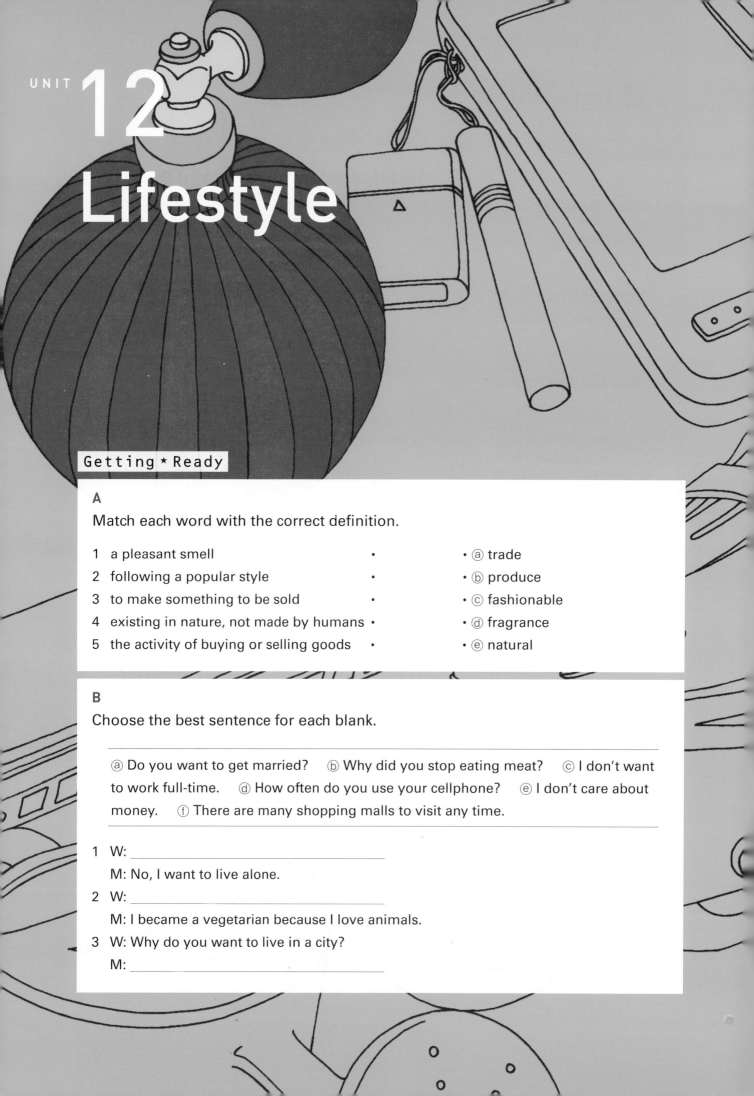

UNIT 12

Lifestyle

Getting ★ Ready

A

Match each word with the correct definition.

1 a pleasant smell   •   • ⓐ trade
2 following a popular style   •   • ⓑ produce
3 to make something to be sold   •   • ⓒ fashionable
4 existing in nature, not made by humans   •   • ⓓ fragrance
5 the activity of buying or selling goods   •   • ⓔ natural

B

Choose the best sentence for each blank.

ⓐ Do you want to get married?   ⓑ Why did you stop eating meat?   ⓒ I don't want
to work full-time.   ⓓ How often do you use your cellphone?   ⓔ I don't care about
money.   ⓕ There are many shopping malls to visit any time.

1 W: _____
   M: No, I want to live alone.
2 W: _____
   M: I became a vegetarian because I love animals.
3 W: Why do you want to live in a city?
   M: _____

1   Choose the two jobs that the woman's sister has now.

    ① a nurse   ② a banker

    ③ a baker   ④ a waitress

+ Listen again and fill in the blanks.

M: I heard there are many people _____ _____ _____ these days.

W: My sister is one of them.

M: Really? What does she do?

W: _____ _____ _____ is as a nurse. But she's working as a waitress on weekends.

M: Wow, then she must earn _____ _____ _____ _____.

W: I think so. She wants to open a bakery after _____ _____ _____.

M: That's nice.

75

2   Why does the woman work part-time?

    ① She couldn't get a full-time job.

    ② She feels too tired to work full-time.

    ③ She needs to study in the afternoons.

    ④ She can work only when she wants to.

+ Listen again and fill in the blanks.

M: What do you do these days?

W: I _____ _____ for a game company. I'm a web designer.

M: Oh, so you work part-time _____ _____ full-time?

W: Yes. I don't want to work full-time.

M: _____ _____?

W: I want to work only when I want to. I don't want to _____ _____ every day.

M: I see. But you can't earn much money.

W: I don't _____ _____ money.

1 Why is the man going to Japan?

① To buy a video game

② To meet his friend

③ To find new fashion trends

④ To go sightseeing

2 Choose the wrong information.

Use Skin Doctor for Your Skin

① Skin Doctor products are made of natural materials.

② You can choose the color of the bottles.

③ You can exchange the empty bottles for samples.

④ You can buy the products both offline and online.

---

3 What are they mainly talking about?

① Why they shop online

② How to buy a good camera

③ Why they write product reviews

④ How to get information about products

4 Which is NOT a way the man saves money?

①    ②    ③    ④

5 Who has the same opinion as the woman?

①

I want to get married so that I won't feel lonely.

Neville

②

Having children is the most important thing in life.

Sandra

③

I want to enjoy my life without getting married.

Mark

6 Which is an example of "digital cocooning"?

① Going to see a movie with friends

② Surfing the Internet at an Internet café

③ Learning about digital technology at school

④ Downloading music and movies at home

7 Which is NOT information that you can get from *Your Style*?

① clothing styles

② best-selling books

③ dating places

④ cosmetics

8 What advice would the woman give to the boy?

① Buy a used cellphone.

② Treat your cellphone carefully.

③ Make a time limit for using your cellphone.

④ Be sure to take your cellphone when you go out.

A - 1   Choose all the food that the man eats.

ⓐ ⓑ ⓒ ⓓ ⓔ

2   Why did the man become a vegetarian?

① He doesn't like meat.

② He wanted to be healthy.

③ He wanted to lose weight.

④ He loves animals so much.

B - 1   What did the woman consider when she bought the chocolate?

① How it tastes

② How much it costs

③ Which company made it

④ How much the farmers were paid

2   What will they probably do next?

① Read the book about chocolate

② Eat some chocolate

③ Go to buy some chocolate

④ Do their homework

 Critical★Thinking

Where to Live

1 Check [✓] if each person prefers to live in a city or in the countryside.

	City	Countryside
(1) Ricky	☐	☐
(2) Mary	☐	☐
(3) Jim	☐	☐

2 Match each person with their opinion.

(1) Ricky ·   · ⓐ There are many interesting places in a city.

(2) Mary ·   · ⓑ Cities have good public transportation systems.

(3) Jim ·   · ⓒ I enjoy living in the countryside because of its clean
                            environment.

What do you think?

1

Check [✓] if you have the same opinion. You can add your own opinion in the blank.

☐ I don't like living in the city because of air and water pollution.

☐ I want to live in the city because I can get a better education and job.

☐ There are more interesting things to do in a city than in the countryside.

_____

2

Talk about the following questions with your partner.

· Do you live in a city or in the countryside? How is your life there?

· What is the most important thing for you when choosing a place to live?

Vocabulary ★ List

UNIT 01

yet
while
cook
fried
rice
vegetable
would like to-v
potato
ready
soon
popular
curry
beef
spicy
a little bit
be famous for
pork
oily
sour
sauce
delicious
dish
noodle
homemade
chocolate
try
special
nut
be allergic to
get sick
grocery store
mango
enough
choose

fresh
sound
soft
hard
smell
bake
reason
carrot
recipe
soup
thin
slightly
taste
region
topping
boiled
green onion
except
downtown
post office
disappointing
meat
tough
tuna
decide
corn
hurry up
order
forget
pasta
bacon
frying pan
fry
boil
add
cover

top
prepare
meal
powder
onion
fajita
traditional
chance
for the first time
wrap
grilled
tortilla
piece
wheat
flour
junk food
fat
gain weight
cause
heart trouble
tooth problem
ban
in order to-v
protect
health
unhealthy

UNIT 02

among
trouble
boring
on the other hand
funny
subject
fashionable

lose
timetable
Japanese
history
science
math
library
make a call
empty
seat
save
snack
terrible
noise
borrow
ID
return
bring
check out
pay
fine
send
text message
focus on
these days
date
guess
prepare
presentation
search for
information
festival
include
present
worth
final

grade	had better-v	tie	grade
paper	cap	join	apply
author	drink	get together	classical music
choose	provide	once	twice
at first	necessary	practice	instrument
change one's mind	upset	gym	put on
vacation	report card	casual	play
facility	cover	running shoes	main role
certain	chapter	website	trip
period	as well	information	museum
gym	a little bit	save	dry
available	midterm	travel	area
language lab	carefully	trumpet	look like
whole	helpful	noisy	stone
reopen	graduate	neighbor	sunlight
as usual	knowledge	teddy bear	water
paint	chance	lovely	makeup
ride	earn	gift	excited
go on a picnic	income	Valentine's Day	act
talent	care	collect	imagine
jog	various	doll	neither
be disappointed with		same	script
advice	UNIT 03	lotion	make a mistake
useful		sunburn	stage
tight	model	wear	rehearsal
decide	take a picture of	sunblock	performance
weak	bookstore	work	costume
spend	downtown	put on	finish
field trip	accessory	avoid	last
desert	sunglasses	midday	extreme sport
farm	costume play	sleeve	run up
plant	dress up	instead	jump off
lake	character	cheering club	letter
tour	princess	attend	climb
anyway	socks	cheer	without
lunch box	shirt	active	rope

spell
fit
amazing
dangerous
train
badly
hurt
be full of
thrill
safe
success
serious

UNIT 04

light
pet
name
piggy
raise
giant
spider
strange
seem
sick
have a runny nose
puppy
catch a cold
dry
enough
reason
medicine
rounded
tail
hardly
useful
climb
bear

carry
back
penguin
prepare
special
event
magician
put on
fantastic
dolphin
amazing
be scared of
snake
make friends with
depressed
have a fight with
die
bark
loudly
fix
training
take care of
earn
part-time job
look for
friendly
walk
feed
cellphone
be interested in
worried
happen
guess
worry
sure
crow
smart
brain

tool
catch
insect
sweet
grow up
hunt
sensitive
careful
wild
indoors
corn
nut
pull
hurt
if possible
dirty
wet
cloth
plane
airline
pay
extra
less than
seat
cage
document
healthy
join
season
accessory

UNIT 05

doorbell
delivery
quick
order
actually

terribly
price
plant
garden
except for
tulip
dead
daisy
colorful
fantastic
have one's photo taken
passport
cost
take a seat
mirror
wash dishes
clean
dish
oily
frying pan
paper towel
smell
heat
microwave
dry-clean
pick up
turn
purple
make a mistake
shape
bakery
heart-shaped
be sold out
instead
address
message
graduation

account

cash card

credit card

ID card

fill out

form

get one's hair cut

cut off

perm

in my opinion

curly

straight

blond

that way

relax

afterwards

worry

prepare

set the table

used to-v

couch potato

badminton

package

several

weight

prefer

regular mail

express mail

half

fruit

market

favorite

feel like v-ing

comic book

strawberry

melon

refrigerator

add

egg roll

fried rice

seafood

correct

noodle

chopstick

housework

share

bathroom

take care of

alone

pleased

try to-v

UNIT 06

musical

wonderful

still

forget

theater

show

sound

ballet

excited

satisfied

part

cancel

reservation

section

available

weekly

over

act

actor

take a break

for a while

hope

play

drawing show

hold

concert hall

art gallery

end

result

beginning

magic

funny

boring

stage set

real

manner

hurry

already

be sold out

adult

teenager

talent

mostly

importance

teamwork

lastly

laugh

showmanship

male

cool

ballerina

hip-hop

powerful

play a big role

version

orchestra

select

video

audition

receive

musician

online

gather

expect

success

main actor

series

lucky

close up

teenage

scream

focus on

go up

UNIT 07

back

hurt

appointment

full

make it

fever

cough

have a runny nose

cold

syrup

file

age

blood type

serious

disease

allergy

allergic

for a second

result

stomach

test

empty

83

dry

contact lenses

for a while

get better

sore throat

lately

good

advice

snowboard

wheelchair

terrible

stomachache

corn

stay

catch a cold

happen

cure

pill

prevent A from v-ing

headache

toast

taste

in a hurry

tooth

dental

clinic

dentist

experience

provide

weekday

offer

checkup

department store

smoke

be likely to-v

punish

catch

punishment

fact

UNIT 08

baseball

stadium

last

bored

amazing

sports day

relay race

basketball

running shoes

uniform

pack

already

sunblock

court

make a reservation

racket

figure skating

championship

skater

record

suggestion

in-line skating

first of all

outside

fresh

sunlight

either A or B

alone

right away

score

golfer

talent

train

strike

knock down

pin

turkey

in a row

marathon

comfortable

finish

at least

be sure to-v

stretch

serious

yoga

position

straight

ahead

forward

ankle

pull

second

opposite

congratulation

MVP

handball

gold medal

the Olympics

someday

skill

Premier League

offer

home stay

sign up

interview

hero

champion

fantastic

point

shot

prove

appear

waste

focus on

improve

earn

cost

natural

UNIT 09

airline

flight

book

tip

alcohol

caffeine

awake

uncomfortable

position

stretch

aisle

youth hostel

mostly

perhaps

provide

private

quite

search

check-out

possible

check out

extra

charge

per

backpack

front desk

direct

tube

subway	shut down	foreigner	decorate
on foot	right away	thousands of	bride
cost	carry	rank	New Year's Day
twin room	useful	proud	item
busy season	download	come to an end	wrap
baggage tag	over and over	e-book	celebrate
make a mistake	record	laptop	firework
airport	review	bookstore	server
terribly	set	search	uniform
contact	regular	reply	luck
online	online	log into	penny
homepage	alien	messenger	ground
counter	character	contact	spider
pack	weapon	valuable	sign
tightly	best of all	own	unlucky
throw away	storyline	get bored with	smell
light	earth	digital camera	badly
plastic bag	melody	work	grade
in that case	repeat	noise	Murphy's Law
screen	turn off	drop	keep v-ing
guidebook	volume	fix	get lost
matter	email	according to	score
sandboard	correct	study	on one's way home
bike	spam	Canadian	fashion designer
sand	mailbox	Israel	marriage
bungee-jump	happen	website	superstition
package tour	storage	visitor	classmate
stressful	space	exchange	necklace
whole	follow	text message	stone
local	netiquette	tool	ruby
culture	chat	dictionary	birthstone
by oneself	guy	connect	be born
waste	a couple of	communicate	emerald
	in the middle of		pass
UNIT 10	recently	UNIT 11	salt
	behave		spill
surf the Internet	Italian	lucky	blind date
Chinese	surprised	ghost	throw

85

shoulder

be tired of

British

wake up

pocket

however

umbrella

inside

four-leaf clover

message

keychain

fortune

break up with

stay

gold

heart-shaped

plain

silver

hockey

hire

company

stomach

careful

get married to

try one's best

sophomore

jinx

effort

successful

writer

publish

hit

wonderful

UNIT 12

main

nurse

waitress

earn

bakery

save

part-time

web designer

rather than

full-time

care about

go sightseeing

surprising

cosmetic

brand

product

natural

material

sensitive

fragrance

environment

empty

bottle

sample

review

share

reason

probably

instant coffee

discount coupon

marry

be able to-v

freely

lonely

various

freedom

someday

need

entertainment

digital

device

allow

chat

cocooning

channel

introduce

romantic

according to

fashionable

miss

nervous

serious

seafood

vegetarian

vegetable

actually

fair

trade

cacao

farmer

produce

receive

amount

lend

countryside

public transportation

get around

everywhere

available

boring

country

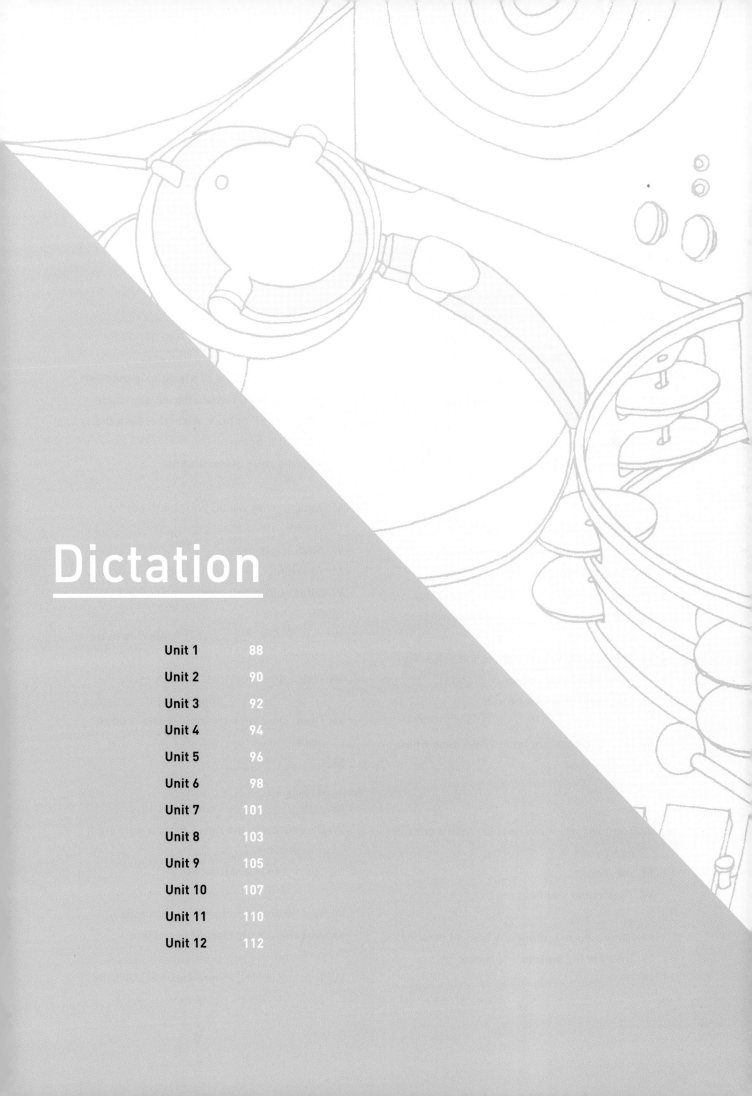

Dictation

UNIT 01 Food

1

M: Hey, Amy. What are those?

W: These are _____ _____ and cookies. I made them.

M: They look delicious. May I try one?

W: Sure. Try this special chocolate. I put _____ _____ _____ in it.

M: Did you say that you put nuts in it?

W: Yes. What's the problem?

M: I'm _____ _____ nuts. If I eat them, I get very sick.

W: Really? Then, try _____ _____. It doesn't have any nuts in it.

M: Okay, thanks.

2

W: Justin, could you go to the _____ _____ and buy some mangoes?

M: Sure, Mom. How many?

W: Five is enough. And choose fresh ones.

M: Oh, that _____ _____. How will I know which ones are fresh?

W: The easiest way is to check the color. The color should be yellow or orange.

M: I see. And should it be soft _____ _____ _____ _____?

W: No. Hard ones are better. And fresh ones smell sweet.

M: Okay.

3

W: Thomas, you know how to make a cake, don't you?

M: Yes, I do.

W: Then could you help me _____ _____ _____?

M: No problem. Is there any special reason?

W: Today is my brother's birthday.

M: Oh, I see. _____ _____ _____

_____ do you want to make for him?

W: Well, he likes carrot cake.

M: Okay. Did you _____ _____ _____?

W: Not yet.

M: How about finding a recipe on the Internet first? _____ _____ _____ a supermarket after that.

W: Okay!

4

W: This is one of _____ _____ _____ Japanese dishes. It is a kind of noodle soup. The noodles are thin and _____ _____. The taste of the soup is different from region to region. It's usually made with chicken or pork. Also, there are many kinds of toppings, _____ _____ a boiled egg or green onions.

5

M: Janice, what would you like to eat for lunch?

W: Anything is okay, _____ _____.

M: You don't like fish? Why not?

W: It has such a bad smell. I really don't like it.

M: Oh, I see.

W: _____ _____ _____, Alex? Is there anything you don't like?

M: Well, I don't like fried chicken. I usually _____ _____ after eating it.

W: Then, shall we eat pizza? I know a good place.

M: _____ _____.

6

M: _____ _____? You look angry.

W: Do you know the new Chinese restaurant downtown?

M: You mean the restaurant _____ _____ _____ _____?

W: Yes. I went there to have lunch today.

M: Was there a problem? I heard that restaurant _____ _____ _____.

W: That's true. They were very kind. But the

food was so disappointing!

M: What was wrong with it?

W: The meat was _____ _____ and the vegetables were not fresh at all.

M: Oh, I'm sorry to hear that. Well, I won't go there.

7

W: Brad, are you going to _____ _____ _____ _____?

M: Um, I haven't decided yet.

W: What? You wanted to _____ _____ to have a tuna sandwich.

M: Yes, I did. But the cheeseburgers _____ _____ _____. How about you?

W: I'm going to have a ham sandwich and corn salad.

M: Oh, my god. That sounds great, too!

W: Please _____ _____ and order. Don't forget that we have only 30 minutes for lunch.

M: Okay. I'll have a tuna sandwich and a Coke.

W: Good.

8

M: _____ _____ *Jamie's Cooking Show.* Today, I'll show you how to make an oven-baked pasta dish. Firstly, _____ _____ and bacon in a frying pan and fry them. Secondly, boil some pasta _____ _____ _____. Next, put the pasta into the frying pan and add some milk or cream. Finally, put all of it into an oven dish and cover the top with cheese. Then cook it in the oven _____ _____ _____.

Listening ★ Challenge   **Answers p. 2**

A [1-2]

W: Do you know that tomorrow is _____ _____?

M: Oh no, I forgot! Do you have any good ideas?

W: What about _____ _____ _____ _____ for dinner tomorrow?

M: That's a good idea!

W: Then, we have to decide what to make.

M: I think we should _____ _____. It's easy to make.

W: Great! For curry, we'll need curry powder, carrots, onions, and potatoes. Anything else?

M: _____ _____ _____ in it. Mom likes that.

W: Okay. Well, we already have curry powder, potatoes and carrots.

M: So, we only need to buy _____ _____ _____. Let's go to buy them.

B [1-2]

M: Have you ever tried "fajitas"? They are a traditional _____ _____. I had a chance to taste them for the first time when I visited my friend's house. They were _____ _____ _____ they became my favorite food. When you eat a fajita, you wrap the grilled meat and fried vegetables in a tortilla. A tortilla is a very thin round _____ _____ _____ made from corn or wheat flour.

Critical ★ Thinking   **Answers p. 2**

W: Junk food usually has _____ _____ _____ fat, salt, or sugar in it. Eating too much fat can make students gain weight. And eating too much salt may cause heart trouble _____ _____ _____. Also, eating sugar can cause tooth problems. I think schools should ban junk foods _____ _____ _____ protect the health of students.

M: Hamburgers, chocolate bars and ice cream are all _____ _____. We can easily get junk food outside school. So, even if schools ban junk food, students will buy it anyway. In my opinion, it is better to teach students _____ _____ those foods are.

UNIT 02 School Life

Listening ∗ Practice   Answers p. 2

1

M1: I'm Alex. Some people _____ _____ _____ _____ in the library. The library is a place to study and read books. They should go outside to _____ _____ _____.

W: I'm Megan. Yesterday, I found an empty seat in the library. But a boy said he was _____ _____ _____ for his friend, so I couldn't sit there.

M2: I'm Colin. I don't understand why some students _____ _____ in the library. As you know, it makes a terrible noise.

2

W: Hi, I'd like to _____ _____ _____.

M: Can I see your student ID?

W: Here it is.

M: _____ _____ you can't borrow a book. You haven't returned *The Little Prince*.

W: Oh, I'll bring it back tomorrow. Can't I just check out this book now?

M: Sorry, you can't.

W: Then I'll _____ _____ to get the book now. I must borrow this book for my homework.

M: Don't forget that you must also _____ _____ _____.

W: Okay.

3

M: How's Mike doing? He doesn't _____

_____ _____ or my wife about his school life.

W: Well, I often see him sending text messages in my class. He doesn't seem to _____ _____ his lessons these days.

M: Maybe it's because he started to date a girl. What should I do?

W: Don't worry. I'll talk with him about it.

M: Thank you. Is he _____ _____ _____ his friends?

W: Yes, he's very popular in his class.

M: I guess that's why many of his friends _____ _____ to the house.

4

M: Listen, class. By _____ _____, you must prepare a group presentation. Make groups of five members and search for information about one of the festivals _____ _____ _____. Include the festival's history, place, and activities. Each group will have 15 minutes to _____ _____ _____. This presentation is worth 20 points, and it'll be included in your _____ _____.

5

(*Telephone rings.*)

M: Hello.

W: Hi, Kevin. This is Sally.

M: Hey, _____ _____?

W: I want to know if there's any homework for English class.

M: We have to write a _____ _____ about our favorite author.

W: Who are you going to write about?

M: I chose Mark Twain at first. But then I _____ _____ _____ to write about Ernest Hemingway.

W: Why?

M: I read his *The Old Man and the Sea* _____ _____ _____ _____, and it was great. What about you?

W: I'm thinking of writing about Emily Brontë.

6

W: Attention, please. _____ _____

_____ , you will not be able to use

school facilities for certain periods of time.

The gym will not be available for two

weeks, from July 6th to _____ _____ .

The language lab will be closed for the

whole vacation. The computer lab will be

closed from July 20th and reopen on July

31st. Students can use the library _____

_____ during the vacation.

7

W: I heard you got an A⁺ in _____ _____ .

Congratulations! Can I see your picture?

M: Sure. This is it.

W: Wow, you painted a boy _____ _____

_____ .

M: He's my brother. This is when my family

went on a picnic _____ _____ .

W: Where did you go?

M: We went to Silver Lake Park and _____

_____ _____ there.

W: You really have a talent for painting.

M: Thanks, Julie. So, what did you paint

_____ _____ _____ ?

W: I painted a woman jogging in the

morning. I got a B.

8

W: I'm disappointed with my grades. Can you

give me some advice?

M: Sure. Let me _____ _____ _____

first. Why do you study?

W: Well... I don't know.

M: You should know why you need to study

first. It helps you _____ _____ _____ .

W: Umm... I see.

M: Making a study plan is also useful. But

don't make it _____ _____ .

W: Okay.

M: Finally, decide what your weakest subject

is and _____ _____ _____ on it.

W: Thanks for your advice.

Listening ⋆ Challenge   Answers p. 3

A [1-2]

W: Mike, we're going on a field trip on the

20th.

M: Really, Ms. Taylor? _____ _____

_____ _____ ?

W: Arizona Desert Garden. It's a farm where

desert plants grow.

M: Sounds interesting. The last field trip to

the lake was boring.

W: Was it? But the _____ _____ _____

was very good.

M: You're right. Anyway, do I need to bring

my lunch box?

W: Yes, you do. Also, _____ _____

_____ your cap. It's hot there.

M: Okay. How about a drink?

W: You don't need to bring one. The school

will _____ _____ .

M: Great. And I'll bring my pen and some

paper.

W: Good boy. They're necessary for _____

_____ about the trip.

B [1-2]

M: You look upset. What's the matter?

W: I just got my report card, and my math

grade is really bad.

M: Didn't you _____ _____ _____ ?

W: Yes, I did. But I thought the exam covered

chapters four, five and six.

M: Oh, the exam included chapter seven

_____ _____ .

W: That's why I got a C! Many questions

came from that chapter.

M: _____ _____ _____ .

W: How about you?

M: I did a little bit better than on the midterm

exam.

W: That's good. You _____ _____ _____ on the midterm exam.

M: I got a B⁺ this time. It's not an A, but I'm happy with my grade.

Critical ★ Thinking   Answers p. 3

M: Mom, I don't know why I have to _____ _____ _____.

W: What are you talking about? It's helpful when getting a job, isn't it?

M: I can get a job after just graduating from high school.

W: But you can _____ _____ _____ of a subject at university. That way, you'll have a better chance to earn a higher income.

M: But I don't _____ _____ money.

W: Hmm... do you think you've prepared enough for your future job?

M: Well... no, _____ _____ _____ _____.

W: That's why you'd better go to university. You can prepare for your future job while studying and meeting various people.

M: I see.

UNIT 03 Hobbies

Listening ★ Practice   Answers p. 3

1

M: Welcome! Do you want to join our dance club?

W: Yes. _____ _____ do you guys get together?

M: We get together once a week. It's every Wednesday at 7 p.m.

W: Okay. Where do you practice?

M: _____ _____. But we usually practice in the school gym.

W: Do I need to wear special dance clothes?

M: No. You can wear casual sports clothes. But you should _____ _____ _____, not running shoes.

W: I see. See you on Wednesday, then.

2

W: These days, I visit many websites about Angkor Wat in Cambodia. I _____ _____ _____ about places to visit, food, and hotels. Then I save the information on my computer. I can't travel around the world now because I'm a student and I don't have _____ _____. But after getting a job, I'll travel to many places. So, I like to find travel information _____ _____ _____ _____.

3

M: _____ _____ _____ buying a trumpet.

W: Really? But aren't trumpets expensive?

M: Yes, but I'll buy an old one, so _____ _____ _____.

W: So, will you play it at home?

M: Yes. I'll practice it every day.

W: I don't think it's a good idea to buy a trumpet.

M: _____ _____?

W: If you play it at home, it'll be very noisy. Your neighbors won't like it.

M: Hmm... that may be a problem.

W: Why don't you _____ _____ _____ and learn to play the trumpet there?

M: That's a good idea.

4

M: What do you do in your free time?

W: I _____ _____ _____.

M: Interesting!

W: Look at this teddy bear. I made it myself.

M: Wow! It's lovely. It's holding a gift box.

W: I'll put chocolates in it. This is a _____ _____ _____ for my boyfriend.

M: Good idea. Can you teach me how to make one?

W: Why?

M: My girlfriend _____ _____.

W: Then how about making a teddy bear with a heart or a flower?

M: They sound fine, but _____ _____ _____ _____ the same teddy bear as you.

5

M: Doctor, look at my arms. They're red.

W: Were you in the sun for a long time?

M: Yes. I _____ _____ yesterday.

W: I'll give you some lotion. It looks like sunburn.

M: I wore sunblock, but maybe _____ _____ _____.

W: Well, you need to put it on every 2 or 3 hours.

M: Oops. I didn't know that. So, how can I _____ _____?

W: Don't play outside around midday. And wear long sleeves.

M: Okay. I'll play tennis _____ _____ _____ instead.

6

M: _____ _____ _____ is looking for new members! We attend every soccer game and cheer for our team. We have song and dance practice at 5 p.m. _____ _____. Are you worried that you don't sing and dance well? No problem! If you are active and love soccer, you'll be welcome. Only 7th and _____ _____ _____ can apply.

7

M: I'm Kevin. There are 25 members in our club. We _____ _____ _____ as a group and we practice together twice a week. My instrument is the violin.

W1: I'm Michele. Our club will _____

_____ _____ _____ next month. I'll play the main role of a baseball player, so I'm practicing hard.

W2: I'm Laura. Our club members will go to Texas _____ _____ next month. This is our 10th trip. Last time, we went to Chicago by plane and _____ _____ _____ and parks.

8

M: Lily, I'm thinking of growing plants _____ _____ _____.

W: Great. How about growing a "lithops" plant?

M: A lithops plant?

W: It's a plant _____ _____ _____ in Southern Africa. It's easy to grow.

M: What does it look like?

W: It looks like a small stone.

M: That's interesting! How can I grow it?

W: Put it where _____ _____. And you just need to water it during spring and fall.

M: How often should I water it then?

W: Every two weeks is enough.

M: Great! _____ _____ _____ _____.

Listening ＊ Challenge Answers p. 3

A [1-2]

W: Thanks for coming, Jay.

M: Wow! You really _____ _____ _____ _____.

W: Thanks. The makeup took over 2 hours.

M: I'm so excited about seeing you act. I never imagined you would join an acting club.

W: _____ _____ _____.

M: But are you okay? You look tired.

W: I stayed up all night studying the script. I'm worried about _____ _____ _____ on stage.

M: Just think of it as a rehearsal.

W: I'm trying, but this is my first performance.

M: Don't worry. You'll do well.

93

W: Thanks. Oh, look at the time! I have to
_____ _____ _____ _____ now.

M: Okay. I'll go take my seat.

B [1-2]

M: Julia, are you still trying to finish that?

W: Wait! I just need to _____ _____
_____ _____.

M: What's the question?

W: 10 down, "It's an extreme sport. Its players
_____ _____ _____ and jump off
buildings."

M: Do you know any of the letters?

W: The word starts with Y and ends with I.

M: Oh, I know.

W: Really? What is it?

M: It's Yamakasi. Yamakasi players also
_____ _____ without ropes.

W: I've never heard of it. How do you spell it?

M: Y-A-M-A-K-A-S-I.

W: _____ _____! How did you know that
word?

M: I saw a TV show about the sport.

Critical ★ Thinking   Answers p. 3

W: Did you watch the show about _____
_____ yesterday?

M: Yes. It's amazing that people go ice
climbing or mountain biking as a hobby.

W: I don't understand why people like
_____ _____ _____.

M: Well, those sports aren't so dangerous if
people train well.

W: But they could still get badly hurt. You're
not thinking about trying extreme sports,
are you?

M: Why not? Extreme sports are _____
_____ _____.

W: Why don't you just play a safe sport?

M: Because extreme sports aren't easy,
doing them will give me _____ _____

_____ _____.

W: Are you serious? You could lose your life!

UNIT 04 Animals

Listening ★ Practice   Answers p. 4

1

M: This animal spends most of its time in
trees and eats leaves. It has a large head
with _____ _____ _____. Its tail is
very short, so you can hardly see it. Its
legs are short too, but they are useful for
_____ _____. Many people think it
looks like a small bear. It carries its babies
_____ _____ _____.

2

M: _____ _____ _____ _____?

W: I'm reading Zoo World. I buy it every
month.

M: Ah, I've seen it before. What animals are
in it this month?

W: There are penguins and many _____
_____ _____ _____.

M: What are the stories about?

W: They're about how fish sleep, and _____
_____ _____ in cold places.

M: Really? How interesting! So, do fish sleep?

W: Yes, they do. But they sleep _____
_____ _____ _____.

3

W: The San Diego Zoo has prepared some
special events for children. On Monday, a
magician will _____ _____ a fantastic
show with animals. Have you ever seen a
pink dolphin? If you want to see _____
_____ _____, visit us on Wednesday.
You can watch them dance to music. Are
you _____ _____ _____? Then
come to the zoo on Saturday. You'll have

a chance to make friends with them.

4

M: You _____ _____. Is something wrong?

W: I had a fight with my mom.

M: What was the problem?

W: My friend's cat just _____ _____. She wanted to give me one, but my mom said no.

M: Why? Does she hate cats?

W: No, she likes them.

M: Then, why?

W: She says that she _____ _____ when a pet dies.

M: Has she had a pet before?

W: Yes. She had a dog for 10 years. But it _____ _____ and died.

M: How sad!

5

M: What a cute puppy! What's her name?

W: Her name is Tinkerbell. She's two years old.

M: What is her biggest problem?

W: She _____ _____ when people visit.

M: I see. Anything else?

W: Yes. She also doesn't eat her food. She only wants _____ _____ _____.

M: Don't worry. We can fix her problems.

W: How long will it take?

M: After a month of training, she'll be better.

W: Okay. Please _____ _____ _____ _____ her.

6

W: Do you like playing with animals? Do you want to _____ _____ and have fun? Here's a fun part-time job. We're looking for a _____ _____ who loves animals. The job is taking care of three dogs, walking and feeding them. You must be older than 18, and have a cellphone. If _____ _____ _____ this job, please send us an email.

7

M: You look so worried. What's wrong?

W: I lost my dog Bo _____ _____ _____ in Central Park.

M: Oh, when did it happen?

W: Two days ago.

M: Wait! I saw a dog running around yesterday. _____ _____ _____?

W: His face is brown, but his body is white.

M: Was he wearing a red ribbon?

W: No, he wasn't wearing a ribbon.

M: Hmm... _____ _____ it wasn't him then.

W: Anyway, please call me if you see him.

M: Don't worry. _____ _____ you'll find him.

8

M: Did you know that crows are _____ _____ _____ in the world? Crows have large brains. They have the highest IQ of any bird. They can _____ _____ to catch insects. Also, crows are sweet birds. After growing up, they take care of their mothers. They bring food to their moms when they are _____ _____ _____ _____.

Listening ⋆ **Challenge**   Answers p. 4

A [1-2]

W: _____ _____ _____ _____?

M: Yes. I want to buy a pet rabbit.

W: Okay. How about this white one?

M: Wow. It's _____ _____.

W: Rabbits are very sensitive animals, so you should be very careful.

M: What should I do?

W: Pet rabbits are _____ _____ wild rabbits, so you should keep them indoors.

M: Anything else?

W: Do not give them corn or nuts. They can _____ _____ _____.

95

M: Okay. I won't.

W: And don't pull their ears. It can hurt them.

M: All right.

W: And don't wash them with water if possible. Just wash their _____ _____ with a wet cloth.

M: Okay.

B [1-2]

M: Do you know how to take an animal _____ _____ _____?

W: Yes, I've done it before.

M: What should I do?

W: First, you should tell the airline about it. You'll have to _____ _____ _____.

M: Can I take her on the plane with me?

W: If she is less than 6 kg, you can put her _____ _____ _____. But she has to be in a cage.

M: Okay. She is only 1 kg.

W: Also, you _____ _____ _____ that says your puppy is healthy.

M: Where can I get one?

W: From any pet clinic.

M: Then I should go get one now. Thank you for your help.

W: _____ _____.

Critical ★ Thinking   Answers p. 4

M: I'm Joe. My dog, Rex, is _____ _____ _____ now. He joined my family when he was one year old. Each season, I buy him new clothes and accessories. Every weekend, I _____ _____ _____ _____ with him. For Christmas, I'm going to buy him a new house. My friend Sally doesn't understand why I _____ _____ _____ _____ on a dog. She says I can help poor people with that money. But he's _____ _____ _____ my family. Is it wrong to spend money on my family?

UNIT 05 Daily Life

Listening ★ Practice   Answers p. 4

1

W: What can I do for you?

M: I'd like to _____ _____ _____ _____ for my passport. How much does it cost?

W: It's $10 for eight pictures.

M: _____ _____ _____ four more pictures?

W: Of course. Then, you should pay $4 more.

M: Okay.

W: Could you please _____ _____ _____ over there?

M: Wait. I want to look in the mirror first.

W: Sure. _____ _____.

2

M: When you wash dishes, use warm water. It helps you clean dirty dishes _____ _____. Also, it's important to wash cleaner dishes first and oily ones last. When you _____ _____ _____, clean off the oil with a paper towel first. And what should you do for dishes with _____ _____ _____ _____? Heat them in the microwave first and then wash them well with warm water.

3

M: What can I do for you?

W: I had my blue shirt dry-cleaned here and _____ _____ _____ yesterday.

M: Is something wrong?

W: Yes. Look at this! When you cleaned it, it _____ _____!

M: Oh, I'm very sorry.

W: Last time, you made my sweater smaller.

And now you've _____ _____ _____.

M: I don't know what to say.

W: I'll never come here again. Next time, the
   shape of my shirt might change.

M: I'm terribly sorry. I'll buy you a new shirt
   _____ _____ _____.

4

(*Telephone rings.*)

M: Happy Bakery. How may I help you?

W: Hello. I want to _____ _____ _____.

M: Okay. What kind of cake do you want?

W: I want a heart-shaped chocolate cake.

M: Sorry, but they're all _____ _____.
   What about a round cake instead?

W: That will be fine.

M: What is your address?

W: 506 Riverside Street.

M: Okay. Also, we can _____ _____
   _____ on the cake. Is this a birthday
   cake?

W: No, it's for _____ _____ _____. He'll
   become a high school student soon.

M: Okay.

5

W: How can I help you?

M: I _____ _____ _____ here, but I
   don't have a cash card. So I'd like to get
   one.

W: If you get a credit card, you can use it
   _____ _____ _____ _____, too.
   What do you think?

M: Well, I just need a cash card.

W: All right. _____ _____ _____
   _____ your ID card?

M: Here it is.

W: Could you please fill out this form?

M: Okay.

W: If you _____ _____ _____ _____,
   I'll go get the card.

6

W: Hi, I want to get my hair cut.

M: Okay. How short?

W: I want really short hair. Please _____
   _____ about 10 cm.

M: All right. Do you also want to _____
   _____ _____?

W: I don't think so.

M: In my opinion, you would look better with
   curly hair.

W: I like my _____ _____, but I want to
   change the color.

M: What color do you want?

W: Brown or blond. Which one would be
   better?

M: Blond would _____ _____ _____
   you.

W: All right.

7

W: I always _____ _____ _____ right
   after I get home from school. That way, I
   can relax afterwards without any worries.
   While I do my homework, my mom
   prepares dinner. Then I help her _____
   _____ _____. I used to watch TV after
   dinner, so my parents called me _____
   _____ _____. But last week I started
   to play badminton with my dad instead.
   It's really _____ _____.

8

W: Can I help you?

M: Yes, please. I want to _____ _____
   _____ to America.

W: What's in it?

M: Just some clothes and _____ _____.

W: Could you put it on here? We need to
   know the weight.

M: All right. Here it is.

W: It's 850 grams. Which would you prefer,
   regular mail or express mail?

M: Is regular mail much cheaper?

W: It's about _____ _____ _____. But it
   takes about six days longer.

M: Then I'll use express mail. How much will it cost?

W: It'll be $100.

A [1-2]

W: Steve, can you go _____ _____ _____ from the market for me?

M: Why me? Can't you ask Jack, instead?

W: Your brother _____ _____ _____ tomorrow. He's too busy.

M: But my favorite drama is on TV right now.

W: I'm sorry, but I need you to do this now. _____ _____ _____, I'll make spaghetti — your favorite.

M: But I don't feel like eating that today.

W: Okay, then I'll buy you a comic book.

M: Thanks, Mom! So, _____ _____ _____ _____?

W: Oranges, strawberries, and melons.

M: Got it.

W: Oh, there are some oranges left _____ _____ _____. Just forget about oranges.

M: Okay.

B [1-2]

(Telephone rings.)

M: Hello, Royal Chinese Restaurant.

W: Hi. I ordered some food _____ _____ _____, and I want to add two egg rolls.

M: Could you tell me your address?

W: My address is _____ _____ _____ _____.

M: And your phone number please?

W: It's 3142–0357.

M: Okay. So you ordered _____ _____ _____ fried rice, one seafood noodle, and two egg rolls, correct?

W: That's right. When can I get my food?

M: In about 30 minutes. It'll take some time

today _____ _____ _____ _____.

W: Okay. Also, I didn't get chopsticks last time. So please don't forget to _____ _____.

M: Don't worry. You'll get them.

M: Do you help your mother do housework?

W: Sure. Our family _____ _____ _____.

M: How do you share it?

W: Well, for example, when mom cooks, I set the table. Then after dinner, dad _____ _____ _____.

M: Really?

W: Yes. I also clean the bathroom and dad sometimes _____ _____.

M: That's surprising. My mom takes care of all the housework.

W: Then your mother _____ _____ _____ _____! Housework is hard to do alone.

M: Is it? I've never thought about it.

W: Your mother will be _____ _____ if you help her.

M: You're right. I'm going to help her from now on.

UNIT 06 Entertainment

(Telephone rings.)

M: Eden Theater. How may I help you?

W: I _____ _____ _____ for tomorrow, but I can't go.

M: Okay. What's your name?

W: Edwards. Betty Edwards.

M: Do you want to _____ _____ _____?

1

W: No. I just want to change the date to next
Saturday.
M: Do you mean _____ _____?
W: Yes. Can the seat still be in the section A?
M: Sorry. Only B section seats are available
then.
W: _____ _____.

2
M: I'm John Wilson from *Weekly Theater*.
_____ _____ _____ _____.
W: Nice to meet you, too.
M: You've just finished the last show. _____
_____ _____ _____?
W: I can't believe that it's over. I was happy to
play the part of Juliet.
M: You _____ _____ Patrick Roberts in
this play. How was that?
W: Patrick is a great actor, so I really enjoyed
it.
M: _____ _____ _____ after this?
W: I'm going to take a break for a while.
M: I see. Well, I hope to see you in another
play soon.

3
M: Do you know what a drawing show is? It
is usually held _____ _____ _____
or a concert hall. When you go to an art
gallery, you can see only _____ _____
_____ of a picture. But at a drawing
show, you can see how a picture is drawn
_____ _____ _____ _____. It
really is like magic.

4
W: How was the play yesterday?
M: I heard it was very funny. But I thought
_____ _____ _____ _____.
W: Really?
M: Yes. But the stage sets were fantastic. It
_____ _____ _____ a real hospital.
W: How were the actors?
M: The actors weren't famous, but they

_____ _____ _____.
W: That's good.
M: But I was angry when some people took
pictures during the show.
W: Oh, I can't believe that! They have
_____ _____.

5
W: Shall we go to see the play *Our Town* this
week?
M: Okay. _____ _____ _____ is it
showing?
W: The Richmond Arts Center. It closes at the
end of this month.
M: Oh, we _____ _____ _____ then.
When do you want to go?
W: How about the 8 p.m. show on the 14th of
May?
M: The 14th is this Friday, right? I already
have plans.
W: Then how about _____ _____? It is
showing at 4 p.m. and 7 p.m.
M: The 4 p.m. show is _____ _____
_____.
W: Okay.

6
(*Telephone rings.*)
W: Thank you for calling Toronto Grand
Theater.
M: Hello. I want to _____ _____ _____
for *Hamlet*.
W: Okay. Which date?
M: May 5th. _____ _____ _____
_____ the 7 p.m. show.
W: I'm sorry. The tickets are sold out.
M: How about May 7th _____ _____
_____ _____?
W: Yes, seats are available then. How many
tickets do you need?
M: I need _____ _____ _____.
W: Okay. May I have your name?
M: My name is Peter Jackson.

W: Okay.

7

W: These days, many teenagers want to be musical actors. But this is not easy, because _____ _____ need many talents. So, what talents are needed? First, it's very important to _____ _____ _____ well. As you know, musicals are mostly singing and dancing. Also, you should know the _____ _____ _____. Musical actors have to work with many people. Lastly, to _____ _____ _____, you should have showmanship.

8

M: _____ _____ _____ _____!

W: Right. I've seen dance shows before, but this one was the best.

M: What did you _____ _____ about it?

W: Well, I liked the male dancers. They were so cool.

M: I agree. The beautiful dances by the ballerina were good, too.

W: That's true. _____ _____ _____ to see both ballet and hip-hop dance on the same stage.

M: But I liked the music best. I think the powerful music _____ _____ _____ _____ in the show.

Listening ★ Challenge Answers p. 5

A [1-2]

W: Have you ever seen the musical *Rent*?

M: No, _____ _____.

W: How about seeing it with me?

M: I'd love to!

W: Then when do you want to go? _____ _____ _____ _____?

M: Isn't it better to see it on Saturday or Sunday?

W: Well... we can only see Daniel Parker _____ _____.

M: Oh, he's your favorite actor, isn't he? Let's see it on Friday, then.

W: Thank you. I'll buy the tickets tomorrow.

M: I heard there is a _____ _____ of the musical. Have you ever seen it?

W: No, but I have the DVD _____ _____. We can go there now and watch it.

M: Great.

B [1-2]

M: On April 2009, a very special orchestra _____ _____ _____ _____ in Carnegie Hall. Its members were selected by video audition. About 4,000 audition tapes from _____ _____ _____ _____ were received. Finally, 90 musicians were chosen to become members of the orchestra. They practiced online together for months. They gathered in New York just three days before the concert, so they had _____ _____ _____ to practice together. Many people expected the performance to be bad. But the concert was _____ _____ _____.

Critical ★ Thinking Answers p. 5

W: Jeremy, what did you do _____ _____?

M: I went to see a musical. Ricky Smith was the main actor.

W: _____ _____ _____ _____ Ricky Smith from the TV series *Vacation*? I didn't know he did musicals.

M: Actually it's _____ _____ _____.

W: I'm sure his performance was very good. How lucky you were to see him close up!

M: Um... it wasn't all that good.

W: _____ _____?

M: Well, so many of his teenage fans were there. They screamed _____ _____ he came on stage.

W: Wasn't it hard to focus on the musical?

M: Yes, it was. Also, the ticket price _____ _____ _____ _____. That's because Ricky gets a lot of money for his performances.

UNIT 07 Health

Listening ∗ Practice   Answers p. 6

1

W: What can I do for you?

M: I have a _____ _____ _____. My name is Ben Smith.

W: Is this your first visit to our hospital?

M: Yes, it is.

W: Could you please answer _____ _____ _____ for your file?

M: Okay.

W: What's your age and blood type?

M: _____ _____, and my blood type is A.

W: Have you ever had a serious disease?

M: No. Never.

W: Do you _____ _____ _____?

M: Yes. I'm allergic to fish.

W: Thank you. Please wait for a second.

2

W: Doctor, what's the result of my tests? _____ _____ _____ with me?

M: You have a problem with your stomach. You need to be tested again.

W: Gee. _____ _____ _____ _____ today?

M: Well, your stomach should be empty when it's taken.

W: I had breakfast. So it can't be taken today?

M: That's right. Please _____ _____ _____ for tomorrow with the nurse.

W: Okay.

M: And don't eat anything before you come.

W: I'll remember.

3

M: Hello, what can I do for you?

W: My eyes are _____ _____. I don't know why.

M: Do they hurt much?

W: A little. They're _____ _____.

M: Then put this in your eyes three times a day.

W: Great. Thank you.

M: Do you _____ _____ _____?

W: Yes, I do. Why?

M: You shouldn't wear them for a while.

W: Okay. I won't. How much is it?

M: It's $4. If it doesn't get better soon, you should _____ _____ _____.

W: Okay, thanks.

4

M: How is your mother? I heard she's _____ _____ _____.

W: Yes. Her leg is getting better, but she has a bad cold.

M: I'm sorry to hear that. Is it bad?

W: Yes. Yesterday, she _____ _____ _____ _____ and coughed a lot.

M: How is she now?

W: She still has a sore throat and isn't _____ _____. She lost some weight.

M: She must be having a hard time.

W: Yes, she is. I hope she _____ _____ _____.

5

W: I can't get enough sleep _____ _____ lately.

M: Why? Are you worried about something?

W: Not really. How can I get a good night's sleep?

M: Drink warm milk before you go to bed.

W: I'm _____ _____ _____.

M: Then how about exercising in the evening? It'll make you tired.

101

W: Okay. I should try that.

M: Also, try not to eat too much before

_____ _____ _____.

W: That'll be difficult, but I'll try that too. Thanks for your advice.

6

M1: I'm Tom. I went snowboarding last winter and _____ _____ _____. So I had to use a wheelchair for a month.

M2: I'm Brad. I had a terrible stomachache _____ _____ _____. So I could only eat corn soup for a week.

M3: I'm Ron. I _____ _____ _____ _____ last month. I had to stay in bed for two days.

7

M: Nancy, you don't look good. What's wrong?

W: I _____ _____ _____ _____. It's killing me.

M: Did you catch a cold?

W: No. It's because of my allergy.

M: _____ _____ _____ _____?

W: I'm allergic to flowers. This happens to me every spring.

M: Oh. Do you have an eye problem, too?

W: Not really. But I _____ _____ _____.

M: I heard that there's no cure for allergies.

W: Right. I just try not to go out often.

M: I feel sorry for you.

8

M: When you _____ _____ _____, don't take it with juice or milk. They can prevent pills from working well. Drink _____ _____ _____ _____ when you take a pill. If you don't drink enough water, pills can hurt your stomach. And there are some pills that you should not take together. When _____ _____ _____, you must ask a doctor about it.

A [1-2]

W: Good afternoon! How can I help you?

M: Doctor, my stomach really hurts.

W: Do you have a fever?

M: No. But I _____ _____ _____. And my hands and feet are really cold.

W: Did you eat anything this morning?

M: Yes. I drank milk and ate some toast. But the milk _____ _____ _____ _____ today.

W: Well, that isn't making you sick. Did you eat them in a hurry?

M: Yes. I was _____ _____ _____. So I ate really fast.

W: I think that made you sick. Don't eat anything today and just _____ _____ _____ _____.

M: Okay. Thank you, doctor.

B [1-2]

W: Have a problem with _____ _____? Come to "Smile Dental Clinic." Our dentists have _____ _____ _____ _____. They'll provide you with the best service. And you don't need to miss work for dental appointments any more. We are open until 9 p.m. _____ _____. Also, if you visit our clinic, we offer you a free checkup every six months. Our clinic is across from the W Department Store. We're waiting for you _____ _____. Please visit us and get the best dental service in town.

W1: Many students are smoking in school. If they _____ _____ early, they are more likely to get serious diseases later. So, schools should do something. What do you think, Mr. Robin?

M: We should _____ _____. If a student

is caught smoking three times, he or she must leave school. They should know that smoking is wrong. Do you _____ _____ _____, Ms. Claire?

W2: Strong punishment is not the answer. We should teach them _____ _____ _____ _____ and that they can die early because of it. If they know the facts, they won't smoke.

UNIT 08 Sports

Listening * Practice Answers p. 6

1

W: Dad, _____ _____ _____ this weekend?

M: No, I'm not. Why?

W: A new sports center with a tennis court opened in Lake City. I want to _____ _____ with you there.

M: Oh, do you know how to play tennis?

W: I'm taking lessons at school these days. It's so much fun.

M: Good. We need to _____ _____ _____ for the court, don't we?

W: Yes, I'll call the center now.

M: Okay. I'll go to _____ _____ _____.

2

W: Dave, what are you watching?

M: _____ _____ _____.

W: The Figure Skating Championships are on TV soon. Let's watch them.

M: Weren't they on yesterday? You _____ _____ _____ last night.

W: Well, it was the short program. In figure skating, skaters must do _____ _____ — a short program and then a free skating program.

M: _____ _____. So will they do the free

skating today?

W: That's right.

M: Then I'll record the baseball game and _____ _____ _____.

W: Great. Thank you.

3

M: I want to _____ _____. Do you have any suggestions?

W: How about in-line skating? It's my favorite sport.

M: What do you like about it?

W: _____ _____ _____, because I do it outside, I get fresh air and sunlight.

M: Okay.

W: Also, there's no need to _____ _____ _____. I mean, I can skate right in front of my house.

M: That's really good.

W: And I can either _____ _____ or together with friends.

M: It sounds perfect. I'll start right away.

4

W: Mike, your scores have been getting worse.

M: You're right, Mrs. Wilson.

W: I don't feel you _____ _____ _____. What's the problem?

M: Well... I'm not sure whether I can become a great golfer.

W: And _____ _____ _____?

M: Well, I was very disappointed with my last game.

W: It's true you didn't do very well last time. But just forget about it and _____ _____.

M: Do you think I can do well?

W: Of course. I can see you _____ _____. I've trained many golfers, you know.

M: Thank you.

5

M: Look, Jerry has just got another strike.

W: Wow. He _____ _____ all ten pins. It's a turkey!

M: A turkey? What do you mean by that?

W: We call three strikes _____ _____ _____ a turkey.

M: That's funny. Anyway, I think Jerry is going to win the game.

W: I agree with that. Tony doesn't seem to be _____ _____.

M: Yes. He knocked down only five pins this time.

6

M: To _____ _____ _____, you must have a comfortable pair of shoes. New shoes can hurt your feet. On the race day, finish your meal at least three hours before the race. And _____ _____ _____ stretch enough just before your race. During a marathon, drink cold water every 15 minutes. If you don't drink enough water, you could have serious _____ _____.

7

W: Now we will do the last yoga position for today. First, look _____ _____.

M: Look straight...

W: Put your left hand forward. And _____ _____ _____ _____ with your right hand.

M: Like this?

W: Good. Then pull it up.

M: Wow, it's hard. _____ _____ should I stay like this?

W: Around 20 to 30 seconds. Then do the same position _____ _____ _____ _____.

M: Okay.

8

W: _____! You were the MVP of today's game.

M: Thank you.

W: But you don't _____ _____. Did you get hurt during the game?

M: No. I'm okay.

W: Then _____ _____ _____?

M: There were only a small number of people in the stadium. I was a bit disappointed.

W: Oh, I see. I guess handball isn't popular.

M: We _____ _____ _____ _____ in the Olympics last year. But nothing changed.

W: Cheer up! Someday people will _____ _____ _____ handball.

M: I hope so.

Listening * **Challenge**   Answers p. 7

A [1-2]

W: Are you interested in _____ _____? Then join the Junior Premier Camp with Chelsea FC in London. In this program, you can _____ _____ _____ from Chelsea Academy coaches. You can also watch and enjoy Premier League games. We even _____ _____ _____ _____ in London. This camp will be held from the 13th to the 30th of January. Any child from 10 to _____ _____ _____ _____ can join. You can sign up online before December 15th. Don't miss this great chance!

B [1-2]

W: Today we're going to _____ _____ _____ _____ a sports hero, Kobe Bryant.

M: Hello. This is Kobe Bryant of the LA Lakers.

W: The LA Lakers became the _____ _____ _____ _____. How do you feel?

M: I feel fantastic!

W: Just before the game ended, your team was losing by one point, 96–95.

M: Right, I thought we would lose the game.

W: But you made a three-point shot _____

_____ _____ _____ _____.

M: Right. Thanks to me, my team won the game 98–96.

W: It was _____ _____! I couldn't believe my eyes.

M: Haha... me neither.

W: You proved that you really are _____

_____ _____ _____.

M: Thank you.

Critical★Thinking Answers p. 7

M1: I'm Jack. Some sports players appear on TV too often. They _____ _____ _____ that they are big movie stars or something. I don't understand why they waste their time. They should focus on improving their skills.

W: I'm Lisa. I heard sports players need _____ _____ _____ _____ for training. By being on TV, they can earn money to pay for their training costs. Then they can do well in their sports.

M2: I'm Chad. Sports players _____ _____ TV shows because many people want to see them. I don't think they're different from movie stars or singers. It is natural for _____ _____ to appear on TV often.

UNIT 09 Travel

Listening ★ Practice Answers p. 7

1

W: Charles, _____ _____ _____ _____ to London this summer.

M: Great!

W: But the hotels are really expensive.

M: How about _____ _____ a youth hostel?

W: Aren't they mostly far from the city center?

M: Perhaps. Then _____ _____ _____ look for a B&B? There are many B&Bs in the city center.

W: What's a B&B?

M: It provides private bedrooms and _____ _____. So, it's called a "Bed and Breakfast," or B&B.

W: Aren't they quite expensive?

M: They're more expensive than a youth hostel, but _____ _____ a hotel.

W: I should search for one, then.

2

M: Hello. I want to know the _____ _____.

W: Our check-out time is 11 o'clock in the morning.

M: 11 a.m.? My flight is at 4 p.m. Is it possible to check out at 1 p.m.?

W: Yes, it's possible. But _____ _____ _____ _____.

M: How much is it?

W: It's $15 per hour.

M: That's expensive. Instead, could you _____ _____ _____ after I check out?

W: Of course. That's free.

M: Then I'll check out at 11 a.m. and leave my backpack _____ _____ _____.

W: Okay.

3

W: How may I help you?

M: I want to know which bus goes to the British Museum.

W: I'm sorry, but there's no direct bus. You need to _____ _____.

M: Well, that won't be easy. This is my first time here.

W: Why don't you _____ _____ _____?

M: The tube? Are you talking about the
   subway?

W: Yes. The nearest station is _____
   _____ _____ _____ on foot.

M: How about a taxi? How much will a taxi
   cost?

W: Taxis are expensive. It will cost _____
   _____ _____.

M: Well... I'll just take the tube.

4

(*Telephone rings.*)

W: Thank you for calling the Hilltop Hotel.

M: Yes. I want to make a reservation _____
   _____ _____ from July 15th.

W: Okay. So you'll be checking out on the
   17th. What type of room do you want?

M: I'd like a twin room. How much is it?

W: _____ _____ for two nights.

M: What? It was $180 last time.

W: That's because July is the busy season.
   Do you still want to make a reservation?

M: _____ _____ _____.

W: Could you please tell me your name?

M: My name is Steve Arnold.

5

M: Excuse me.

W: Yes. What can I do for you?

M: I've been waiting _____ _____
   _____ for my bag, but it hasn't come out.

W: Okay. Could you please tell me your flight
   number?

M: It's GT210.

W: Could you show me your baggage tag?

M: Yes. _____ _____ _____.

W: Wait for a second... oh, our airline made a
   mistake. Your bag was sent to Hong Kong
   airport.

M: What? What should I do, then?

W: I'm terribly sorry about this. I'll _____
   _____ _____ _____ to get your bag.

6

M: DB Airlines is offering an _____ _____
   _____ starting this month. With this
   service, you can choose your seat on the
   DB airlines homepage. Plus, you can use
   a special counter for _____ _____ at
   the airport. This means you can save time
   at the airport. This service is offered from
   48 hours to 3 hours _____ _____
   _____.

7

W: When you travel, packing your bags is
   _____ _____ _____ planning the
   trip. So, how should you pack? First, don't
   pack your bag tightly. Usually, bags become
   heavier with things you buy _____
   _____ _____. And take old clothes.
   That way, you can wear them and then
   throw them away. It will make your bag
   lighter. Also, _____ _____ _____
   _____ to put wet or dirty clothes in.
   That way, you can keep your bag clean.

8

W: Do you want a _____ _____ or an
   aisle seat?

M: Aisle, please. It's a long flight, so a
   window seat wouldn't be comfortable.

W: Okay. There are two aisle seats left.

M: Oh, _____ _____ _____, can I get a
   seat near the front?

W: That seat is right _____ _____
   _____ the screen. Is that okay?

M: Well, I don't want that one. It'll make my
   eyes feel tired.

W: Then, do you want the seat in the back?

M: Yes. _____ _____ _____.

W: Okay. Here's your ticket. Your seat is 24C.

M: Thanks.

Listening ★ Challenge Answers p. 7

A [1-2]

M: Jessica, _____ _____ _____
_____?

W: I'm reading a travel guidebook.

M: Are you still planning your trip?

W: Yes. I haven't decided how to get from Paris to Barcelona.

M: Why don't you _____ _____ _____?

W: Lion Airlines? I've never heard of it.

M: It only flies in Europe. _____ _____ _____ low prices.

W: That's good!

M: But the ticket price goes up as more people _____ _____ _____.

W: So, if I buy a ticket early, it will be cheaper.

M: That's right.

W: Wow! I'll book a ticket _____ _____ _____ now.

M: But there are no extra services like drinks or meals.

W: That doesn't matter. Thanks for the tip.

B [1-2]

W: _____ _____ _____ _____ this summer?

M: I want to go to Turkey.

W: Turkey is a beautiful country. But I visited Turkey and Greece last year.

M: Then where do you want to go?

W: _____ _____ Australia? There are many things we can do there.

M: I've been there, but it wasn't fun.

W: Did you ride a sandboard?

M: No. I just swam and _____ _____.

W: I heard riding a board on the sand is really fun. Also, we can go bungee-jumping.

M: I never want to try bungee-jumping. But riding a sandboard _____ _____.

W: There you go. Let's try it.

M: All right. Maybe I can go to Turkey _____ _____.

Critical ★ Thinking Answers p. 7

W1: I'm May. I always _____ _____ _____. Planning a trip takes time, and it's very stressful. But I don't need to _____ _____ _____ _____ when I take a package tour.

M: I'm Chris. When you travel on a package tour, you travel with the same people the whole time. But travel is about meeting local people and _____ _____ _____ _____.

W2: I'm Tina. I went to France last summer. I planned the tour all by myself, but I wasted time trying to _____ _____. Having a tour guide can save time.

UNIT 10 IT

Listening ★ Practice Answers p. 8

1

M: Hello?

W: Hey, Chris. I can see you now.

M: Wow. It's exciting to see you _____ _____ _____ _____.

W: I agree. You look different today.

M: I changed my glasses. How do I look?

W: You look good. It doesn't feel like you're in Canada.

M: I know. I like _____ _____ _____ _____ while we talk.

W: So do I. And it costs nothing.

M: Why don't we _____ _____ _____ _____ to talk online?

W: Okay. Fridays are good for me.

M: Let's talk every Friday afternoon, then.

2

M: In my free time, I _____ _____ _____ _____ called Aliens. It has so many cute characters in it. It's fun to change

107

their clothes and weapons. _____
_____ _____, the storyline of saving
the earth from aliens is exciting. But my
friend Jenny thinks _____ _____.
For me, the problem with this game is the
sound. The same melody is _____
_____ _____ _____, so I sometimes
turn the volume off.

3

W: I sent you the photos of us _____
_____. Did you get the file?

M: No. When did you send it?

W: I sent it _____ _____ _____.

M: I just checked my mail, but there was no
new mail. Did you send it to the correct
address?

W: Isn't it micky@kkmail.com?

M: That's right. _____ _____.

W: Did you check your spam mailbox?

M: I did, but it wasn't there. Oh, I know
_____ _____.

W: What?

M: I don't have enough storage space in my
mailbox.

4

M: I'm angry that so many people don't
_____ _____.

W: What happened?

M: I was chatting with some guy a couple of
days ago.

W: And?

M: He just left in the middle of chatting.

W: _____ _____ _____?

M: Right. And that wasn't the first time.

W: Really?

M: I was playing an online game with some
girl recently and she said really _____
_____ when she lost.

W: That's not nice.

M: I think people should _____ _____
online.

W: Right. Too many people think they can do
anything online.

5

W: I found something interesting on YouTube
recently. An Italian man was teaching
people _____ _____ _____ Korean
bulgogi. I was surprised to see a foreigner
making it. He also said that he _____
_____ Korean songs. He even said he's
good at taekwondo. Thousands of people
_____ _____ _____. It was ranked
the top video of the week. I was so proud
to be Korean.

6

M: The days of paper books are _____
_____ _____ _____. That's because
of e-books. Now you don't need to carry
heavy books. You can read e-books on
laptops, PMPs, MP3 players, and even
cellphones. You can easily download
e-books _____ _____ _____. They're
cheaper than paper books. And if you
need to know something while reading an
e-book, you can use the search program
to _____ _____ _____ _____ in
the e-book.

7

M: Have you _____ _____ Jennifer
recently?

W: No, I haven't. Why?

M: I called her, but she didn't _____
_____ _____.

W: Really? Maybe she's busy.

M: Well, I also sent her an email, but I didn't
_____ _____ _____.

W: Jennifer doesn't check her email very
often. But I saw she was logged into
messenger today.

M: Really?

W: Yes. She was on around lunchtime. Why
don't you _____ _____ through

M: I guess I should do that.

8

W: Alex, what's _____ _____ _____ _____ you own?

M: It's this.

W: Wow. It has a really nice design.

M: It does. I never _____ _____ _____ it.

W: Do you talk on the phone a lot?

M: Yes. I also watch TV on the subway.

W: Can you surf the Internet with it?

M: Sure. I send emails and _____ _____ with it.

W: Great. Does the camera work well, too?

M: Yes. I don't even need to carry a digital camera when I go out.

W: Wow. I should _____ _____ like that, too.

Listening ★ Challenge Answers p. 8

A [1-2]

M: How may I help you?

W: My cellphone _____ _____ _____. I often can't hear the other person.

M: Anything else?

W: Yes. There's _____ _____ _____ _____ when I'm on the phone.

M: Have you dropped it before?

W: Yes, once.

M: That could be the reason. Can you see the letters _____ _____ _____?

W: Yes. Do you think you can fix it?

M: I think I can.

W: Great. When can I _____ _____ _____?

M: It'll take about two days. Today is Tuesday, so come back on Thursday.

W: But I really need to use my phone every day. Could you fix it _____ _____, please?

M: Okay, I will.

B [1-2]

W: How much time do you spend _____ _____ _____ each day?

M: About an hour. Why?

W: According to a study, Canadians use the Internet the most per month.

M: Really? _____ _____ do they spend on it?

W: They spend around 40 hours on it.

M: Wow. How about the United States?

W: The USA was ranked fourth. _____ _____ _____ and Korea was third.

M: I didn't think that Canada would be first.

W: Me, neither. Do you know _____ _____ has the most visitors?

M: Maybe Google or Yahoo?

W: _____ _____. It was the Microsoft homepage.

M: Really? I've never visited it before, but maybe I should.

109

Critical ★ Thinking Answers p. 8

M1: I'm Mike. I believe that students should not _____ _____. Do they really need to have them? I don't think so. They just _____ _____ _____ in class. It means they can't focus on studying.

W: I'm Judy. I think cellphones are great tools for studying. Many cellphones have dictionaries and can _____ _____ _____ _____. They are useful during class and also for homework.

M2: I'm Alex. These days, students _____ _____ _____ _____ by exchanging text messages. They need cellphones to connect with friends.

UNIT 11 Superstitions

1

M: Did you study a lot for the exam?

W: Not much, so _____ _____.

M: Oh, when did you last wash your hair? It smells.

W: _____ _____ _____.

M: Why?

W: I can't help it. If I wash my hair, I'll _____ _____ _____ _____ _____.

M: What?

W: It's true. I washed my hair before the last exam and got a low grade.

M: I want to change my seat!

W: Come on, it's not _____ _____.

M: Oh, no. The teacher is coming. It's time to sit down.

W: Let's talk again after the exam.

2

W: Murphy's Law means that bad things _____ _____. Today was my Murphy's Law day. I took a taxi because I was late for school. But the taxi driver got lost! I was _____ _____! Then, I got a bad score on a test. Most of the questions were from the only part I didn't study. Plus, _____ _____ _____ _____, I left my cellphone on the bus and I couldn't find it. What a terrible day!

3

W: Steven, I can't _____ _____ _____ _____ I like.

M: But you're a fashion designer. Why don't you make one yourself?

W: I want to. But if the bride _____ _____ _____ _____, the marriage will be unhappy.

M: Do you believe that superstition?

W: Of course.

M: Then how about asking Jane Williams to make it for you?

W: Jane Williams, our _____ _____ _____?

M: Yes. I heard she became a famous wedding dress designer.

W: Really? I didn't know that.

M: Just tell her _____ _____ _____ _____ you want.

W: That's a good idea.

4

W: David, _____ _____ _____ _____. Isn't it pretty?

M: Wow, it is pretty. I like the red stone.

W: Yes, it's a ruby. It's _____ _____.

M: What's a birthstone?

W: _____ _____ has a birthstone. Good things will come to you if you wear your birthstone.

M: I _____ _____ _____ May. Do you know the birthstone of May?

W: It's emerald.

M: You mean the green stone?

W: Yes. Why don't you wear one? You might _____ _____ _____.

M: Really? I should wear one!

5

W: Ted, could you _____ _____ _____ _____?

M: Here. Oops! Sorry.

W: Oh, you spilled it. Spilling salt is bad luck.

M: Oh, no! I _____ _____ _____ _____ today.

W: Don't worry. If you throw some salt over your left shoulder, you will be fine.

M: Then _____ _____ _____ _____ again.

W: Do you want a girlfriend that badly?

M: Of course! I'm tired of going to the movies with my friends.

W: (*laughs*) Here's the salt. _____ _____ on your date!

6

M: When some British people _____ _____ on the first morning of the month, they say "white rabbits" three times. They believe it brings good luck for the month. They also think that _____ _____ in the pocket of new clothes brings good luck. However, British people never _____ _____ _____ inside the house. They think it's bad luck. And when a bird flies into a house, it's a sign that _____ _____ _____.

7

W: What are you doing?
M: I'm _____ _____ to buy a present for my girlfriend.
W: Is it her birthday?
M: No. She's taking an important exam.
W: Why don't you get her a necklace with four-leaf clovers on it?
M: I want to give her _____ _____ _____.
W: How about a ring with a message on it?
M: Well...
W: Oh, _____ _____ _____ _____ with a rabbit foot on it?
M: A rabbit foot?
W: In England, people believe that a rabbit foot _____ _____ _____.
M: Interesting! I think I'll get one.

8

M: I _____ _____ _____ for this year, but it was bad.
W: What did it say?
M: I'm going to get bad grades and _____ _____ _____ my girlfriend.
W: Why do you believe that? You will get good scores if you study hard!
M: I don't know...

W: And if you're nice to your girlfriend, you'll _____ _____.
M: Maybe. But I'm still worried.
W: Look, if something bad happens, it's not _____ _____ your fortune. It's because of you.

Listening ∙ **Challenge**   Answers p. 8

A [1-2]
M: You _____ _____. What's up?
W: I lost my ring. Have you seen a ring around here?
M: I _____ _____ _____ _____ on the desk. Is it a heart-shaped ring?
W: No, it's just a plain silver ring.
M: I guess that one isn't yours, then.
W: Oh, no. It's _____ _____ to me. I must find it.
M: Did your boyfriend give it to you?
W: No. But I need it to _____ _____ _____ _____ tomorrow.
M: How can a ring help you win a hockey game?
W: You might not believe it, but each time I didn't wear it, I lost the game.
M: Well, cheer up. I'll _____ _____ _____ _____.

B [1-2]
W: What do you want to know?
M: I want to know whether I'll _____ _____ _____ this year.
W: All right. When is your birthday?
M: It's December 15th, 1982.
W: Yes, you'll have good luck getting a job _____ _____. You'll soon be hired by a large company.
M: Wow, that's great!
W: Yes. However, you'll _____ _____ _____ with your health.
M: Oh, no! Which part of my body?
W: Your stomach. So _____ _____

_____ what kind of food you eat.

M: Okay. Also, I have a girlfriend. Will I _____ _____ _____ her?

W: Actually, I see you breaking up with her.

M: Oh, no!

Critical ★ Thinking   Answers p. 9

M: How's your practice going?

W: I'm _____ _____ _____ . But I'm worried about having the sophomore jinx.

M: The sophomore jinx? What's that?

W: It's when your first effort is successful, but _____ _____ _____ isn't.

M: For example?

W: When a writer publishes a first book successfully but _____ _____ the second one, that's the sophomore jinx.

M: I see. But your new song is really good. It'll be _____ _____ _____ .

W: Do you really think so?

M: Yes, I do. Cheer up!

W: Okay. If this becomes a big hit, I'll buy you a _____ _____ !

UNIT 12 Lifestyle

Listening ★ Practice   Answers p. 9

1

W: What are you doing this weekend?

M: I'm going to Japan.

W: Really? Are you _____ _____ ?

M: No. I'm going to buy a new video game. It's only sold in Japan.

W: Only for that? But airplane tickets are expensive. Also, you need to find _____ _____ _____ _____ .

M: I'll stay at my friend's house. And many people visit other countries to shop _____ _____ .

W: Really?

M: My friend goes to Hong Kong to buy clothes every year.

W: Oh, _____ _____ .

2

W: A new _____ _____ called "Skin Doctor" has just come into stores. Skin Doctor products are made from natural materials, so they're good for people _____ _____ _____ . When you visit our stores, you can choose the color and fragrance of your cosmetics. And Skin Doctor cares about our environment. If you _____ _____ your empty cosmetic bottles, we'll give you free samples. It's also possible to order products online.

3

W: What are you doing?

M: I'm _____ _____ _____ _____ about my new camera.

W: Do you often write product reviews?

M: I _____ _____ _____ after buying a product.

W: So do I. I like to share information about products with other people.

M: That's right. That helps people buy good products.

W: Do you write reviews _____ _____ _____ ?

M: Yes. But I also believe that product reviews help companies make better products.

W: I agree. They won't want any bad reviews, so they'll _____ _____ _____ good products.

4

W: Jerry, I heard you saved a lot of money. You must be _____ _____ .

M: Not really. You probably earn more than me. But I just try not to _____ _____ .

W: How?

M: Well, I carry a lunch box instead of eating

at restaurants.

W: Oh, really?

M: And I don't drink _____ _____. I usually drink instant coffee.

W: But you sometimes go to expensive restaurants.

M: That's only when I have discount coupons. Then I can enjoy good food for _____ _____.

5

M: _____ _____ _____ _____ do you want to marry?

W: Well, I haven't thought about it. I don't want to _____ _____.

M: Really? Why not?

W: If I get married, I won't be able to _____ _____ because of my new family.

M: But don't you think you'll be lonely?

W: No. I can enjoy various hobbies with many friends.

M: What about kids? Don't you want any?

W: Yes, I do. But my freedom is _____ _____ than having children.

M: That's interesting. But I still want to get married someday.

6

W: These days, some people spend most of their _____ _____ at home. They don't feel any need to go out because they can enjoy various kinds of entertainment at home. _____ _____ like computers and DVD players allow this. These people play games, listen to music, chat and shop online using their computers. They may also _____ _____ _____ on home theater systems. This kind of lifestyle is called "digital cocooning."

7

M: The YBC Channel is _____ _____ _____ _____ for men called *Your Style*. It shows the newest styles of men's clothing and accessories. Also, you can get information about wonderful restaurants for _____ _____. It'll even give you tips for choosing cosmetics according to your skin type. If you want to become a cool, fashionable guy, _____ _____ *Your Style*. This program is on Friday nights at 10 p.m.

8

M: Mom, I have a big problem.

W: _____ _____ _____?

M: Yesterday, I didn't take my cellphone to school, and I couldn't _____ _____ anything.

W: Do you feel nervous when you don't have your cellphone?

M: Yes. I _____ _____ _____ without it.

W: How often do you use it during a day?

M: I think I use my cellphone _____ _____ _____, listening to music, sending text messages, and talking.

W: I didn't know your problem was _____ _____.

Listening ∗ Challenge   Answers p. 9

A [1-2]

W: Jason, are you _____ _____ now?

M: Yes. What's the matter?

W: You're a vegetarian. Don't vegetarians only eat vegetables?

M: Well, actually, there are _____ _____ _____ _____ vegetarians.

W: Really? My sister is a vegetarian, and she only eats vegetables.

M: I'm a _____ _____ _____ _____. I don't eat meat, but I eat seafood.

W: What about eggs or milk?

M: I eat eggs and drink milk.

W: I see. By the way, why did you _____ _____ _____?

M: I became a vegetarian for my health.

W: Did you? My sister became a vegetarian because she _____ _____ so much.

B [1-2]

W: Do you want to try some of my "_____ _____" chocolate?

M: What's that?

W: Well, do you know chocolate is made from cacao?

M: Yes, I do.

W: Many farmers work hard to _____ _____. But they receive a very small amount of money.

M: That's not fair.

W: But this chocolate is made after _____ _____ to the farmers.

M: I see. How did you know that?

W: I read a book about chocolate _____ _____.

M: Please lend me the book later. I want to read it.

W: Okay.

M: And where did you _____ _____ _____? I want to buy some too.

W: The shop is near here. Let's go together.

Critical ★ Thinking   **Answers p. 9**

M1: I'm Ricky. The countryside doesn't have much _____ _____, so it's hard to get around without a car. But in the city, I can go everywhere easily. It's better to live in the city than _____ _____ _____.

W: I'm Mary. In the city, there are many shopping malls and theaters to _____ _____ _____. But these aren't available in the countryside, so life there would be really boring.

M2: I'm Jim. I really love country life because I can live in a _____ _____. I was often sick in the city. But since I moved to the country, I feel much healthier.

JUNIOR
LISTENING EXPERT

A Theme-Based Listening Course for Young EFL Learners

Level 2

Answer Key

JUNIOR
LISTENING EXPERT

A Theme-Based Listening Course for Young EFL Learners

Answer Key

Level **2**

★ ★

UNIT 01 Food

Getting ★ Ready p. 8
A 1 ⓑ 2 ⓓ 3 ⓒ B 1 ⓒ 2 ⓐ 3 ⓑ
C 1 ⓒ 2 ⓐ 3 ⓑ

Listening ★ Start p. 9
1 ③ / wait a while, how about fried rice, what
  would you like, be ready
2 (1) ⓑ (2) ⓓ / popular restaurants, as well
  as, is famous for, My favorite dish

Listening ★ Practice p. 10
1 ② 2 ④ 3 ④ 4 ③ 5 (1) ⓐ (2) ⓓ 6 ③
7 Tuna sandwich, Coke 8 ① → ④ → ③ → ②

Listening ★ Challenge p. 12
A 1 ③ 2 ②, ④ B 1 ② 2 ③

Critical ★ Thinking p. 13
1 ① 2 (1) F (2) T (3) F

Dictation
Listening ★ Practice p. 88
1 homemade chocolates, many different
  nuts, allergic to, this cookie
2 grocery store, sounds difficult, when I
  touch it
3 bake a cake, What kind of cake, find a
  recipe, Let's go to
4 the most popular, slightly yellow, such as
5 except fish, What about you, feel sick,
  Sounds great
6 What's wrong, near the post office, gives
  good service, very tough
7 have a tuna sandwich, come here, look so
  delicious, hurry up
8 Welcome to, put potatoes, in hot water, for
  ten minutes

Listening ★ Challenge p. 89
A Mom's birthday, preparing a delicious
  meal, make curry, Let's put chicken,
  chicken and onions
B Mexican food, so good that, piece of bread

Critical ★ Thinking p. 89
a lot of, later in life, in order to, around us,
how unhealthy

UNIT 02 School Life

Getting ★ Ready p. 14
A 1 ⓖ 2 ⓒ 3 ⓕ 4 ⓗ 5 ⓑ
B 1 ⓐ 2 ⓓ 3 ⓑ

Listening ★ Start p. 15
1 (1) ⓓ (2) ⓒ / Among all my teachers,
  we're in trouble, On the other hand, not
  fashionable at all
2 ③ / exam timetable, at 3 o'clock, when the
  science exam is, On Tuesday

Listening ★ Practice p. 16
1 (1) ⓑ (2) ⓒ (3) ⓐ 2 ④ 3 ② 4 ③ 5 ②
6 ③ 7 ② 8 ①

Listening ★ Challenge p. 18
A 1 ② 2 ③ B 1 ② 2 ②

Critical ★ Thinking p. 19
1 ③ 2 ①, ②

Dictation
Listening ★ Practice p. 90
1 talk on the phone, make a call, saving the
  seat, eat snacks
2 borrow this book, I'm afraid, go home, pay
  a fine

3 talk to me, focus on, doing well with, come over

4 next Thursday, around the world, present their information, final grade

5 what's up, three-page paper, changed my mind, a few days ago

6 During the vacation, July 19th, as usual

7 art class, riding a bicycle, last month, rode a boat, for the homework

8 ask you something, focus on studying, too tight, spend more time

Listening ★ Challenge p. 91

A Where are we going, history museum tour, you'd better bring, provide drinks, taking notes

B study math hard, as well, That's too bad, got a C⁺

Critical ★ Thinking p. 92

go to university, get deeper knowledge, care about, I don't think so

ᵁᴺᴵᵀ**03** Hobbies

Getting ★ Ready p. 20

A 1 ⓒ **2** ⓔ **3** ⓑ **4** ⓓ **5** ⓐ

B 1 ⓔ **2** ⓕ **3** ⓓ

Listening ★ Start p. 21

1 ① / have any plans, take pictures of, Places like, That sounds fun

2 ④ / is going to, painted my face green, blue skirt, with a tie

Listening ★ Practice p. 22

1 ④ **2** ④ **3** ③ **4** ④ **5** (1) T (2) F (3) T

6 ③ **7** (1) ⓐ (2) ⓓ (3) ⓕ **8** ④

Listening ★ Challenge p. 24

A 1 ③ **2** ④ **B 1** ④ **2** ②

Critical ★ Thinking p. 25

1 ①, ④ **2** ①

Dictation

Listening ★ Practice p. 92

1 How often, It depends, wear dance shoes

2 look for information, much money, in my free time

3 I'm thinking about, it won't be, Why not, join a club

4 make teddy bears, Valentine's Day gift, collects dolls, I'd like to make

5 played tennis, it didn't work, avoid sunburn, in the mornings

6 The cheering club, every Thursday, 8th grade students

7 play classical music, put on a play, by bicycle, visited famous museums

8 as a hobby, from dry areas, there's sunlight, Thanks for your advice

Listening ★ Challenge p. 93

A look like a princess, Neither did I, making a mistake, change into my costume

B get this last word, run up walls, climb buildings, It fits

Critical ★ Thinking p. 94

extreme sports, such dangerous sports, full of thrills, a feeling of success

ᵁᴺᴵᵀ**04** Animals

Getting ★ Ready p. 26

A 1 ⓓ **2** ⓑ **3** ⓔ **4** ⓐ **5** ⓒ

B 1 ⓓ **2** ⓐ **3** ⓕ

★　★

Listening ★ Start p. 27
1 ② / Look at, light brown color, raising a pig, call it Piggy, how cute he is
2 ③ / has a runny nose, dry her well, some medicine

Listening ★ Practice p. 28
1 ③　2 ②　3 (1) Wednesday　(2) Saturday (3) Monday　4 ④　5 ②　6 ④　7 ①　8 (1) T (2) T　(3) F

Listening ★ Challenge p. 30
A 1 ④　2 ④　B 1 ②　2 ③

Critical ★ Thinking p. 31
1 ①　2 (1) ⓒ　(2) ⓑ

Dictation
Listening ★ Practice p. 94
1 two rounded ears, climbing trees, on its back
2 What are you doing, different kinds of fish, how penguins live, with their eyes open
3 put on, these amazing animals, scared of snakes
4 look depressed, had babies, feels terrible, got sick
5 barks loudly, what I eat, take good care of
6 earn money, friendly person, you're interested in
7 while walking him, Is he brown, I guess, I'm sure
8 the smartest birds, use tools, too old to hunt

Listening ★ Challenge p. 95
A May I help you, so cute, different from, make them sick, dirty parts
B on a plane, pay extra money, under your seat, need a document, No problem

Critical ★ Thinking p. 96
three years old, go to dog cafés, spend so much money, a member of

UNIT 05 Daily Life

Getting ★ Ready p. 32
A 1 dry-clean　2 microwave　3 refrigerator 4 passport
B 1 ⓐ　2 ⓓ　3 ⓕ

Listening ★ Start p. 33
1 ③ / Who is it, How much is it, Didn't you order, don't worry
2 ②, ④ / plant some flowers, Except for, What kind of, you're right, look fantastic

Listening ★ Practice p. 34
1 ④　2 ②　3 ③　4 ①　5 ②　6 ④　7 ④　8 ③

Listening ★ Challenge p. 36
A 1 ④　2 ③, ④　B 1 ①　2 ③

Critical ★ Thinking p. 37
1 ①　2 ②, ④

Dictation
Listening ★ Practice p. 96
1 have my photo taken, Can I order, take a seat, Go ahead
2 more quickly, wash frying pans, a bad fish smell
3 picked it up, turned purple, made another mistake, if you want
4 order a cake, sold out, write a message, my son's graduation
5 have an account, as a cash card, Could you show me, wait for a second
6 cut off, get a perm, straight hair, look better on

7 do my homework, set the table, a couch potato, good exercise

8 send this package, several books, half the price

Listening ★ Challenge p. 98

A get some fruit, has a test, If you go, what do you need, in the refrigerator

B five minutes ago, 135 New York Street, two boxes of, because of the rain, bring chopsticks

Critical ★ Thinking p. 98

shares the work, washes the dishes, prepares lunch, must have hard time, very pleased

UNIT 06 Entertainment

Getting ★ Ready p. 38

A 1 ⓑ 2 ⓓ 3 ⓖ 4 ⓐ 5 ⓕ

B 1 ⓕ 2 ⓒ 3 ⓔ

Listening ★ Start p. 39

1 ③ / going to a musical, can't forget, heard a lot, sounds more interesting

2 ④ / so excited, seem satisfied, played the part, my favorite

Listening ★ Practice p. 40

1 ③ **2** ③ **3** ② **4** (1) Bad (2) Good (3) Good (4) Bad **5** ③ **6** ② **7** ③ **8** ④

Listening ★ Challenge p. 42

A 1 ② 2 ② **B** 1 ① 2 (1) T (2) F (3) T

Critical ★ Thinking p. 43

1 ③ **2** ③, ④

Dictation

Listening ★ Practice p. 98

1 bought a ticket, cancel the reservation, July 23rd, That's okay

2 Nice to meet you, How do you feel, acted with, What's your plan

3 in a theater, the end result, from beginning to end

4 the story was boring, looked just like, acted really well, no manners

5 At which theater, have to hurry, this Saturday, better for me

6 make a reservation, I'd like to see, at the same time, two adult tickets

7 musical actors, sing and dance, importance of teamwork, make people laugh

8 What an interesting show, like most, It was exciting, played a big role

Listening ★ Challenge p. 100

A not yet, How about this Friday, on Fridays, movie version, at home

B gave its first performance, all over the world, only two days, a big success

Critical ★ Thinking p. 100

last weekend, Are you talking about, his first musical, Why not, every time, went up a lot

UNIT 07 Health

Getting ★ Ready p. 44

A 1 ⓑ 2 ⓓ 3 ⓔ 4 ⓒ

B 1 ⓑ 2 ⓒ 3 ⓔ

Listening ★ Start p. 45

1 ③ / make an appointment, come in, make it, see you then

2 ①, ② / What's the matter, can't sleep,

What's wrong with him, some cough syrup

Listening ★ Practice p. 46
1 ② **2** ④ **3** ② **4** ② **5** ②, ④ **6** (1) ⓑ (2) ⓒ
(3) ⓐ **7** ② **8** ①

Listening ★ Challenge p. 48
A 1 ② **2** ④ **B 1** ③ **2** (1) T (2) T (3) F

Critical ★ Thinking p. 49
1 ③ **2** (1) ⓐ (2) ⓒ

Listening ★ Practice p. 101

1 3 o'clock appointment, a few questions, I'm 27, have any allergies

2 Is something wrong, Can it be done, make an appointment

3 really dry, getting red, wear contact lenses, see your doctor

4 in the hospital, had a sore throat, eating much, gets better soon

5 at night, allergic to milk, going to bed

6 broke my leg, because of stress, had a bad cold

7 have a runny nose, What kind of allergy, cough a lot

8 take a pill, a cup of water, you're not sure

Listening ★ Challenge p. 102

A have a headache, tasted a little different, late for school, drink some warm water

B your teeth, a lot of experience, on weekdays, with smiles

Critical ★ Thinking p. 102

start smoking, punish students, agree with me, how bad smoking is

UNIT 08 Sports

Getting ★ Ready p. 50
A 1 ⓐ **2** ⓒ **3** ⓔ **4** ⓑ **5** ⓓ
B 1 ⓑ **2** ⓒ **3** ⓕ

Listening ★ Start p. 51
1 ② / watch a baseball game, so close up, wasn't bored

2 ③ / sports day, play basketball, I've packed it, wear my cap

Listening ★ Practice p. 52
1 ④ **2** ③ **3** ② **4** ① **5** ③ **6** ① **7** ③ **8** ④

Listening ★ Challenge p. 54
A 1 ① **2** ② **B 1** ③ **2** ②

Critical ★ Thinking p. 55
1 (1) Against (2) For (3) For
2 (1) ⓑ (2) ⓒ (3) ⓐ

Listening ★ Practice p. 103

1 are you busy, play tennis, make a reservation, find my racket

2 A baseball game, watched figure skating, two programs, I see, watch it later

3 start exercising, First of all, go far away, skate alone

4 practice hard enough, why is that, keep practicing, have talent

5 knocked down, in a row, playing well

6 run a marathon, be sure to, health problems

7 straight ahead, hold your right ankle, How long, on the opposite side

8 Congratulations, look happy, what's the matter, won the gold medal, be interested in

Listening ★ Challenge p. 104
A playing football, learn football skills, offer home stay services, 13 years of age
B have an interview with, champions of the NBA, at the very last minute, really amazing, the best basketball player

Critical ★ Thinking p. 105
seem to think, a lot of money, appear on, popular players

UNIT 09 Travel

Getting ★ Ready p. 56
A 1 ⓒ 2 ⓓ 3 ⓐ 4 ⓔ 5 ⓖ
B 1 ⓒ 2 ⓑ 3 ⓔ

Listening ★ Start p. 57
1 ④ / made a flight reservation, Which date, all booked, I'll take that one
2 ④ / travel by plane, lots of water, keep you awake, walk around the aisles

Listening ★ Practice p. 58
1 ② 2 ① 3 ③ 4 ④ 5 ④ 6 (1) F (2) T (3) F 7 ③ 8 ④

Listening ★ Challenge p. 60
A 1 ② 2 ① B 1 ④ 2 ③

Critical ★ Thinking p. 61
1 (1) For (2) Against (3) For
2 (1) ⓑ (2) ⓓ (3) ⓒ

Dictation

Listening ★ Practice p. 105
1 I'm going to travel, staying at, why don't you, offers breakfast, cheaper than
2 check-out time, there's an extra charge,

keep my backpack, at the front desk
3 change buses, try the tube, only five minutes away, about 15 pounds
4 for two nights, It's $200, I guess so
5 a long time, Here it is, contact Hong Kong airport
6 online check-in service, service users, before the flight
7 as important as, during the trip, take some plastic bags
8 window seat, in that case, in front of, It'll be better

Listening ★ Challenge p. 107
A what are you doing, take Lion Airlines, It's famous for, book the flight, on the website
B Where should we travel, How about, went biking, sounds fun, next year

Critical ★ Thinking p. 107
take package tours, worry about a thing, learning about new cultures, find places

UNIT 10 IT

Getting ★ Ready p. 62
A 1 ⓑ 2 ⓐ 3 ⓒ B 1 ⓒ 2 ⓐ 3 ⓓ
C 1 ⓒ 2 ⓑ 3 ⓐ

Listening ★ Start p. 63
1 ① / surfing the Internet, What's wrong, shut down, didn't save it, right away
2 ③ / bought this for me, download English files, record classes

Listening ★ Practice p. 64
1 ① 2 (1) Good (2) Good (3) Bad 3 ④
4 ① 5 ① 6 ③ 7 ④ 8 ④

Listening ★ Challenge p. 66

A 1 ①, ③ 2 ③   B 1 (1) ⓑ (2) ⓓ (3) ⓐ 2 ③

Critical ★ Thinking p. 67

1 (1) Against (2) For (3) For

2 (1) ⓒ (2) ⓑ (3) ⓓ

Dictation

Listening ★ Practice p. 107

1 on a computer screen, looking at your face, set a regular time

2 play a computer game, Best of all, it's boring, repeated over and over

3 by email, around 1 p.m., How strange, what happened

4 follow netiquette, Without saying goodbye, bad words, behave well

5 how to cook, loves singing, watched this video

6 coming to an end, from online bookstores, look for more information

7 talked to, answer the phone, get any reply, contact her

8 the most valuable thing, get bored with, chat online, get one

Listening ★ Challenge p. 109

A doesn't work well, a lot of noise, on the screen, pick it up, by tomorrow

B on the Internet, How long, Israel was second, which website, You're wrong

Critical ★ Thinking p. 109

carry cellphones, exchange text messages, connect to the Internet, communicate with each other

UNIT 11 Superstitions

Getting ★ Ready p. 68

A 1 ⓑ 2 ⓓ 3 ⓒ 4 ⓐ 5 ⓔ

B 1 ⓑ 2 ⓔ 3 ⓐ

Listening ★ Start p. 69

1 ② / as a lucky color, decorate the wedding hall, wrapped in red, wear red uniforms

2 ③ / a black cat, find a penny, see a spider, an unlucky sign

Listening ★ Practice p. 70

1 ③ 2 ① 3 ④ 4 ③ 5 ③ 6 ② 7 ④ 8 ②

Listening ★ Challenge p. 72

A 1 ① 2 ②   B 1 ④ 2 (1) T (2) T (3) F

Critical ★ Thinking p. 73

1 ④ 2 ②

Dictation

Listening ★ Practice p. 110

1 I'm nervous, Four days ago, do badly on my exam, that bad

2 keep happening, so late, on my way home

3 find a wedding dress, makes her own dress, high school classmate, what kind of dress

4 look at this necklace, my birthstone, Each month, was born in, find a girlfriend

5 pass me the salt, have a blind date, give me the salt, Good luck

6 wake up, putting money, open an umbrella, someone will die

7 shopping online, something more special, how about a keychain, brings good luck

8 read my fortune, break up with, stay together, because of

Listening ★ Challenge p. 111

A look worried, saw a gold ring, very

important, win the hockey game, help you find it

B get a job, this year, have some problems, be careful about, get married to

Critical ★ Thinking p. 112

trying my best, your second effort, fails with, a big hit, wonderful dinner

UNIT 12 Lifestyle

Getting ★ Ready p. 74
A 1 ⓓ 2 ⓒ 3 ⓑ 4 ⓔ 5 ⓐ
B 1 ⓐ 2 ⓑ 3 ⓕ

Listening ★ Start p. 75
1 ①, ④ / with two jobs, Her main job, a lot of money, saving enough money
2 ④ / work part-time, rather than, Why not, work hard, care about

Listening ★ Practice p. 76
1 ① 2 ② 3 ③ 4 ② 5 ③ 6 ④ 7 ② 8 ③

Listening ★ Challenge p. 78
A 1 ⓐ, ⓑ, ⓓ, ⓔ 2 ② B 1 ④ 2 ③

Critical ★ Thinking p. 79
1 (1) City (2) City (3) Countryside
2 (1) ⓑ (2) ⓐ (3) ⓒ

Dictation
Listening ★ Practice p. 112
1 going sightseeing, a place to stay, these days, that's surprising
2 cosmetic brand, with sensitive skin, bring back
3 writing a product review, always write them, for that reason, try to make

4 well paid, spend money, expensive coffee, less money
5 What kind of man, get married, live freely, more important
6 free time, Digital devices, watch various movies
7 introducing a new program, romantic dates, don't miss
8 What is it, focus on, can't do anything, all day long, so serious

Listening ★ Challenge p. 113
A eating seafood, a few types of, different kind of vegetarian, stop eating meat, loves animals
B fair trade, produce cacao, paying enough money, for homework, buy this chocolate

Critical ★ Thinking p. 114
public transportation, in the countryside, visit any time, clean environment

9

UNIT 01 Food

Getting ★ Ready p. 8

A 1 ⓑ 2 ⓓ 3 ⓒ B 1 ⓒ 2 ⓐ 3 ⓑ
C 1 ⓒ 2 ⓐ 3 ⓑ

C 1 여: 네 저녁 여기 있어. 어떠니?
　　남: <u>맛있어 보여요.</u>
　2 여: <u>무엇을 먹고 싶으세요?</u>
　　남: 햄 샌드위치로 할게요.
　3 여: '파이타(fajita)'를 먹어 본 적 있어요?
　　남: <u>아뇨, 처음 먹는 거예요.</u>

Listening ★ Start p. 9

1 ③ / wait a while, how about fried rice,
what would you like, be ready
2 (1) ⓑ (2) ⓓ / popular restaurants, as well
as, is famous for, My favorite dish

1

M: Mom, I'm hungry.
W: I'm sorry. I haven't started dinner yet.
　　You'll have to wait a while.
M: Okay. What are you going to cook?
W: Hmm... how about fried rice and
　　vegetable soup?
M: Again? We had fried rice yesterday.
W: Then, what would you like to have for
　　dinner?
M: I'd like to have chicken and potatoes.
W: Okay. It will be ready soon.
M: Thank you, Mom.

남: 엄마, 배고파요.
여: 미안. 아직 저녁 준비를 시작하지 않았어. 잠시 기다려야
　　한단다.
남: 알겠어요. 뭘 요리하실 거예요?
여: 흠… 볶음밥과 야채 수프는 어때?
남: 또요? 어제 볶음밥 먹었잖아요.
여: 그럼, 저녁으로 뭘 먹고 싶어?
남: 치킨과 감자를 먹고 싶어요.
여: 알았어. 금방 될 거야.
남: 고마워요, 엄마.

어휘

yet[jet] 윗 아직 while[hwail] 명 잠시 cook[kuk]
동 요리하다 fried[fraid] 형 튀긴; *볶은 rice[rais] 명
밥 vegetable[védʒitəbl] 명 채소 would like to-v
~하고 싶다 potato[pətéitou] 명 감자 ready[rédi]
형 준비가 된 soon[suːn] 윗 곧, 금방

문제 해설

Q: 그들은 저녁으로 무엇을 먹을 것인가?
　　소년이 원하는 대로 치킨과 감자를 먹을 것이다.

2

M: In my town, there are two popular
restaurants, Real India and Hello China.
Real India has many kinds of curry on the
menu, as well as Tandoori chicken. I like
beef curry the most. It is very spicy and a
little bit sweet. Hello China is famous for
its fried pork. It is quite oily, but the sweet
and sour sauce on it is really delicious.
My favorite dish there is fried noodles.

남: 저희 동네에는 Real India와 Hello China라는 두 개의
인기 있는 음식점이 있어요. Real India에는 탄두리 치
킨뿐만 아니라 여러 종류의 카레 메뉴가 있어요. 저는 쇠
고기 카레를 가장 좋아해요. 그건 아주 맵고 약간 달콤
하죠. Hello China는 튀긴 돼지고기로 유명해요. 상당히
기름지지만 새콤달콤한 소스가 아주 맛있어요. 그곳에서
제가 제일 좋아하는 요리는 볶음면이에요.

어휘

popular[pápjulər] 형 인기 있는 curry[kə́ːri] 명 카레
beef[biːf] 명 쇠고기 spicy[spáisi] 형 매운, 향이 강한
a little bit 조금 be famous for ~으로 유명하다
pork[pɔːrk] 명 돼지고기 oily[ɔ́ili] 형 기름진 sour
[sauər] 형 신 sauce[sɔːs] 명 소스 delicious[dilíʃəs]
형 맛있는 dish[diʃ] 명 음식, 요리 noodle[núːdl] 명
면, 국수

문제 해설

Q: 각 음식점에서 남자가 가장 좋아하는 음식은?
　　Real Inida에서는 쇠고기 카레가, Hello China에서는 볶
음면이 가장 좋다고 했다.

Listening ★ Practice p. 10

1 ② 2 ④ 3 ④ 4 ③ 5 (1) ⓐ (2) ⓓ 6 ③
7 Tuna sandwich, Coke 8 ① → ④ → ③ → ②

10

1

M: Hey, Amy. What are those?

W: These are homemade chocolates and cookies. I made them.

M: They look delicious. May I try one?

W: Sure. Try this special chocolate. I put many different nuts in it.

M: Did you say that you put nuts in it?

W: Yes. What's the problem?

M: I'm allergic to nuts. If I eat them, I get very sick.

W: Really? Then, try this cookie. It doesn't have any nuts in it.

M: Okay, thanks.

남: 이봐, Amy. 그것들이 뭐야?

여: 집에서 만든 초콜릿과 쿠키야. 내가 만들었어.

남: 맛있어 보여. 하나 먹어 봐도 돼?

여: 물론이지. 이 특별한 초콜릿을 먹어 봐. 여러 견과류를 넣었어.

남: 여기에 견과류를 넣었다고 했니?

여: 응. 무슨 문제가 있어?

남: 난 견과류에 알레르기가 있어. 먹으면 심하게 병이 나거든.

여: 정말? 그렇다면 이 쿠키를 먹어 봐. 거긴 견과류가 안 들어 있어.

남: 알았어. 고마워.

어휘

homemade[hóumméid] 형 가정에서 만든 chocolate[tʃɔ́ːkəlit] 명 초콜릿 try[trai] 동 시도하다; *먹어 보다 special[spéʃəl] 형 특별한 nut[nʌt] 명 견과류 be allergic to ~에 알레르기가 있다 get sick 병이 나다 [문제] be on a diet 다이어트를 하고 있다

문제 해설

Q: 남자가 초콜릿을 먹지 않은 이유는?

① 다이어트 중이어서

② 견과류를 먹으면 안 되어서

③ 초콜릿을 좋아하지 않아서

④ 좀 전에 초콜릿을 너무 많이 먹어서

초콜릿 안에 남자가 알레르기 반응을 보이는 견과류가 들어 있어서 먹지 않았다.

2

W: Justin, could you go to the grocery store and buy some mangoes?

M: Sure, Mom. How many?

W: Five is enough. And choose fresh ones.

M: Oh, that sounds difficult. How will I know which ones are fresh?

W: The easiest way is to check the color. The color should be yellow or orange.

M: I see. And should it be soft when I touch it?

W: No. Hard ones are better. And fresh ones smell sweet.

M: Okay.

여: Justin, 망고 좀 사러 식료품점에 좀 다녀올 수 있겠니?

남: 물론이죠, 엄마. 몇 개나요?

여: 다섯 개면 충분해. 그리고 신선한 걸로 골라.

남: 아, 어려울 것 같은데요. 어느 것이 신선한지 어떻게 알 수 있죠?

여: 가장 쉬운 방법은 색깔을 보는 거야. 노란색이거나 오렌지색이어야 해.

남: 알았어요. 만졌을 때 부드러워야 해요?

여: 아니. 딱딱한 것이 더 좋아. 그리고 신선한 것은 향이 달콤해.

남: 알았어요.

어휘

grocery store 식료품점 mango[mǽŋgou] 명 망고 enough[inʌ́f] 형 충분한 choose[tʃuːz] 동 고르다 (choose-chose-chosen) fresh[freʃ] 형 신선한 sound[saund] 동 생각되다, ~인 것 같다 soft[sɔ(ː)ft] 형 부드러운 hard[haːrd] 형 딱딱한 smell[smel] 동 ~한 냄새가 나다

문제 해설

Q: 틀린 정보를 고르시오.

신선한 망고는 만졌을 때 딱딱한 것이라고 했다.

3

W: Thomas, you know how to make a cake, don't you?

M: Yes, I do.

W: Then could you help me bake a cake?

M: No problem. Is there any special reason?

W: Today is my brother's birthday.

M: Oh, I see. What kind of cake do you want to make for him?

W: Well, he likes carrot cake.

M: Okay. Did you find a recipe?

W: Not yet.

11

M: How about finding a recipe on the Internet first? Let's go to a supermarket after that.
W: Okay!

여: Thomas, 케이크 만드는 법 알지, 그렇지?
남: 응, 알아.
여: 그럼 케이크 굽는 것 좀 도와 줄래?
남: 좋아. 특별한 이유라도 있어?
여: 오늘이 남동생 생일이야.
남: 아, 그렇구나. 어떤 종류의 케이크를 만들어 주고 싶어?
여: 음, 그 앤 당근 케이크를 좋아해.
남: 좋아. 요리법은 찾았어?
여: 아직.
남: 우선 인터넷에서 요리법을 찾아보는 게 어때? 그런 다음에 슈퍼마켓에 가자.
여: 좋아!

어휘
bake[beik] 통 굽다   reason[ríːzən] 명 이유   carrot [kǽrət] 명 당근   recipe[résəpìː] 명 요리법   Not yet. 아직 아니야.   [문제] information[ìnfərméiʃən] 명 정보

문제 해설
Q: 그들이 다음에 할 일은?
인터넷에서 요리법을 찾고 나서 장을 보러 가자고 했으므로, 먼저 인터넷을 검색할 것이다.

12

4

W: This is one of the most popular Japanese dishes. It is a kind of noodle soup. The noodles are thin and slightly yellow. The taste of the soup is different from region to region. It's usually made with chicken or pork. Also, there are many kinds of toppings, such as a boiled egg or green onions.

여: 이것은 가장 인기 있는 일본 요리 중의 하나입니다. 국물이 있는 면 종류인데요. 면은 가늘고 약간 노란색입니다. 국물의 맛은 지역마다 다릅니다. 주로 닭고기나 돼지고기로 만들어집니다. 또한, 삶은 달걀이나 파와 같은 여러 종류의 토핑이 있습니다.

어휘
soup[suːp] 명 수프   thin[θin] 형 *가는; 얇은 slightly[sláitli] 부 약간   taste[teist] 명 맛   region [ríːdʒən] 명 지역   topping[tápiŋ] 명 토핑, 요리 위에 얹는 것   boiled[bɔild] 형 삶은   green onion 파

문제 해설
Q: 여자가 이야기하고 있는 음식을 고르시오.
국물이 있는 면에 여러 가지의 토핑을 얹은 음식은 라면이다.

5

M: Janice, what would you like to eat for lunch?
W: Anything is okay, except fish.
M: You don't like fish? Why not?
W: It has such a bad smell. I really don't like it.
M: Oh, I see.
W: What about you, Alex? Is there anything you don't like?
M: Well, I don't like fried chicken. I usually feel sick after eating it.
W: Then, shall we eat pizza? I know a good place.
M: Sounds great.

남: Janice, 점심으로 뭐 먹고 싶어?
여: 뭐든 좋아, 생선만 빼면.
남: 생선을 싫어해? 왜?
여: 너무 안 좋은 냄새가 나잖아. 그게 너무 싫어.
남: 아, 그렇구나.
여: 넌 어때, Alex? 싫어하는 게 있어?
남: 음, 난 프라이드 치킨을 좋아하지 않아. 먹고 나면 보통 아프거든.
여: 그렇다면 피자를 먹을까? 좋은 곳을 알아.
남: 그거 좋겠다.

어휘
except[iksépt] 전 ~을 빼고   [문제] taste[teist] 동 *~한 맛이 나다; 맛보다   salty[sɔ́ːlti] 형 짠   raw[rɔː] 형 날 것인

문제 해설
Q: 각 인물이 특정한 음식을 싫어하는 이유로 맞는 것을 고르시오.
(1) Janice는 생선이 냄새가 좋지 않아서 싫어한다.
(2) Alex는 프라이드 치킨을 먹으면 병이 나서 싫어한다.

6

M: What's wrong? You look angry.
W: Do you know the new Chinese restaurant downtown?

M: You mean the restaurant near the post office?

W: Yes. I went there to have lunch today.

M: Was there a problem? I heard that restaurant gives good service.

W: That's true. They were very kind. But the food was so disappointing!

M: What was wrong with it?

W: The meat was very tough and the vegetables were not fresh at all.

M: Oh, I'm sorry to hear that. Well, I won't go there.

남: 무슨 일 있어? 화가 난 것 같은데.

여: 시내에 새로 생긴 중국 음식점 알아?

남: 우체국 근처에 있는 음식점 말하는 거야?

여: 응. 오늘 거기에 점심을 먹으러 갔었어.

남: 문제가 있었어? 그 음식점이 서비스가 좋다고 들었는데.

여: 그건 사실이야. 아주 친절했어. 하지만 음식은 너무나 실망스러웠어!

남: 음식이 어떻게 실망스러웠는데?

여: 고기는 아주 질기고 야채는 전혀 신선하지 않았어.

남: 아, 그거 유감이네. 음, 난 거기 가지 말아야겠다.

어휘

downtown[dáuntáun] 분 시내에   post office 우체국
disappointing[dìsəpɔ́intiŋ] 형 실망스러운   meat[miːt]
명 고기   tough[tʌf] 형 질긴   [문제] crowded
[kráudid] 형 붐비는   terrible[térəbl] 형 끔찍한
expensive[ikspénsiv] 형 비싼

문제 해설

Q: 여자가 음식점에 대해 화가 난 이유는?
   음식이 형편없었다고 했다.

7

W: Brad, are you going to have a tuna sandwich?

M: Um, I haven't decided yet.

W: What? You wanted to come here to have a tuna sandwich.

M: Yes, I did. But the cheeseburgers look so delicious. How about you?

W: I'm going to have a ham sandwich and corn salad.

M: Oh, my god. That sounds great, too!

W: Please hurry up and order. Don't forget

that we have only 30 minutes for lunch.

M: Okay. I'll have a tuna sandwich and a Coke.

W: Good.

여: Brad, 참치 샌드위치 먹을 거야?

남: 음. 아직 결정하지 못했어.

여: 뭐라고? 너 참치 샌드위치 먹으려고 여기 오고 싶어 했잖아.

남: 응, 그랬지. 그런데 치즈버거가 아주 맛있어 보여서. 넌 어때?

여: 난 햄 샌드위치와 콘 샐러드 먹을 거야.

남: 아, 이런. 그것도 좋겠다!

여: 제발 서둘러 주문해. 점심 먹을 시간이 30분밖에 없다는 걸 잊지 마.

남: 알았어. 참치 샌드위치와 콜라 먹을래.

여: 그래.

어휘

tuna[tjúːnə] 명 참치   decide[disáid] 동 결정하다
corn[kɔːrn] 명 옥수수   hurry up 서두르다   order
[ɔ́ːrdər] 동 주문하다   forget[fərgét] 동 잊다 (forget-
forgot-forgotten)   [문제] potato chips 감자 튀김
iced tea 아이스티

문제 해설

Q: 남자가 주문할 메뉴 항목에 √표 하시오.
   남자는 참치 샌드위치와 콜라를 골랐다.

8

M: Welcome to *Jamie's Cooking Show*. Today, I'll show you how to make an oven-baked pasta dish. Firstly, put potatoes and bacon in a frying pan and fry them. Secondly, boil some pasta in hot water. Next, put the pasta into the frying pan and add some milk or cream. Finally, put all of it into an oven dish and cover the top with cheese. Then cook it in the oven for ten minutes.

남: 'Jamie의 요리 쇼'에 오신 것을 환영합니다. 오늘은 오븐에 구운 파스타 요리를 만드는 법을 보여 드리도록 할게요. 우선, 감자와 베이컨을 프라이팬에 넣고 볶으세요. 두 번째로, 뜨거운 물에 파스타를 삶으세요. 그 다음엔, 파스타를 프라이팬에 넣고 우유나 크림을 좀 넣으세요. 마지막으로 오븐 그릇에 모두를 담고 위를 치즈로 덮으세요. 그리고 오븐에서 10분 동안 구워주세요.

13

어휘

pasta[pάːstə] 몡 파스타   bacon[béikən] 몡 베이컨
frying pan 프라이팬   fry[frai] 툉 튀기다; *기름에 볶다
boil[bɔil] 툉 끓이다; *삶다   add[æd] 툉 더하다
cover[kʌ́vər] 툉 덮다   top[tɑp] 몡 윗면

문제 해설

Q: 사진을 알맞은 순서대로 정렬하시오.

　처음엔 감자와 베이컨을 볶고 파스타를 삶은 뒤, 프라이팬에 파스타와 우유 또는 크림을 넣은 다음, 오븐 그릇에 담고 치즈로 덮어서 오븐에 넣는다.

Listening ★ Challenge   p. 12

A 1 ③   2 ②, ④   B 1 ② 2 ③

A [1-2]

W: Do you know that tomorrow is Mom's birthday?

M: Oh no, I forgot! Do you have any good ideas?

W: What about preparing a delicious meal for dinner tomorrow?

M: That's a good idea!

W: Then, we have to decide what to make.

M: I think we should make curry. It's easy to make.

W: Great! For curry, we'll need curry powder, carrots, onions, and potatoes. Anything else?

M: Let's put chicken in it. Mom likes that.

W: Okay. Well, we already have curry powder, potatoes and carrots.

M: So, we only need to buy chicken and onions. Let's go to buy them.

여: 내일이 엄마 생신인 거 알아?

남: 아, 이런, 잊고 있었어! 뭐 좋은 생각 있어?

여: 내일 저녁에 맛있는 식사를 준비해 드리는 거 어때?

남: 좋은 생각이야!

여: 그럼 무얼 만들지 결정해야지.

남: 카레를 만드는 게 좋을 거 같아. 만들기가 쉽잖아.

여: 좋아! 카레에는 카레 가루와 당근, 양파, 그리고 감자가 필요해. 또 뭐가 있나?

남: 닭고기를 넣자. 엄마가 좋아하시잖아.

여: 좋아. 음, 카레 가루랑 감자와 당근은 있어.

남: 그럼 닭고기와 양파만 사야겠네. 사러 가자.

어휘

prepare[pripέər] 툉 준비하다   meal[miːl] 몡 식사
powder[páudər] 몡 가루   onion[ʌ́njən] 몡 양파

문제 해설

Q1: 그들은 왜 내일 저녁을 요리하기로 했나?

　엄마 생신이어서 엄마를 위해 식사를 준비하기로 했다.

Q2: 그들이 살 물건 두 개를 고르시오.

　이미 있는 재료들은 제외하고 양파와 닭고기를 사야 한다고 했다.

B [1-2]

M: Have you ever tried "fajitas"? They are a traditional Mexican food. I had a chance to taste them for the first time when I visited my friend's house. They were so good that they became my favorite food. When you eat a fajita, you wrap the grilled meat and fried vegetables in a tortilla. A tortilla is a very thin round piece of bread made from corn or wheat flour.

남: '파이타(fajitas)'를 먹어 본 적이 있으세요? 그것은 멕시코의 전통 음식이에요. 제가 친구 집에 갔을 때 처음으로 맛을 볼 기회가 있었죠. 아주 맛이 좋아 제가 가장 좋아하는 음식이 되었어요. 파이타를 먹을 때는 구운 고기와 볶은 야채를 토르티야(tortilla)에 싸서 먹어요. 토르티야는 옥수수나 밀가루로 만든 아주 얇고 둥근 빵이에요.

어휘

fajita[fəhíːtə] 몡 파이타   traditional[trədíʃənəl] 혱 전통적인   chance[tʃæns] 몡 기회   for the first time 처음으로   wrap[ræp] 툉 싸다   grilled[grild] 혱 구운   tortilla[tɔːrtíːə] 몡 토르티야   piece[piːs] 몡 한 개   wheat[hwiːt] 몡 밀   flour[fláuər] 몡 밀가루; *곡물 가루

문제 해설

Q1: 남자는 주로 무엇에 대해 이야기하고 있나?

　① 파이타를 만드는 그의 특별 요리법

　② 그가 가장 좋아하는 음식

　③ 다양한 종류의 멕시코 음식

　④ 그가 가장 좋아하는 멕시코 음식점

　자신이 가장 좋아하는 음식인 파이타를 소개하고 있다.

Q2: 남자는 어디에서 처음 파이타를 먹어 보았나?

　친구네 집에서 처음 먹었다고 했다.

Critical ★ Thinking   p. 13

1 ①   2 (1) F (2) T (3) F

W: Junk food usually has a lot of fat, salt, or sugar in it. Eating too much fat can make students gain weight. And eating too much salt may cause heart trouble later in life. Also, eating sugar can cause tooth problems. I think schools should ban junk foods in order to protect the health of students.

M: Hamburgers, chocolate bars and ice cream are all around us. We can easily get junk food outside school. So, even if schools ban junk food, students will buy it anyway. In my opinion, it is better to teach students how unhealthy those foods are.

여: 정크푸드에는 보통 많은 지방과 소금, 설탕이 들어 있습니다. 지방을 너무 많이 먹으면 학생들이 살찌게 됩니다. 그리고 소금을 너무 많이 먹으면 나이가 들어서 심장병을 일으킬 수 있습니다. 또한 설탕을 먹는 것은 치아 질환을 일으킬 수 있습니다. 저는 학교가 학생들의 건강을 보호하기 위해서 정크푸드를 금지해야 한다고 생각합니다.

남: 햄버거, 초콜릿 바, 아이스크림은 우리 주변에 많이 있습니다. 우리는 학교 밖에서 쉽게 정크푸드를 구할 수 있습니다. 그래서 학교가 정크푸드를 금지한다고 하더라도 학생들은 어떻게든 사 먹을 것입니다. 제 의견은 학생들에게 그런 음식들이 얼마나 건강에 좋지 않은지 가르치는 것이 더 좋을 거라는 것입니다.

어휘
junk food 정크푸드, 인스턴트 음식   fat [fæt] 형 지방
gain weight 체중이 늘다   cause [kɔːz] 통 ~의 원인이 되다. ~을 일으키다   heart trouble 심장병   tooth problem 치아 질환   ban [bæn] 통 금지하다   in order to-v ~하기 위해서   protect [prətékt] 통 보호하다
health [helθ] 명 건강   unhealthy [ʌnhélθi] 형 건강에 좋지 않은 [문제] diet [dáiət] 명 식단   advertisement [ædvərtáizmənt] 명 광고   danger [déindʒər] 명 위험
harmful [háːrmfəl] 형 해로운

문제 해설
Q1: 그들은 주로 무엇에 대해 이야기하고 있나?
   ① 교내에서 정크푸드를 금지하는 것

② 학생들의 식단을 더 건강에 좋게 만드는 것
③ TV에서 정크푸드의 광고를 금지하는 것
④ 정크푸드의 위험성을 학생들에게 가르치는 것
학교 내에서 정크푸드를 금지해야 하는지에 대한 의견을 말하고 있다.

Q2: 사실이면 T, 사실이 아니면 F를 쓰시오.
   (1) 소녀는 학생들이 정크푸드가 얼마나 유해한지 알아야 한다고 생각한다.
   (2) 소년은 학생들이 학교 밖에서 정크푸드를 쉽게 살 수 있다고 생각한다.
   (3) 소년은 약간의 정크푸드를 먹는 것은 우리 건강에 그렇게 나쁘지는 않다고 생각한다.

UNIT 02 School Life

Getting ★ Ready   p. 14

A 1 ⓖ 2 ⓒ 3 ⓕ 4 ⓗ 5 ⓑ
B 1 ⓐ 2 ⓓ 3 ⓑ

B 1 여: 이 책을 대출할 수 있나요?
      남: 아니요. 책 한 권을 반납하지 않았네요.
   2 여: 우리 현장 학습 언제 가니?
      남: 6월 4일이야.
   3 여: 수학 시험은 잘 봤니?
      남: 중간고사 때보다 조금 더 잘했어.

Listening ★ Start   p. 15

1 (1) ⓓ (2) ⓒ / Among all my teachers, we're in trouble, On the other hand, not fashionable at all
2 ③ / exam timetable, at 3 o'clock, when the science exam is, On Tuesday

1

M: Among all my teachers, I like Ms. Simpson and Ms. Fox the most. Ms. Simpson is very kind to us. She helps us when we're in trouble. But her classes are very boring and make me sleepy. On the other hand, Ms. Fox teaches us in a very interesting way. She often tells us funny stories about the subject. But her clothes and hairstyle are not fashionable at all.

남: 저는 모든 선생님들 중에서 Simpson 선생님과 Fox 선생님을 가장 좋아해요. Simpson 선생님께서는 저희들에게 아주 친절하세요. 문제가 생겼을 때면 도와 주시죠. 하지만 선생님 수업은 아주 지루하고 졸려요. 반면, Fox 선생님은 아주 재미있게 가르쳐 주세요. 주제에 대해 종종 재미있는 이야기를 들려주신답니다. 하지만 선생님의 옷과 헤어 스타일은 전혀 유행에 맞지 않아요.

어휘
among[əmʌ́ŋ] 전 ~ 중에서   trouble[trʌ́bl] 명 곤란, 어려움   boring[bɔ́:riŋ] 형 지루한   on the other hand 반면에   funny[fʌ́ni] 형 재미있는   subject [sʌ́bdʒikt] 명 과목; *주제   fashionable[fǽʃənəbl] 형 최신 유행에 따른   [문제] personality[pɔ̀rsənǽləti] 명 성격   appearance[əpí(:)ərəns] 명 외모

문제 해설
Q: 각 선생님에 대해 소년이 좋아하지 않는 점을 고르시오.
   Simpson 선생님의 수업 방식과 Fox 선생님의 패션 스타일을 좋아하지 않는다고 했다.

2

M: I lost my exam timetable. Is the Japanese test at 1 p.m. on Monday?
W: No, it isn't. It's at 2 p.m.
M: Really? I have a history exam at 3 o'clock.
W: Right after the Japanese exam? That's too bad!
M: Also, do you know when the science exam is? Isn't it at 4 p.m. on Tuesday?
W: No, it's on Wednesday at 4 p.m. On Tuesday at 4 p.m., we have a math exam.

남: 시험 시간표를 잃어 버렸어. 일본어 시험이 월요일 오후 1시에 있니?
여: 아니, 그렇지 않아. 오후 2시야.
남: 정말? 난 3시에 역사 시험이 있어.
여: 일본어 시험 바로 후에? 안됐구나!
남: 또, 과학 시험이 언제인지 알아? 화요일 오후 4시 아닌가?
여: 아니, 수요일 오후 4시야. 화요일 오후 4시에는 수학 시험이 있어.

어휘
lose[lu:z] 동 잃어버리다 (lose-lost-lost)   timetable

[táimtèibl] 명 시간표   Japanese[dʒæ̀pəní:z] 명 일본어   history[hístəri] 명 역사   science[sáiəns] 명 과학   math[mæθ] 명 수학

문제 해설
Q: 소년의 시험 시간표에 관해 사실이 아닌 것은?
   수학 시험은 화요일 오후 4시라고 했다.

Listening ★ Practice p. 16

1 (1) ⓑ (2) ⓒ (3) ⓐ   2 ④   3 ②   4 ③   5 ②
6 ③   7 ②   8 ①

1

M1: I'm Alex. Some people talk on the phone in the library. The library is a place to study and read books. They should go outside to make a call.
W: I'm Megan. Yesterday, I found an empty seat in the library. But a boy said he was saving the seat for his friend, so I couldn't sit there.
M2: I'm Colin. I don't understand why some students eat snacks in the library. As you know, it makes a terrible noise.

남1: 난 Alex야. 어떤 사람들은 도서관에서 전화 통화를 해. 도서관은 공부를 하고 책을 읽는 장소야. 전화는 밖으로 나가서 해야 해.
여: 난 Megan이야. 어제 도서관에서 빈 자리를 하나 찾았어. 그런데 한 남자애가 친구 자리를 맡아 두고 있는 거라고 해서 거기 앉을 수 없었어.
남2: 난 Colin이야. 왜 도서관에서 몇몇 애들이 간식을 먹는지 이해가 안 돼. 알다시피, 심한 소음을 내게 되잖아.

어휘
library[láibrèri] 명 도서관   make a call 전화를 하다   empty[ém/pti] 형 빈   seat[si:t] 명 좌석   save[seiv] 동 맡아 두다   snack[snæk] 명 스낵, 간식   terrible [térəbl] 형 끔찍한   noise[nɔiz] 명 소음

문제 해설
Q: 각 인물과 그들이 이야기하고 있는 도서관 예절을 연결하시오.
   (1) Alex는 전화 통화는 도서관 밖에서 해야 한다고 했다.
   (2) Megan은 친구의 자리를 맡아 주면 안 된다고 했다.
   (3) Colin은 음식물을 먹지 말아야 한다고 했다.

2

W: Hi, I'd like to borrow this book.
M: Can I see your student ID?
W: Here it is.
M: I'm afraid you can't borrow a book. You haven't returned *The Little Prince*.
W: Oh, I'll bring it back tomorrow. Can't I just check out this book now?
M: Sorry, you can't.
W: Then I'll go home to get the book now. I must borrow this book for my homework.
M: Don't forget that you must also pay a fine.
W: Okay.

여: 안녕하세요, 이 책을 빌리고 싶어요.
남: 학생증 좀 보여 주실래요?
여: 여기요.
남: 유감이지만 책을 빌릴 수 없어요. 〈어린 왕자〉를 반납하지 않았어요.
여: 아, 내일 반납할게요. 그냥 지금 이 책을 대출할 수 없을까요?
남: 죄송하지만, 안 됩니다.
여: 그럼 집에 가서 지금 책을 가져올게요. 숙제 때문에 이 책을 빌려야 하거든요.
남: 벌금도 내야 한다는 거 잊지 말아요.
여: 알겠어요.

어휘
borrow[bárou] 통 빌리다   ID[àidíː] 명 신분증
(= identification)   return[ritə́ːrn] 통 반납하다   bring
[briŋ] 통 가져오다 (bring–brought–brought)   check out
대출하다   pay[pei] 통 지불하다   fine[fain] 명 벌금

문제 해설
Q: 소녀가 다음에 할 일은?
　소녀는 책을 대출하기 위해 집에 가서 반납하지 않은 〈어린 왕자〉를 가져오겠다고 했다.

3

M: How's Mike doing? He doesn't talk to me or my wife about his school life.
W: Well, I often see him sending text messages in my class. He doesn't seem to focus on his lessons these days.
M: Maybe it's because he started to date a girl. What should I do?

W: Don't worry. I'll talk with him about it.
M: Thank you. Is he doing well with his friends?
W: Yes, he's very popular in his class.
M: I guess that's why many of his friends come over to the house.

남: Mike는 어떻게 지내나요? 그 애는 학교 생활에 관해 저나 제 아내에게 말을 안 해요.
여: 음, 제 수업 시간에 문자 메세지를 보내는 걸 자주 봐요. 요즘 수업에 집중하지 않는 것 같아요.
남: 아마도 여자애와 데이트를 시작해서 그럴 거예요. 어떻게 해야 할까요?
여: 걱정 마세요. 제가 얘기 좀 해 볼게요.
남: 감사해요. 친구들과는 잘 지내고 있나요?
여: 네, 반에서 아주 인기가 있어요.
남: 그래서 친구들이 집으로 많이 놀러 오는가 봐요.

어휘
send[send] 통 보내다 (send–sent–sent)   text
message 문자 메세지   focus on ～에 집중하다
these days 요즘   date[deit] 통 ～와 데이트하다
guess[ges] 통 짐작하다

문제 해설
Q: 화자 간의 관계는?
　Mike의 학교 생활에 대해 Mike의 아버지와 선생님이 대화를 나누고 있다.

17

4

M: Listen, class. By next Thursday, you must prepare a group presentation. Make groups of five members and search for information about one of the festivals around the world. Include the festival's history, place, and activities. Each group will have 15 minutes to present their information. This presentation is worth 20 points, and it'll be included in your final grade.

남: 학생 여러분, 잘 들으세요. 다음 주 목요일까지 그룹 발표를 준비해야 해요. 5명씩 그룹을 만들어서 세계의 축제 중 하나에 대한 정보를 찾으세요. 축제의 역사와 장소, 활동을 포함시키세요. 각 그룹은 정보에 대해 15분간 발표를 할 거예요. 이 발표는 20점짜리이고 기말 성적에 포함될 거예요.

어휘

prepare[pripέər] 통 준비하다　presentation [prèzəntéiʃən] 명 발표　search for ~을 찾다 information[ìnfərméiʃən] 명 정보　festival[féstəvəl] 명 축제　include[inklúːd] 통 포함하다　present [prizént] 통 주다; *발표하다　worth[wəːrθ] 형 ~의 가치가 있는　final[fáinəl] 형 기말의　grade[greid] 명 점수, 성적

문제 해설

Q: 틀린 정보를 고르시오.

발표 시간은 20분이 아니라 15분이라고 했다.

5

(Telephone rings.)

M: Hello.

W: Hi, Kevin. This is Sally.

M: Hey, what's up?

W: I want to know if there's any homework for English class.

M: We have to write a three-page paper about our favorite author.

W: Who are you going to write about?

M: I chose Mark Twain at first. But then I changed my mind to write about Ernest Hemingway.

W: Why?

M: I read his *The Old Man and the Sea* a few days ago, and it was great. What about you?

W: I'm thinking of writing about Emily Brontë.

18

(전화벨이 울린다.)

남: 여보세요.

여: 안녕, Kevin. 나 Sally야.

남: 그래, 무슨 일이야?

여: 영어 수업 숙제가 있는지 알고 싶어.

남: 제일 좋아하는 작가에 대해서 세 페이지짜리 보고서를 써야 해.

여: 넌 누구에 대해서 쓸 거야?

남: 처음엔 Mark Twain을 골랐어. 하지만 Ernest Hemingway에 대해서 쓰기로 마음을 바꿨지.

여: 왜?

남: 그가 쓴 〈노인과 바다〉를 며칠 전에 읽었는데 아주 좋았어. 넌 어때?

여: 난 Emily Brontë에 대해서 쓸 생각이야.

어휘

what's up? 무슨 일이야?　paper[péipər] 명 보고서 author[ɔ́ːθər] 명 작가　choose[tʃuːz] 통 고르다 (choose-chose-chosen)　at first 처음에는 change one's mind 마음을 바꾸다

문제 해설

Q: 소년의 보고서 제목은 무엇이 될까?

소년은 Hemingway에 관한 보고서를 쓸 것이라고 했다.

6

W: Attention, please. During the vacation, you will not be able to use school facilities for certain periods of time. The gym will not be available for two weeks, from July 6th to July 19th. The language lab will be closed for the whole vacation. The computer lab will be closed from July 20th and reopen on July 31st. Students can use the library as usual during the vacation.

여: 안내 말씀 드립니다. 방학 동안에 특정 기간 동안 학교 시설을 사용할 수 없게 됩니다. 체육관은 7월 6일부터 19일까지 2주 동안 사용할 수 없습니다. 어학 실습실은 방학 내내 닫혀져 있을 것입니다. 컴퓨터 실습실은 7월 20일부터 닫았다가 7월 31일에 다시 개방합니다. 학생들은 방학 동안 도서관을 평소처럼 이용할 수 있습니다.

어휘

Attention, please. 안내 말씀 드리겠습니다. vacation[veikéiʃən] 명 방학　facility[fəsíləti] 명 시설 certain[sə́ːrtən] 형 특정한　period[pí(ː)əriəd] 명 기간 gym[dʒim] 명 체육관　available[əvéiləbl] 형 사용 가능한　language lab 어학 실습실　whole[houl] 형 전체의　reopen[riːóupn] 통 다시 열다　as usual 평소처럼

문제 해설

Q: 틀린 정보를 고르시오.

컴퓨터 실습실은 7월 20일부터 닫았다가 31일에 다시 개방한다고 하였다.

7

W: I heard you got an A⁺ in art class. Congratulations! Can I see your picture?

M: Sure. This is it.

W: Wow, you painted a boy riding a bicycle.

M: He's my brother. This is when my family went on a picnic last month.

W: Where did you go?

M: We went to Silver Lake Park and rode a boat there.

W: You really have a talent for painting.

M: Thanks, Julie. So, what did you paint for the homework?

W: I painted a woman jogging in the morning. I got a B.

여: 너 미술 수업에서 A⁺를 받았다고 들었어. 축하해! 네 그림을 보여줄 수 있니?

남: 물론이지. 이거야.

여: 와, 자전거를 타는 남자애를 그렸구나.

남: 내 남동생이야. 우리 가족이 지난 달에 소풍 갔을 때야.

여: 어디로 갔어?

남: Silver Lake Park에 가서 배를 탔어.

여: 너 정말 그림에 재능이 있구나.

남: 고마워, Julie. 그럼 넌 숙제로 뭘 그렸어?

여: 난 아침에 조깅하는 여자를 그렸어. 난 B를 받았어.

어휘

Congratulations! 축하해! paint[peint] 통 그리다 ride[raid] 통 타다 (ride-rode-ridden) go on a picnic 소풍을 가다 talent[tǽlənt] 명 재능 jog[dʒɑg] 통 조깅하다

문제 해설

Q: 소녀의 그림은?

소녀는 아침에 조깅하는 여자 그림을 그렸다고 했다.

8

W: I'm disappointed with my grades. Can you give me some advice?

M: Sure. Let me ask you something first. Why do you study?

W: Well... I don't know.

M: You should know why you need to study first. It helps you focus on studying.

W: Umm... I see.

M: Making a study plan is also useful. But don't make it too tight.

W: Okay.

M: Finally, decide what your weakest subject is and spend more time on it.

W: Thanks for your advice.

여: 내 성적에 실망했어. 나에게 조언을 좀 해 줄 수 있겠니?

남: 물론이지. 우선 뭘 좀 물어볼게. 넌 왜 공부를 하니?

여: 음… 모르겠어.

남: 왜 공부를 해야 하는지 우선 알아야 해. 그게 공부에 집중하는 데 도움이 되거든.

여: 흠… 알겠어.

남: 공부 계획을 세우는 것도 유용해. 하지만 너무 빡빡하게 세우진 마.

여: 알았어.

남: 마지막으로 가장 약한 과목이 무엇인지 정하고 그것에 더 많은 시간을 할애해.

여: 조언해줘서 고마워.

어휘

be disappointed with ~에 실망하다 advice [ədváis] 명 충고, 조언 useful[júːsfəl] 형 유용한 tight[tait] 형 꽉 짜인 decide[disáid] 통 결정하다 weak[wiːk] 형 취약한 spend[spend] 통 (시간을) 쓰다 (spend-spent-spent) [문제] major[méidʒər] 명 전공 enter[éntər] 통 들어가다 university[jùːnəvə́ːrsəti] 명 대학교

문제 해설

Q: 소년의 충고는 무엇에 관한 것인가?

① 좋은 성적을 얻는 방법

② 공부 계획을 세우는 방법

③ 전공을 정하는 방법

④ 좋은 대학교에 들어가는 방법

좋은 성적을 얻을 수 있는 방법에 대한 내용이다.

Listening ★ Challenge p. 18

A 1 ② 2 ③ B 1 ② 2 ②

A [1-2]

W: Mike, we're going on a field trip on the 20th.

M: Really, Ms. Taylor? Where are we going?

W: Arizona Desert Garden. It's a farm where desert plants grow.

M: Sounds interesting. The last field trip to the lake was boring.

W: Was it? But the history museum tour was very good.

M: You're right. Anyway, do I need to bring my lunch box?

W: Yes, you do. Also, you'd better bring your cap. It's hot there.

M: Okay. How about a drink?

W: You don't need to bring one. The school will provide drinks.

M: Great. And I'll bring my pen and some paper.

W: Good boy. They're necessary for taking notes about the trip.

여: Mike, 우리는 20일에 현장 학습을 갈 거야.

남: 정말이요, Taylor 선생님? 어디로 가나요?

여: Arizona Desert Garden이야. 사막 식물이 자라는 농장이지.

남: 재미있겠어요. 지난번 호수로 간 현장 학습은 지루했어요.

여: 그랬니? 하지만 역사 박물관 투어는 아주 좋았잖아.

남: 맞아요. 그런데, 도시락을 가지고 가야 하나요?

여: 응, 그래야 해. 또, 모자를 가져가는 게 좋아. 거긴 더워.

남: 알겠어요. 마실 것은요?

여: 가져갈 필요가 없어. 학교에서 마실 것을 줄 거야.

남: 좋아요. 그리고 펜과 종이를 가져가야겠어요.

여: 착하구나. 여행에 관해서 필기를 할 때 필요하지.

어휘

field trip 현장 학습 desert[dézərt] 몡 사막 farm [faːrm] 몡 농장 plant[plænt] 몡 식물 lake[leik] 몡 호수 tour[tuər] 몡 짧은 여행, 소풍 anyway[éniwèi] 뷔 어쨌든 lunch box 도시락 had better-v ~하는 것이 낫다 cap[kæp] 몡 (테 없는) 모자 drink[driŋk] 몡 음료수 provide[prəváid] 통 주다 necessary [nésəsèri] 혱 필요한

문제 해설

Q1: 그들은 어디로 현장 학습을 가는가?

　사막 식물이 있는 농장에 갈 것이라고 했다.

Q2: 소년이 현장 학습에 가져가지 않을 것은?

　음료수는 학교에서 준비해 주겠다고 했으므로 가지고 가지 않을 것이다.

B [1-2]

M: You look upset. What's the matter?

W: I just got my report card, and my math grade is really bad.

M: Didn't you study math hard?

W: Yes, I did. But I thought the exam covered chapters four, five and six.

M: Oh, the exam included chapter seven as well.

W: That's why I got a C! Many questions came from that chapter.

M: That's too bad.

W: How about you?

M: I did a little bit better than on the midterm exam.

W: That's good. You got a C+ on the midterm exam.

M: I got a B+ this time. It's not an A, but I'm happy with my grade.

남: 너 기분이 안 좋아 보여. 무슨 일이야?

여: 지금 막 성적표를 받았는데 수학 점수가 정말 나빠.

남: 수학을 열심히 공부하지 않았어?

여: 아니, 했어. 그런데 난 시험 범위가 4장, 5장, 6장인 줄 알았어.

남: 아, 시험에 7장도 포함되었잖아.

여: 그래서 C를 받았어! 많은 문제가 그 장에서 나왔어.

남: 정말 안됐다.

여: 넌 어때?

남: 난 중간고사 때보다는 좀 나아졌어.

여: 잘됐다. 중간고사에서는 C+를 받았었지.

남: 이번에 B+를 받았어. A는 아니지만 내 점수에 만족해.

어휘

upset[ʌpsét] 혱 화가 난 report card 성적표 cover[kʌ́vər] 통 (어떤 범위에) 걸치다, 포함하다 chapter[tʃǽptər] 몡 (책의) 장 as well 역시 a little bit 약간 midterm[mídtəːrm] 혱 (학기) 중간의 [문제] carefully[kɛ́ərfəli] 뷔 주의 깊게

문제 해설

Q1: 소녀는 왜 수학 시험에서 나쁜 점수를 받았나?

　① 시험 시간에 잤다.

　② 한 장을 공부하지 않았다.

　③ 깜빡 잊고 몇 문제에 답하지 않았다.

　④ 문제를 주의 깊게 읽지 않았다.

　시험은 4장부터 7장까지였는데 여자는 6장까지라고 생각했다.

Q2: 소년이 이번에 받은 점수는?

　소년은 지난 중간고사 때에는 C+를 받았고 이번에는 B+를 받았다.

Critical ★ Thinking p. 19

1 ③ 2 ①, ②

20

M: Mom, I don't know why I have to go to university.

W: What are you talking about? It's helpful when getting a job, isn't it?

M: I can get a job after just graduating from high school.

W: But you can get deeper knowledge of a subject at university. That way, you'll have a better chance to earn a higher income.

M: But I don't care about money.

W: Hmm... do you think you've prepared enough for your future job?

M: Well... no, I don't think so.

W: That's why you'd better go to university. You can prepare for your future job while studying and meeting various people.

M: I see.

남: 엄마, 저는 왜 대학에 가야만 하는지 모르겠어요.

여: 무슨 얘기를 하는 거야? 취업을 하는 데 도움이 되지. 그렇지 않니?

남: 고등학교만 졸업하고도 취업을 할 수 있어요.

여: 하지만 대학에서 한 학과에 대해 더 깊은 지식을 얻을 수 있잖니. 그래야 더 많은 수입을 벌 더 좋은 기회를 갖게 되는 거야.

남: 하지만 전 돈에 신경 쓰지 않아요.

여: 흠… 네가 장래의 직업에 대해 충분히 준비가 되어 있다고 생각하니?

남: 음… 아니, 그렇게 생각하진 않아요.

여: 그래서 대학에 가는 게 더 낫다는 거야. 공부하고 다양한 사람들을 만나면서 장래의 직업을 위한 준비를 할 수 있어.

남: 알겠어요.

어휘

helpful[hélpfəl] 혱 도움이 되는 graduate[grǽdʒuèit] 동 졸업하다 knowledge[nɑ́lidʒ] 명 지식 chance [tʃæns] 명 기회 earn[əːrn] 동 벌다 income[ínkʌm] 명 수입 care[kɛər] 동 신경 쓰다 various[vɛ́(ː)əriəs] 혱 다양한 [문제] waste[weist] 명 낭비 experience [ikspí(ː)əriəns] 명 경험

문제 해설

Q1: 그들은 주로 무엇에 대해 이야기하고 있나?

① 어떻게 좋은 직장을 얻는지

② 대학교에서 무엇을 배우는지

③ 왜 대학교에 갈 필요가 있는지

④ 왜 좋은 대학교에 들어갈 필요가 있는지

대학교에 가야 하는 이유에 대한 대화이다.

Q2: 대학 생활에 대한 여자의 의견 두 개를 고르시오.

① 장래 직업을 준비하는 데 도움이 된다.

② 더 많은 돈을 벌 수 있는 기회를 준다.

③ 돈과 시간을 낭비하는 것이다.

④ 현장에서의 경험보다 더 중요하다.

여자는 대학에 가는 것이 장래 직업을 위한 준비에 도움이 되며 더 많은 수입을 벌 수 있는 기회를 준다고 했다.

UNIT 03 Hobbies

Getting ★ Ready   p. 20

A 1 ⓒ 2 ⓔ 3 ⓑ 4 ⓓ 5 ⓐ

B 1 ⓔ 2 ⓕ 3 ⓓ

B 1 남: 넌 여가 시간에 뭘 하니?
　　여: 산악 자전거 타러 가는 걸 좋아해.
　2 남: 동아리 회원들은 얼마나 자주 모이니?
　　여: 일주일에 한 번.
　3 남: 동아리에서 넌 무엇을 하니?
　　여: 나는 우리 축구팀을 응원해.

Listening ★ Start   p. 21

1 ① / have any plans, take pictures of, Places like, That sounds fun

2 ④ / is going to, painted my face green, blue skirt, with a tie

1

M: Catherine, what are you doing this weekend?

W: I don't have any plans yet.

M: Then, could you be my model?

W: Model? What are you talking about?

M: Well, you know I like taking pictures. I want to take pictures of you this time.

W: I see. So where do you want to take my picture?

M: Places like shopping malls, bookstores and coffee shops downtown.

21

W: That sounds fun. Should I bring anything?
M: Just bring some accessories, like hats or sunglasses.

남: Catherine, 이번 주말에 뭐 할 거야?
여: 아직 아무 계획이 없어.
남: 그럼, 내 모델이 되어줄 수 있니?
여: 모델? 무슨 얘기야?
남: 음, 내가 사진 찍는 거 좋아하는 거 알잖아. 이번엔 네 사진을 찍고 싶어.
여: 알았어. 그럼 어디서 내 사진을 찍고 싶니?
남: 시내의 쇼핑몰이나 서점, 커피숍 같은 장소에서.
여: 재미있을 것 같다. 내가 뭘 가져와야 하니?
남: 모자나 선글라스 같은 액세서리를 좀 가져와.

어휘
model[mάdəl] 명 모델 take a picture of ~의 사진을 찍다 bookstore[búkstɔ̀ːr] 명 서점 downtown [dáuntáun] 부 도심에 accessory[əksésəri] 명 액세서리, 장신구 sunglasses[sʌ́nglæ̀siz] 명 선글라스

문제 해설
Q: 그들은 이번 주말에 무엇을 할 것인가?
    남자는 여자를 모델로 해서 사진을 찍기로 했다.

2

W: Our costume play club is going to meet tomorrow. At every meeting, our club members dress up like characters from movies. Last month, I was Princess Fiona. I painted my face green and wore a long dress. Tomorrow, I'll be Pippi Longstocking. I'll wear a blue skirt and long socks. Also, my hair will be red. My friend Sarah will be Hermione. She'll be wearing a coat and a white shirt with a tie.

여: 우리 코스프레 동아리는 내일 모일 거예요. 모임 때마다 우리 동아리 회원들은 영화의 캐릭터처럼 옷을 차려 입죠. 지난 달에 저는 Fiona 공주였어요. 저는 얼굴을 녹색으로 칠하고 긴 드레스를 입었어요. 내일 저는 Pippi Longstocking이 될 거예요. 파란 치마를 입고 긴 양말을 신을 거죠. 또 머리는 빨간색일 거예요. 제 친구 Sarah는 Hermione가 될 거랍니다. 그 애는 코트와 흰 셔츠를 입고 넥타이를 맬 거예요.

어휘
costume play 코스프레(코스튬 플레이) dress up 옷을 차려 입다 character[kǽriktər] 명 인물, 캐릭터 princess[prínses] 명 공주 socks[saks] 명 양말 shirt[ʃəːrt] 명 셔츠, 남방 tie[tai] 명 넥타이

문제 해설
Q: 소녀는 내일 어떤 캐릭터가 될 것인가?
    파란 치마를 입고 긴 양말을 신은 Pippi Longstocking 처럼 복장을 꾸밀 것이다.

Listening ★ Practice p. 22

1 ④ 2 ④ 3 ③ 4 ④ 5 (1) T (2) F (3) T
6 ③ 7 (1) ⓐ (2) ⓓ (3) ① 8 ④

1

M: Welcome! Do you want to join our dance club?
W: Yes. How often do you guys get together?
M: We get together once a week. It's every Wednesday at 7 p.m.
W: Okay. Where do you practice?
M: It depends. But we usually practice in the school gym.
W: Do I need to wear special dance clothes?
M: No. You can wear casual sports clothes. But you should wear dance shoes, not running shoes.
W: I see. See you on Wednesday, then.

남: 환영해! 우리 댄스 동아리에 들고 싶니?
여: 응. 너희들 얼마나 자주 모이니?
남: 우린 일주일에 한 번씩 모여. 매주 수요일 오후 7시야.
여: 알겠어. 어디서 연습하니?
남: 때에 따라 달라. 하지만 보통 학교 체육관에서 연습해.
여: 특별한 댄스복을 입어야 하니?
남: 아니. 캐주얼한 체육복을 입으면 돼. 그렇지만 운동화가 아니라 댄스화를 신어야 해.
여: 알겠어. 그럼 수요일에 보자.

어휘
join[dʒɔin] 동 가입하다 get together 모이다 once[wʌns] 부 한 번 practice[prǽktis] 동 연습하다; 명 연습 It depends. 때에 따라 다르다. gym[dʒim] 명 체육관 casual[kǽʒuəl] 형 캐주얼한, 평상복의 running shoes 운동화

문제 해설
Q: 틀린 정보를 고르시오.

22

신발은 운동화가 아니라 댄스화를 신어야 한다.

2

W: These days, I visit many websites about Angkor Wat in Cambodia. I look for information about places to visit, food, and hotels. Then I save the information on my computer. I can't travel around the world now because I'm a student and I don't have much money. But after getting a job, I'll travel to many places. So, I like to find travel information in my free time.

여: 요즘, 저는 캄보디아에 있는 앙코르와트에 대한 여러 웹 사이트를 찾아다녀요. 가볼 만한 곳과 음식, 호텔에 대한 정보를 찾는답니다. 그리고 나서 컴퓨터에 정보를 저장해요. 지금 저는 학생이고 돈이 많지 않기 때문에 세계를 여행할 수 없어요. 하지만 취직을 한 후에는 여러 곳을 여행할 거예요. 그래서 시간이 날 때 여행 정보를 찾아보는 것을 좋아해요.

어휘
website[wébsàit] 명 웹사이트 information [ìnfərméiʃən] 명 정보 save[seiv] 동 저장하다 travel [trǽvəl] 동 여행하다; 명 여행 [문제] search for ~을 찾다

문제 해설
Q: 여자의 취미는?
여자는 시간이 날 때 미래의 여행을 위해 여행 정보를 찾는 것을 좋아한다고 했다.

3

M: I'm thinking about buying a trumpet.
W: Really? But aren't trumpets expensive?
M: Yes, but I'll buy an old one, so it won't be.
W: So, will you play it at home?
M: Yes. I'll practice it every day.
W: I don't think it's a good idea to buy a trumpet.
M: Why not?
W: If you play it at home, it'll be very noisy. Your neighbors won't like it.
M: Hmm... that may be a problem.
W: Why don't you join a club and learn to play the trumpet there?
M: That's a good idea.

남: 나 트럼펫을 살까 생각 중이야.
여: 정말? 그런데 트럼펫은 비싸지 않니?
남: 그렇지, 하지만 중고를 살 거라서 비싸지 않을 거야.
여: 그럼 집에서 연주할 거야?
남: 응. 매일 연습할 거야.
여: 트럼펫을 사는 건 좋은 생각이 아닌 것 같아.
남: 왜?
여: 집에서 트럼펫을 연주하면 아주 시끄러울 거라고. 이웃들이 좋아하지 않을 거야.
남: 흠… 그건 문제가 될 수 있겠다.
여: 동아리에 가입해서 거기서 트럼펫 연주하는 걸 배우지 그래?
남: 그거 좋은 생각이다.

어휘
trumpet[trʌ́mpit] 명 트럼펫 noisy[nɔ́izi] 형 시끄러운 neighbor[néibər] 명 이웃 [문제] price[prais] 명 가격 loud[laud] 형 소리가 큰; *시끄러운 interest[íntərəst] 명 흥미

문제 해설
Q: 남자가 트럼펫을 사는 것에 여자가 반대하는 이유는?
① 트럼펫의 가격이 너무 비싸다.
② 트럼펫을 배우는 것은 어렵다.
③ 트럼펫은 소리가 너무 시끄러울 것이다.
④ 남자는 트럼펫을 연주하는 것에 금방 관심을 잃을 것이다.
여자는 트럼펫 소리가 시끄러워 이웃들이 좋아하지 않을 것이라고 했다.

4

M: What do you do in your free time?
W: I make teddy bears.
M: Interesting!
W: Look at this teddy bear. I made it myself.
M: Wow! It's lovely. It's holding a gift box.
W: I'll put chocolates in it. This is a Valentine's Day gift for my boyfriend.
M: Good idea. Can you teach me how to make one?
W: Why?
M: My girlfriend collects dolls.
W: Then how about making a teddy bear with a heart or a flower?
M: They sound fine, but I'd like to make the same teddy bear as you.

23

남: 넌 여가 시간에 뭘 하니?

여: 테디 베어를 만들어.

남: 재밌네!

여: 이 테디 베어 좀 봐. 내가 만들었어.

남: 와! 예쁘다. 선물 상자를 들고 있네.

여: 그 안에 초콜릿을 넣을 거야. 내 남자 친구를 위한 발렌타인 데이 선물이야.

남: 좋은 생각이야. 어떻게 만드는지 알려 줄래?

여: 왜?

남: 내 여자 친구가 인형을 모으거든.

여: 그럼 하트나 꽃을 들고 있는 테디 베어를 만드는 게 어때?

남: 그것도 좋은데, 너랑 똑같은 테디 베어를 만들고 싶어.

어휘

teddy bear 봉제 곰 인형, 테디 베어 lovely[lʌ́vli] 형 예쁜, 사랑스러운 gift[gift] 명 선물 Valentine's Day 발렌타인 데이 collect[kəlékt] 동 모으다, 수집하다 doll[dɑl] 명 인형 same[seim] 형 똑같은

문제 해설

Q: 남자가 만들 테디 베어를 고르시오.
남자는 여자와 똑같이 선물 상자를 들고 있는 테디 베어를 만들고 싶다고 했다.

5

M: Doctor, look at my arms. They're red.

W: Were you in the sun for a long time?

M: Yes. I played tennis yesterday.

W: I'll give you some lotion. It looks like sunburn.

M: I wore sunblock, but maybe it didn't work.

W: Well, you need to put it on every 2 or 3 hours.

M: Oops. I didn't know that. So, how can I avoid sunburn?

W: Don't play outside around midday. And wear long sleeves.

M: Okay. I'll play tennis in the mornings instead.

남: 선생님, 제 팔 좀 보세요. 빨개요.

여: 햇볕에 오랜 시간 있었나요?

남: 네. 어제 테니스를 쳤거든요.

여: 로션을 좀 드리죠. 햇볕에 화상을 입은 것 같아요.

남: 자외선 차단제를 발랐는데 그게 효과가 없었나 봐요.

여: 음, 그것을 2시간이나 3시간마다 발라줘야 한답니다.

남: 저런. 그건 몰랐네요. 그렇다면 어떻게 햇볕 화상을 피할

수 있을까요?

여: 정오쯤에는 밖에서 운동하지 마세요. 그리고 긴 소매 옷을 입으세요.

남: 알겠어요. 대신 아침에 테니스를 쳐야겠네요.

어휘

lotion[lóuʃən] 명 로션 sunburn[sʌ́nbə̀ːrn] 명 햇볕 화상 wear[wɛər] 동 바르다 (wear-wore-worn) sunblock[sʌ́nblɑ̀k] 명 자외선 차단제 work[wəːrk] 동 효과가 있다 put on ~을 바르다 avoid[əvɔ́id] 동 피하다 midday[míddèi] 명 한낮 sleeve[sliːv] 명 (옷의) 소매 instead[instéd] 부 대신에

문제 해설

Q: 사실이면 T, 사실이 아니면 F를 쓰시오.

(1) 그는 팔에 햇볕 화상을 입었다.

(2) 그는 테니스를 칠 때 자외선 차단제를 바르지 않았다.

(3) 그는 정오쯤에는 테니스를 치지 않을 것이다.

6

M: The cheering club is looking for new members! We attend every soccer game and cheer for our team. We have song and dance practice at 5 p.m. every Thursday. Are you worried that you don't sing and dance well? No problem! If you are active and love soccer, you'll be welcome. Only 7th and 8th grade students can apply.

남: 응원 동아리가 새 회원을 찾습니다! 저희는 축구 경기마다 참가해서 우리 팀을 응원합니다. 매주 목요일 오후 5시에 노래와 춤 연습을 합니다. 노래와 춤 실력이 뛰어나지 않아서 걱정이세요? 문제 없습니다! 활동적이고 축구를 좋아하기만 하면 환영입니다. 7학년과 8학년 학생만 지원할 수 있습니다.

어휘

cheering club 응원 동아리 attend[əténd] 동 참가하다 cheer[tʃiər] 동 응원하다 active[ǽktiv] 형 활동적인 grade[greid] 명 학년 apply[əplái] 동 지원하다

문제 해설

Q: 동아리에 들어갈 수 없는 사람을 고르시오.

① Steve: 난 매주 목요일 저녁에 시간이 있어.

② Mary: 난 축구를 좋아하지만, 춤을 잘 못 춰.

③ Ryan: 난 9학년이야.

지원자는 7학년이나 8학년 학생이어야 한다고 했다.

7

M: I'm Kevin. There are 25 members in our club. We play classical music as a group and we practice together twice a week. My instrument is the violin.

W1: I'm Michele. Our club will put on a play next month. I'll play the main role of a baseball player, so I'm practicing hard.

W2: I'm Laura. Our club members will go to Texas by bicycle next month. This is our 10th trip. Last time, we went to Chicago by plane and visited famous museums and parks.

남: 난 Kevin이야. 우리 동아리에는 25명의 회원이 있지. 우리는 단체로 클래식 음악을 연주하고 일주일에 두 번씩 함께 연습해. 내 악기는 바이올린이야.

여1: 난 Michele이야. 우리 동아리는 다음 달에 연극을 공연할 거야. 난 주연인 야구 선수역을 맡아서 열심히 연습 중이야.

여2: 난 Laura야. 우리 동아리 회원들은 다음 달에 자전거로 텍사스에 갈 거야. 이번이 10번째 여행이지. 지난 번에는 비행기로 시카고에 가서 유명한 박물관과 공원을 방문했어.

어휘

classical music 클래식 음악, 고전 음악 twice[twais] 위 두 번 instrument[ínstrəmənt] 명 악기 put on 상연하다 play[plei] 명 연극; 동 ~의 역을 맡아 하다 main role 주연 trip[trip] 명 여행 museum [mju(ː)zí(ː)əm] 명 박물관 [문제] orchestra[ɔ́ːrkəstrə] 명 오케스트라, 관현악단 cycling[sáikliŋ] 명 사이클링, 자전거 타기

문제 해설

Q: 각 인물에 맞는 동아리를 고르시오.

(1) Kevin은 단체로 클래식 음악을 연주하므로 학교 오케스트라 단원일 것이다.

(2) Michele은 연극을 공연하는 연극 동아리 회원일 것이다.

(3) Laura는 여행을 다니는 여행 동아리 회원일 것이다.

8

M: Lily, I'm thinking of growing plants as a hobby.

W: Great. How about growing a "lithops" plant?

M: A lithops plant?

W: It's a plant from dry areas in Southern Africa. It's easy to grow.

M: What does it look like?

W: It looks like a small stone.

M: That's interesting! How can I grow it?

W: Put it where there's sunlight. And you just need to water it during spring and fall.

M: How often should I water it then?

W: Every two weeks is enough.

M: Great! Thanks for your advice.

남: Lily, 나 취미로 식물을 키워볼까 생각 중이야.

여: 좋지. '리톱스'라는 식물을 키워보는 게 어때?

남: 리톱스?

여: 남아프리카의 건조 지대에서 나는 식물이야. 키우기 쉬워.

남: 어떻게 생겼는데?

여: 작은 돌처럼 생겼어.

남: 흥미로운걸! 어떻게 키워야 해?

여: 햇빛이 있는 곳에 놓아둬. 그리고 봄과 가을에 물을 주기만 하면 돼.

남: 그때 얼마나 자주 물을 줘야 해?

여: 2주에 한 번이면 충분해.

남: 좋은걸! 조언해 줘서 고마워.

어휘

dry[drai] 형 건조한 area[έəriə] 명 지역 look like ~처럼 보이다 stone[stoun] 명 돌 sunlight[sʌ́nlàit] 명 햇빛 water[wɔ́ːtər] 동 물을 주다

문제 해설

Q: 리톱스라는 식물에 관해 언급된 것이 <u>아닌</u> 것은?
원산지와 생김새, 재배 방법은 나왔지만 얼마나 오래 사는지는 언급되지 않았다.

Listening ★ Challenge p. 24

A 1 ③ 2 ④ B 1 ④ 2 ②

A [1-2]

W: Thanks for coming, Jay.

M: Wow! You really look like a princess.

W: Thanks. The makeup took over 2 hours.

M: I'm so excited about seeing you act. I never imagined you would join an acting club.

W: Neither did I.

M: But are you okay? You look tired.

★　★

W: I stayed up all night studying the script. I'm worried about making a mistake on stage.

M: Just think of it as a rehearsal.

W: I'm trying, but this is my first performance.

M: Don't worry. You'll do well.

W: Thanks. Oh, look at the time! I have to change into my costume now.

M: Okay. I'll go take my seat.

M: Do you know any of the letters?

W: The word starts with Y and ends with I.

M: Oh, I know.

W: Really? What is it?

M: It's Yamakasi. Yamakasi players also climb buildings without ropes.

W: I've never heard of it. How do you spell it?

M: Y-A-M-A-K-A-S-I.

W: It fits! How did you know that word?

M: I saw a TV show about the sport.

여: Jay, 와 줘서 고마워.

남: 왜! 너 정말 공주 같아.

여: 고마워. 분장하는 데 2시간이 넘게 걸렸어.

남: 네가 연기하는 걸 보다니 아주 흥분된다. 네가 연극 동아리에 들어갈 거라고 상상 못 했거든.

여: 나 역시 못 했어.

남: 그런데 괜찮니? 피곤해 보여.

여: 대본을 익히느라 밤을 새웠거든. 무대에서 실수할까 봐 걱정돼.

남: 그냥 리허설이라고 생각해.

여: 노력하고 있긴 한데, 첫 공연이라서 말이야.

남: 걱정하지 마. 넌 잘 할거야.

여: 고마워. 아, 시간 좀 봐! 이제 의상을 갈아입어야겠어.

남: 그래. 난 가서 자리에 앉을게.

어휘

makeup[méikʌ̀p] 몡 *분장; 화장   excited[iksáitid] 혱 흥분한   act[ækt] 동 연기하다   imagine[imǽdʒin] 동 상상하다   neither[ní:ðər] 부 ~도 …아니다   script [skript] 몡 대본   make a mistake 실수하다   stage [steidʒ] 몡 무대   rehearsal[rihə́:rsəl] 몡 리허설, 총연습   performance[pərfɔ́:rməns] 몡 공연   costume [kástju:m] 몡 복장, 의상

문제 해설

Q1: 여자의 현재 기분은?

　첫 공연을 앞두고 실수할까 봐 걱정하고 있으므로 긴장한 상태이다.

Q2: 여자가 다음에 할 일은?

　시간이 되어서 의상을 갈아입겠다고 했다.

B [1-2]

M: Julia, are you still trying to finish that?

W: Wait! I just need to get this last word.

M: What's the question?

W: 10 down, "It's an extreme sport. Its players run up walls and jump off buildings."

남: Julia, 아직까지 그걸 끝내려고 하고 있는 거야?

여: 기다려! 이 마지막 단어만 찾으면 돼.

남: 질문이 뭔데?

여: 10의 세로야. '이것은 익스트림 스포츠이다. 플레이어들은 벽을 뛰어오르고 건물에서 뛰어내린다.'

남: 철자 하나라도 알아?

여: 이 단어는 Y로 시작하고 I로 끝나.

남: 아, 알겠다.

여: 그래? 뭐야?

남: Yamakasi야. Yamakasi 플레이어들은 로프 없이 건물을 오르기도 해.

여: 들어본 적이 없는데. 철자가 어떻게 돼?

남: Y-A-M-A-K-A-S-I.

여: 맞네! 그 단어를 어떻게 알았어?

남: 그 스포츠에 대한 TV 쇼를 봤어.

어휘

finish[fíniʃ] 동 끝내다   last[læst] 혱 마지막의   extreme sport 극한 스포츠, 익스트림 스포츠   run up 뛰어오르다   jump off 뛰어내리다   letter[létər] 몡 글자   climb[klaim] 동 오르다   without[wiðáut] 전 ~없이   rope[roup] 몡 로프, 밧줄   spell[spel] 동 철자를 쓰다   fit[fit] 동 들어맞다, 적합하다   [문제] solve[salv] 동 풀다   crossword puzzle 크로스워드 퍼즐, 글자 맞추기 게임

문제 해설

Q1: 그들은 무엇을 하고 있나?

　단어에 대한 설명을 보고 가로 세로의 퍼즐에 맞는 단어를 맞추는 게임을 하고 있다.

Q2: Yamakasi를 가장 잘 묘사한 것은?

　벽을 뛰어오르고 빌딩에서 뛰어내리는 스포츠이다.

Critical ★ Thinking　p. 25

1 ①, ④   2 ①

26

W: Did you watch the show about extreme sports yesterday?

M: Yes. It's amazing that people go ice climbing or mountain biking as a hobby.

W: I don't understand why people like such dangerous sports.

M: Well, those sports aren't so dangerous if people train well.

W: But they could still get badly hurt. You're not thinking about trying extreme sports, are you?

M: Why not? Extreme sports are full of thrills.

W: Why don't you just play a safe sport?

M: Because extreme sports aren't easy, doing them will give me a feeling of success.

W: Are you serious? You could lose your life!

여: 어제 익스트림 스포츠에 관한 프로그램 봤니?

남: 응. 취미로 빙벽 등반을 하거나 산악 자전거를 타러 간다는 게 놀랍더라.

여: 난 사람들이 왜 그렇게 위험한 스포츠를 좋아하는지 이해가 안 돼.

남: 음, 그런 스포츠도 훈련을 잘 하면 그렇게 위험하지 않아.

여: 하지만 그래도 심하게 부상을 입을 수 있잖아. 너 익스트림 스포츠를 해 볼 생각은 아니지, 그렇지?

남: 왜 안 돼? 익스트림 스포츠는 스릴이 넘쳐.

여: 그냥 안전한 스포츠를 하는 게 어때?

남: 익스트림 스포츠는 쉽지 않기 때문에 그걸 하면 성취감을 느끼게 될 거야.

여: 진심이야? 목숨을 잃을 수도 있어!

어휘

amazing[əméiziŋ] 형 놀라운 dangerous[déindʒərəs] 형 위험한 train[trein] 동 훈련하다 badly[bǽdli] 부 심하게 hurt[həːrt] 형 상처를 입은 be full of ~으로 가득하다 thrill[θril] 명 스릴, 전율 safe[seif] 형 안전한 success[səksés] 명 성공 serious[sí(ː)əriəs] 형 진지한, 진담의 [문제] thrilling[θríliŋ] 형 스릴 만점의 offer[ɔ́(ː)fər] 동 제공하다 require[rikwáiər] 동 필요로 하다 clothing[klóuðiŋ] 명 의류

문제 해설

Q1: 남자에 따르면 익스트림 스포츠의 좋은 점 두 가지는?

① 스릴이 넘친다.

② 배우기가 쉽다.

③ 몸을 더 튼튼하게 만든다.

④ 성취감을 준다.

스릴이 넘쳐서 좋고, 성취감을 준다고 말했다.

Q2: 여자가 익스트림 스포츠를 반대하는 이유는?

① 너무 위험하다.

② 배우는 데 시간이 오래 걸린다.

③ 비싼 옷이 필요하다.

④ 할 장소를 찾기가 어렵다.

부상을 당하거나 목숨을 잃을 수도 있다는 말을 통해 여자가 위험하기 때문에 익스트림 스포츠에 반대하는 것을 알 수 있다.

UNIT 04 Animals

Getting ★ Ready p. 26

A 1 ⓓ 2 ⓑ 3 ⓔ 4 ⓐ 5 ⓒ
B 1 ⓓ 2 ⓐ 3 ⓕ

B 1 남: 너 애완동물 있어?

여: 응. Happy라는 이름의 고양이가 있어.

2 남: 전에 애완동물 기른 적 있니?

여: 응, 토끼를 2년 동안 키웠어.

3 남: 네 개는 뭐가 문제니?

여: 사람들이 집에 오면 크게 짖어.

Listening ★ Start p. 27

1 ② / Look at, light brown color, raising a pig, call it Piggy, how cute he is
2 ③ / has a runny nose, dry her well, some medicine

1

W: Look at this picture. Isn't my cat cute?

M: Yes, she is. She's a nice light brown color.

W: Do you have a pet, too?

M: I have a pet named Piggy.

W: Are you raising a pig?

M: No. Piggy is a giant spider.

W: Then why do you call it Piggy? That's strange.

M: I call it that because he eats too much.

W: Wow. How can you raise a spider?

M: You don't know how cute he is.

여: 이 사진 좀 봐. 내 고양이 귀엽지 않니?

남: 응, 그러네. 멋진 밝은 갈색이로구나.

여: 너도 애완동물이 있어?

남: Piggy라는 이름의 애완동물이 있어.

여: 돼지를 기르는 거야?

남: 아니. Piggy는 왕거미야.

여: 그럼 왜 Piggy라고 부르는 거야? 이상해.

남: 그 녀석이 너무 많이 먹어서 그렇게 불러.

여: 와. 어떻게 거미를 키울 수 있지?

남: 얼마나 귀여운지 넌 모를 거야.

어휘

light[lait] 형 *밝은; 가벼운 pet[pet] 명 애완동물
name[neim] 통 이름을 붙이다 piggy[pígi] 명 《(유아
어)》 (새끼) 돼지 raise[reiz] 통 기르다 giant[ʤáiənt]
형 거대한 spider[spáidər] 명 거미 strange[streinʤ]
형 이상한

문제 해설

Q: 어떤 동물이 남자의 애완동물인가?

　　남자는 왕거미를 기르고 있다고 했다.

2

W: My pet seems sick.

M: What's wrong with her?

W: She has a runny nose and she doesn't
　　eat anything.

M: Let me see. It looks like she caught a cold.

W: Do puppies catch colds?

M: Yes, they do. Did you dry her well after
　　washing her?

W: Maybe I didn't dry her enough last
　　Tuesday.

M: That could be the reason. I'll give you
　　some medicine for her.

W: Okay. Thank you.

여: 제 애완동물이 아픈 것 같아요.

남: 무슨 문제가 있는데요?

여: 콧물이 나고 아무것도 먹질 않아요.

남: 어디 보자. 감기에 걸린 것 같네요.

여: 강아지가 감기에 걸리나요?

남: 네, 그래요. 목욕을 시킨 후에 잘 말려줬나요?

여: 아마 지난 화요일에 충분히 말려주지 않나 봐요.

남: 그게 이유일지 몰라요. 강아지에게 줄 약을 드릴게요.

여: 네. 감사합니다.

어휘

seem[siːm] 통 ~인 것 같다 sick[sik] 형 아픈 have
a runny nose 콧물이 나다 puppy[pʌ́pi] 명 강아지
catch a cold 감기에 걸리다 dry[drai] 통 말리다
enough[inʌ́f] 부 충분히 reason[ríːzən] 명 이유
medicine[médəsin] 명 약 [문제] drugstore
[drʌ́gstɔ̀ːr] 명 약국 clinic[klínik] 명 진료소, 병원

문제 해설

Q: 이 대화가 이루어지고 있는 장소는?

　　강아지의 건강 상태를 묻고 진찰하는 내용의 대화이므로
　　동물 병원이다.

Listening ★ Practice p. 28

1 ③ 2 ② 3 (1) Wednesday (2) Saturday
(3) Monday 4 ④ 5 ② 6 ④ 7 ① 8 (1) T
(2) T (3) F

1

M: This animal spends most of its time in
　　trees and eats leaves. It has a large head
　　with two rounded ears. Its tail is very
　　short, so you can hardly see it. Its legs are
　　short too, but they are useful for climbing
　　trees. Many people think it looks like a
　　small bear. It carries its babies on its back.

남: 이 동물은 대부분의 시간을 나무에서 보내고 잎을 먹습니
　　다. 2개의 둥근 귀가 있고 머리가 큽니다. 꼬리는 아주 짧
　　아서 거의 보이지 않습니다. 다리 역시 짧지만 나무를 오
　　를 때 유용합니다. 많은 사람들이 이 동물이 작은 곰처럼
　　생겼다고 생각합니다. 새끼를 등에 업고 다닙니다.

어휘

rounded[ráundid] 형 둥근 tail[teil] 명 꼬리
hardly[háːrdli] 부 거의 ~하지 않다 useful[júːsfəl] 형
쓸모 있는 climb[klaim] 통 오르다 bear[bɛər] 명 곰
carry[kǽri] 통 나르다; *업고 가다 back[bæk] 명 등

문제 해설

Q: 남자는 어떤 동물에 대해 말하고 있는가?

　　나무 위에서 살면서 잎을 먹고, 둥근 귀와 큰 머리, 짧은
　　꼬리를 가졌고 새끼를 등에 업고 다니는 동물은 코알라
　　이다.

2

M: What are you doing?
W: I'm reading *Zoo World*. I buy it every month.
M: Ah, I've seen it before. What animals are in it this month?
W: There are penguins and many different kinds of fish.
M: What are the stories about?
W: They're about how fish sleep, and how penguins live in cold places.
M: Really? How interesting! So, do fish sleep?
W: Yes, they do. But they sleep with their eyes open.

남: 뭐 하고 있니?
여: 〈Zoo World〉를 읽고 있어. 매달 사거든.
남: 아, 전에 본 적이 있어. 이번 달에는 어떤 동물이 나오니?
여: 펭귄과 여러 종류의 물고기들이야.
남: 무슨 이야기인데?
여: 물고기들이 어떻게 잠을 자는지, 펭귄이 추운 곳에서 어떻게 사는지에 대한 거야.
남: 정말? 재미있겠다! 그래서 물고기가 잠을 잔대?
여: 응, 그래. 그런데 눈을 뜨고 잔대.

어휘
penguin[péŋgwin] 명 펭귄 [문제] documentary [dàkjuméntəri] 명 다큐멘터리

문제 해설
Q: 그들은 무엇에 대해 이야기하고 있나?
  〈Zoo World〉라는 동물잡지에 실린 내용에 대한 대화이다.

3

W: The San Diego Zoo has prepared some special events for children. On Monday, a magician will put on a fantastic show with animals. Have you ever seen a pink dolphin? If you want to see these amazing animals, visit us on Wednesday. You can watch them dance to music. Are you scared of snakes? Then come to the zoo on Saturday. You'll have a chance to make friends with them.

여: 샌디에이고 동물원은 어린이들을 위한 특별 행사를 준비했습니다. 월요일에는 마술사가 동물들과 함께 환상적인

쇼를 상연할 것입니다. 분홍 돌고래를 본 적이 있으세요? 이 놀라운 동물을 보고 싶으시면 수요일에 오세요. 음악에 맞춰 춤추는 모습을 볼 수 있습니다. 뱀이 무서우신가요? 그렇다면 토요일에 동물원에 오세요. 그들과 친구가 될 수 있는 기회가 될 거예요.

어휘
prepare[pripέər] 동 준비하다 special[spéʃəl] 형 특별한 event[ivént] 명 행사 magician[mədʒíʃən] 명 마술사 put on 상연하다 fantastic[fæntǽstik] 형 환상적인 dolphin[dálfin] 명 돌고래 amazing[əméiziŋ] 형 놀라운 be scared of ~을 무서워하다 snake [sneik] 명 뱀 make friends with ~와 친구가 되다

문제 해설
Q: 각 인물이 동물원에 갈 요일을 쓰시오.
  (1) 분홍 돌고래의 춤을 볼 수 있는 쇼는 수요일에 한다.
  (2) 뱀을 볼 수 있는 행사는 토요일에 있다.
  (3) 마술쇼가 있는 날은 월요일이다.

4

M: You look depressed. Is something wrong?
W: I had a fight with my mom.
M: What was the problem?
W: My friend's cat just had babies. She wanted to give me one, but my mom said no.
M: Why? Does she hate cats?
W: No, she likes them.
M: Then, why?
W: She says that she feels terrible when a pet dies.
M: Has she had a pet before?
W: Yes. She had a dog for 10 years. But it got sick and died.
M: How sad!

남: 너 우울해 보이는구나. 무슨 일 있어?
여: 엄마와 다투었어.
남: 문제가 뭐였는데?
여: 친구네 고양이가 새끼를 낳았거든. 그 애가 한 마리를 주겠다는데 엄마가 안 된다고 하셨어.
남: 왜? 엄마가 고양이를 싫어하셔?
여: 아니, 좋아하셔.
남: 그럼, 왜지?
여: 애완동물이 죽으면 기분이 안 좋으시대.
남: 전에 애완동물을 기른 적이 있으셔?
여: 응. 10년 동안 강아지를 기르셨는데 병들어 죽었대.
남: 정말 슬프다!

어휘

depressed[diprést] 형 우울한   have a fight with
～와 다투다, 싸우다   die[dai] 동 죽다   [문제] prefer
[prifə́:r] 동 더 좋아하다   be tired of 싫증이 나다

문제 해설

Q: 여자의 엄마는 왜 고양이를 기르고 싶어 하지 <u>않는가</u>?
　　기르던 애완동물이 죽으면 기분이 안 좋으셔서 싫다고
　　했다.

5

M: What a cute puppy! What's her name?

W: Her name is Tinkerbell. She's two years
　old.

M: What is her biggest problem?

W: She barks loudly when people visit.

M: I see. Anything else?

W: Yes. She also doesn't eat her food. She
　only wants what I eat.

M: Don't worry. We can fix her problems.

W: How long will it take?

M: After a month of training, she'll be better.

W: Okay. Please take good care of her.

남: 귀여운 강아지네요! 이름이 뭐죠?

여: Tinkerbell이에요. 2살이고요.

남: 무엇이 제일 문제인가요?

여: 집에 사람들이 오면 크게 짖어요.

남: 알겠어요. 또 다른 게 있나요?

여: 네. 또, 자기 먹이를 안 먹어요. 제가 먹는 것만 먹으려
　　해요.

남: 걱정 마세요. 문제를 고쳐 드릴 수 있어요.

여: 얼마나 걸릴까요?

남: 한 달 동안 훈련하고 나면 좋아질 거예요.

여: 알겠어요. 잘 돌봐 주세요.

어휘

bark[bɑːrk] 동 짖다   loudly[láudli] 부 크게, 시끄럽게
fix[fiks] 동 고치다   training[tréiniŋ] 명 훈련   take
care of ～을 돌보다   [문제] zookeeper[zúːkìːpər]
명 동물원 사육사   trainer[tréinər] 명 조련사, 트레이너
owner[óunər] 명 주인, 소유자

문제 해설

Q: 남자의 직업은?
　　강아지의 문제점을 훈련으로 교정해주는 개 조련사이다.

6

W: Do you like playing with animals? Do
　you want to earn money and have fun?
　Here's a fun part-time job. We're looking
　for a friendly person who loves animals.
　The job is taking care of three dogs,
　walking and feeding them. You must be
　older than 18, and have a cellphone. If
　you're interested in this job, please send
　us an email.

여: 동물과 노는 것을 좋아하세요? 돈을 벌면서 재미도 있길
　　바라세요? 여기 재미있는 아르바이트가 있습니다. 동물
　　을 사랑하는 상냥한 사람을 찾습니다. 세 마리의 개를 산
　　책시키고 먹이를 주면서 돌보는 일입니다. 18세 이상이어
　　야 하고 휴대전화가 있어야 합니다. 이 일에 관심이 있으
　　시면 저희에게 이메일을 보내주세요.

어휘

earn[əːrn] 동 (돈을) 벌다   part-time job 아르바이트,
시간제 일   look for ～을 찾다   friendly[fréndli] 형
상냥한   walk[wɔːk] 동 산책시키다   feed[fiːd] 동 먹이
를 주다   cellphone[sélfòun] 명 휴대전화   be
interested in ～에 관심이 있다   [문제] apply[əplái]
동 지원하다

문제 해설

Q: 잘못된 정보를 고르시오.
　　지원하려면 이메일을 보내라고 했다.

7

M: You look so worried. What's wrong?

W: I lost my dog Bo while walking him in
　Central Park.

M: Oh, when did it happen?

W: Two days ago.

M: Wait! I saw a dog running around
　yesterday. Is he brown?

W: His face is brown, but his body is white.

M: Was he wearing a red ribbon?

W: No, he wasn't wearing a ribbon.

M: Hmm... I guess it wasn't him then.

W: Anyway, please call me if you see him.

M: Don't worry. I'm sure you'll find him.

남: 걱정이 있어 보여. 무슨 문제 있어?

여: 내 개 Bo를 센트럴 파크에서 산책시키던 중에 잃어버렸어.

남: 아, 언제 그런 일이 있었어?

여: 이틀 전이야.

남: 잠깐만! 어제 개가 돌아다니는 걸 봤어. 갈색이니?

여: 얼굴은 갈색인데 몸은 하얀색이야.

남: 빨간 리본을 달았니?

여: 아니, 리본을 달지 않았어.

남: 흠… 그렇다면 그 개가 네 개가 아니었나 봐.

여: 어쨌든, 보게 되면 전화 좀 해 줘.

남: 걱정 마. 꼭 찾게 될 거야.

어휘

worried[wɔ́:rid] ⑲ 걱정스러운   happen[hǽpən] ⑧
일어나다   guess[ges] ⑧ 짐작하다   worry[wɔ́:ri] ⑧
걱정하다   sure[ʃuər] ⑲ 확신하는

문제 해설

Q: Bo의 사진을 고르시오.

몸은 하얗고 얼굴은 갈색인 개가 Bo이다.

8

M: Did you know that crows are the smartest birds in the world? Crows have large brains. They have the highest IQ of any bird. They can use tools to catch insects. Also, crows are sweet birds. After growing up, they take care of their mothers. They bring food to their moms when they are too old to hunt.

남: 까마귀가 세상에서 가장 영리한 새라는 것을 알고 있었나요? 까마귀는 뇌가 큽니다. 그들은 새 중에 가장 IQ가 높습니다. 곤충을 잡기 위해 도구를 사용할 수 있습니다. 또한, 까마귀는 다정한 새입니다. 성장한 이후에는 어미를 돌봅니다. 어미 새가 너무 나이가 들어 사냥을 할 수 없을 때에는 먹이를 물어다 줍니다.

어휘

crow[krou] ⑲ 까마귀   smart[smɑːrt] ⑲ 영리한
brain[brein] ⑲ 뇌   tool[tuːl] ⑲ 도구   catch[kætʃ]
⑧ 잡다 (catch-caught-caught)   insect[ínsekt] ⑲ 곤
충   sweet[swiːt] ⑲ 단; *다정한   grow up 성장하다
hunt[hʌnt] ⑧ 사냥하다   [문제] for life 평생

문제 해설

Q: 까마귀에 대해 사실이면 T, 사실이 아니면 F를 쓰시오.

(1) 가장 영리한 새이다.

(2) 사냥을 할 때 도구를 사용할 수 있다.

(3) 새끼들을 평생 돌본다.

A 1 ④ 2 ④   B 1 ② 2 ③

A [1-2]

W: May I help you?

M: Yes. I want to buy a pet rabbit.

W: Okay. How about this white one?

M: Wow. It's so cute.

W: Rabbits are very sensitive animals, so you should be very careful.

M: What should I do?

W: Pet rabbits are different from wild rabbits, so you should keep them indoors.

M: Anything else?

W: Do not give them corn or nuts. They can make them sick.

M: Okay. I won't.

W: And don't pull their ears. It can hurt them.

M: All right.

W: And don't wash them with water if possible. Just wash their dirty parts with a wet cloth.

M: Okay.

여: 무엇을 도와드릴까요?

남: 네. 애완용 토끼를 사고 싶어요.

여: 알겠습니다. 이 흰 토끼는 어때요?

남: 와. 아주 귀엽네요.

여: 토끼는 아주 예민한 동물이라서 아주 조심해야 해요.

남: 어떻게 해야 하나요?

여: 애완용 토끼는 야생 토끼와는 달라서 실내에 두어야 해요.

남: 또 다른 것은요?

여: 옥수수나 견과류를 주면 안 돼요. 병이 나게 할 수도 있거든요.

남: 알겠어요. 그러지 않을게요.

여: 그리고 귀를 잡아당기면 안 돼요. 아플 수 있어요.

남: 알겠어요.

여: 그리고 가능한 한 물로 씻기지 마세요. 더러운 부분만 젖은 천으로 닦아 주세요.

남: 알겠어요.

어휘

sensitive[sénsətiv] ⑲ 예민한   careful[kɛ́ərfəl] ⑲ 신
경을 쓰는, 유의하는   wild[waild] ⑲ 야생의   indoors
[indɔ́ːrz] ⑨ 실내에   corn[kɔːrn] ⑲ 옥수수   nut[nʌt]
⑲ 견과류   pull[pul] ⑧ 잡아당기다   hurt[həːrt] ⑧

아프게 하다 (hurt–hurt–hurt) **if possible** 가능하면
dirty[dɔ́ːrti] 휑 더러운 **wet**[wet] 휑 젖은 **cloth**
[klɔːθ] 몡 천, 헝겊 [문제] **treat**[triːt] 통 다루다

문제 해설

Q1: 화자 간의 관계는?

애완용 토끼를 사러 온 고객과 애완동물 가게 주인의 대
화이다.

Q2: 토끼를 잘 다루고 있는 사람은?

토끼는 더러워진 부분만 젖은 천으로 닦아 주어야 한다.

B [1-2]

M: Do you know how to take an animal on a
plane?

W: Yes, I've done it before.

M: What should I do?

W: First, you should tell the airline about it.
You'll have to pay extra money.

M: Can I take her on the plane with me?

W: If she is less than 6 kg, you can put her
under your seat. But she has to be in a
cage.

M: Okay. She is only 1 kg.

W: Also, you need a document that says
your puppy is healthy.

M: Where can I get one?

W: From any pet clinic.

M: Then I should go get one now. Thank you
for your help.

W: No problem.

남: 동물을 비행기에 어떻게 데리고 타는지 알아?

여: 응, 전에 해 봤어.

남: 어떻게 해야 해?

여: 우선, 항공사에 얘기를 해야 해. 추가 비용을 지불해야
할 거야.

남: 비행기에 같이 데리고 탈 수 있는 거야?

여: 6kg보다 적게 나가면 좌석 아래에 놓아도 돼. 하지만 우
리 안에 있어야 해.

남: 알겠어. 1kg밖에 안 돼.

여: 또 네 강아지가 건강하다는 것을 말해 줄 서류가 필요해.

남: 어디서 그걸 얻을 수 있지?

여: 아무 동물 병원에서나.

남: 그럼, 지금 받으러 가야겠어. 도와줘서 고마워.

여: 천만에.

32

어휘

plane[plein] 몡 비행기 (= airplane) **airline**[ɛ́ərlàin]
몡 항공사 **pay**[pei] 통 지불하다 **extra**[ékstrə] 휑
추가의 **less than** ~보다 적은 **seat**[siːt] 몡 좌석
cage[keidʒ] 몡 우리, 장 **document**[dɑ́kjumənt] 몡
서류 **healthy**[hélθi] 휑 건강한

문제 해설

Q1: 그들은 무엇에 대해 이야기하고 있나?

① 애완동물을 건강하게 기르는 방법

② 비행기에 애완동물을 데리고 타는 방법

③ 애완동물에게 좋은 우리의 종류

④ 아픈 애완동물이 비행기에 탈 수 없는 이유

비행기에 애완동물을 데리고 타는 방법에 대한 내용이다.

Q2: 남자가 다음에 할 일은?

강아지의 건강을 증명하는 서류를 구하기 위해 동물 병
원에 갈 것이다.

Critical ★ Thinking   p. 31

1 ① 2 (1) © (2) ⓑ

M: I'm Joe. My dog, Rex, is three years old
now. He joined my family when he was
one year old. Each season, I buy him new
clothes and accessories. Every weekend,
I go to dog cafés with him. For Christmas,
I'm going to buy him a new house. My
friend Sally doesn't understand why I
spend so much money on a dog. She
says I can help poor people with that
money. But he's a member of my family.
Is it wrong to spend money on my family?

남: 저는 Joe입니다. 제 개 Rex는 현재 3살이에요. Rex가
1살이었을 때에 저희 가족이 되었지요. 저는 계절마다
Rex에게 새 옷과 액세서리들을 사줍니다. 주말마다 함
께 애견 카페에 가고요. 성탄절에는 새 집을 사주려고 해
요. 제 친구 Sally는 제가 개에게 왜 그렇게 많은 돈을
쓰는지 이해하지 못해요. 그 애는 그 돈으로 불우한 사람
들을 도울 수 있다고 합니다. 그렇지만 Rex는 우리 가족
의 일원이에요. 가족에게 돈을 쓰는 것이 잘못된 건가요?

어휘

join[dʒɔin] 통 합류하다 **season**[síːzən] 몡 계절
accessory[əksésəri] 몡 액세서리, 장신구 [문제]
own[oun] 통 소유하다 **present**[prézənt] 몡 선물

문제 해설
Q1: 사실이 아닌 것은?
　① Joe는 Rex를 3년 동안 키웠다.
　② Rex는 옷을 입고 액세서리를 한다.
　③ Joe와 Rex는 애견 카페에 자주 간다.
　④ Joe는 Rex에게 선물을 줄 계획이다.
　Rex가 1살 때 키우기 시작해 현재 3살이므로 2년 동안
　키웠다.

Q2: 각 인물의 의견을 고르시오.
　ⓐ 애완동물은 옷이나 액세서리가 필요하지 않다.
　ⓑ 애완동물에 많은 돈을 쓰지 말아야 한다.
　ⓒ 애완동물을 위해 물건을 사는 것은 가족에게 돈을 쓰
　　는 것과 같다.
　(1) Joe는 애완동물을 가족으로 생각하고 돈을 쓴다.
　(2) Sally는 애완동물에 많은 돈을 쓰는 것을 이해하지
　　못하므로 그러지 말아야 한다고 생각한다.

UNIT 05 Daily Life

Getting ★ Ready　p. 32

A 1 dry-clean　2 microwave　3 refrigerator
　4 passport
B 1 ⓐ　2 ⓓ　3 ⓕ

B 1 남: 사진을 네 장 더 주문할 수 있을까요?
　　여: 물론이죠. 그러면 4달러를 더 내셔야 합니다.
　2 남: 어떤 머리 색이 더 좋을까요?
　　여: 검은색이 당신에게 더 잘 어울릴 것 같아요.
　3 남: 보통 우편과 빠른 우편 중에 어떤 것이 더 좋으세요?
　　여: 보통 우편이요.

Listening ★ Start　p. 33

1 ③ / Who is it, How much is it, Didn't you
　order, don't worry
2 ②, ④ / plant some flowers, Except for,
　What kind of, you're right, look fantastic

1

(*Doorbell rings.*)
W: Who is it?

M: Pizza Hot delivery.
W: Wow. That was quick. How much is it?
M: It's $20.
W: Okay, but did you only bring one cola?
M: Didn't you order a large pizza and a cola?
W: Actually, I ordered two colas.
M: Oh, I'm terribly sorry. I'll come back with
　it soon.
W: No, don't worry about it. I'll just take the
　one cola.
M: Then the price is just $17. Again, I'm sorry
　about that.

(초인종이 울린다.)
여: 누구세요?
남: Pizza Hot 배달입니다.
여: 와. 빠르네요. 얼마인가요?
남: 20달러예요.
여: 알겠어요, 그런데 콜라를 하나만 가져왔나요?
남: 라지 사이즈 피자 하나와 콜라 하나를 주문하지 않으셨
　나요?
여: 사실, 콜라 2개를 주문했는데요.
남: 아, 정말 죄송합니다. 가서 바로 가져오겠습니다.
여: 아니, 걱정하지 마세요. 그냥 콜라 한 개만 할게요.
남: 그러면 가격이 17달러입니다. 다시 한 번 죄송합니다.

어휘
doorbell[dɔ́ːrbèl] 명 초인종　delivery[dilívəri] 명 배
달　quick[kwik] 형 빠른　order[ɔ́ːrdər] 동 주문하다
actually[ǽktʃuəli] 부 사실은　terribly[térəbli] 부 몹시,
굉장히　price[prais] 명 가격

문제 해설
Q: 남자는 왜 미안해했나?
　여자가 콜라를 2개 주문했는데 실수로 1개만 가져왔다.

2

W: Honey, we should plant some flowers in
　the garden.
M: Flowers?
W: It's going to be spring soon. Except for
　the white tulips, all the flowers in the
　garden are dead.
M: What kind of flowers do you want?
W: I was thinking of pink daisies.
M: Wouldn't red ones be better?
W: Oh, you're right. They'd be more colorful.

M: And how about some yellow roses? You know I love yellow flowers.

W: Good idea. Our garden will look fantastic with those flowers.

여: 여보, 정원에 꽃을 좀 심어야겠어요.

남: 꽃이요?

여: 곧 봄이 되잖아요. 하얀 튤립 빼고는 정원에 있는 꽃들이 다 죽었어요.

남: 어떤 종류의 꽃을 원해요?

여: 분홍 데이지를 생각하고 있었어요.

남: 빨간 것이 낫지 않을까요?

여: 아, 그러네요. 그게 더 화려할 거예요.

남: 그리고 노란색 장미는 어때요? 알다시피 내가 노란색 꽃들 좋아하잖아요.

여: 좋은 생각이에요. 우리 정원이 그 꽃들로 인해 멋지게 될 거예요.

어휘

plant[plænt] 동 심다 garden[gɑ́ːrdən] 명 정원
except for ~을 빼고 tulip[tjúːlip] 명 튤립 dead
[ded] 형 죽은 daisy[déizi] 명 데이지 colorful
[kʌ́lərfəl] 형 화려한, 색채가 풍부한 fantastic[fæntǽstik]
형 환상적인, 멋진

문제 해설

Q: 그들이 심을 꽃 두 종류를 고르시오.
　　빨간색 데이지와 노란색 장미를 심기로 했다.

Listening ★ Practice　　p. 34

1 ④　2 ②　3 ③　4 ①　5 ②　6 ④　7 ④　8 ③

1

W: What can I do for you?

M: I'd like to have my photo taken for my passport. How much does it cost?

W: It's $10 for eight pictures.

M: Can I order four more pictures?

W: Of course. Then, you should pay $4 more.

M: Okay.

W: Could you please take a seat over there?

M: Wait. I want to look in the mirror first.

W: Sure. Go ahead.

여: 무엇을 도와드릴까요?

남: 여권에 필요한 사진을 찍으려고 해요. 얼마인가요?

여: 사진 8장에 10달러예요.

남: 4장을 더 주문할 수 있을까요?

여: 물론이죠. 그러면 4달러를 더 내셔야 합니다.

남: 알겠습니다.

여: 저기 앉으시겠어요?

남: 잠시만요. 우선 거울을 보고 싶어요.

여: 네. 그러세요.

어휘

have one's photo taken 사진을 찍다 passport
[pǽspɔːrt] 명 여권 cost[kɔ(ː)st] 동 (비용이 얼마) 들다
(cost-cost-cost) take a seat 자리에 앉다 mirror
[mírər] 명 거울 Go ahead. 그렇게 하세요.

문제 해설

Q: 남자가 지불할 돈은 얼마인가?
　　기본 8장이 10달러인데 추가로 4장을 더 주문했다. 추가
　　분은 4달러이므로 총 14달러를 지불해야 한다.

2

M: When you wash dishes, use warm water. It helps you clean dirty dishes more quickly. Also, it's important to wash cleaner dishes first and oily ones last. When you wash frying pans, clean off the oil with a paper towel first. And what should you do for dishes with a bad fish smell? Heat them in the microwave first and then wash them well with warm water.

남: 설거지를 할 때에는 따뜻한 물을 사용하세요. 더러운 식기를 더 빨리 닦는 데 도움이 됩니다. 또한, 더 깨끗한 식기들을 먼저 씻고 마지막에 기름기가 있는 것들을 씻는 것이 중요합니다. 프라이팬을 닦을 때는 키친타올로 먼저 기름을 닦아내세요. 그리고 나쁜 생선 냄새가 나는 식기들은 어떻게 해야 할까요? 전자레인지에서 먼저 가열하고 난 다음 따뜻한 물로 잘 씻으세요.

어휘

wash dishes 설거지하다 clean[kliːn] 동 깨끗하게 하
다, 닦다 dish[diʃ] 명 식기 oily[ɔ́ili] 형 기름기 많은
frying pan 프라이팬 paper towel 키친타올
smell[smel] 명 냄새 heat[hiːt] 동 가열하다
microwave[máikrəwèiv] 명 전자레인지 [문제] tip[tip]
명 비결, 비법 difficulty[dífikʌ̀lti] 명 어려움 save
[seiv] 동 절약하다

문제 해설

Q: 남자는 무엇에 대해 이야기하고 있나?
　　① 부엌을 청소하는 방법

② 설거지를 잘하는 요령

③ 기름기가 많은 식기들을 씻는 것의 어려움

④ 설거지할 때 물을 절약하는 방법

설거지를 잘하는 몇 가지 요령에 대한 내용이다.

3

M: What can I do for you?

W: I had my blue shirt dry-cleaned here and picked it up yesterday.

M: Is something wrong?

W: Yes. Look at this! When you cleaned it, it turned purple!

M: Oh, I'm very sorry.

W: Last time, you made my sweater smaller. And now you've made another mistake.

M: I don't know what to say.

W: I'll never come here again. Next time, the shape of my shirt might change.

M: I'm terribly sorry. I'll buy you a new shirt if you want.

남: 무엇을 도와드릴까요?

여: 제 푸른색 셔츠를 여기에 드라이클리닝 맡겼다가 어제 찾아갔어요.

남: 무슨 문제가 있나요?

여: 네. 이것 좀 보세요! 세탁을 하면서 보라색이 되었잖아요!

남: 아, 정말 죄송합니다.

여: 지난번엔 스웨터가 줄어들었어요. 그리고 이제 또 다른 실수를 하셨군요.

남: 드릴 말씀이 없네요.

여: 다신 여기 오지 않겠어요. 다음 번엔 셔츠 모양이 바뀔지도 모르잖아요.

남: 정말 죄송합니다. 원하신다면 새 셔츠를 사드릴게요.

어휘

dry-clean[dráiklíːn] 동 드라이클리닝 하다 pick up 찾아오다 turn[təːrn] 동 변하다 purple[pə́ːrpl] 형 보라색의 make a mistake 실수하다 shape[ʃeip] 명 모양

문제 해설

Q: 여자의 셔츠에는 어떤 문제가 있나?

푸른색 셔츠가 보라색으로 바뀌었다.

4

(*Telephone rings.*)

M: Happy Bakery. How may I help you?

W: Hello. I want to order a cake.

M: Okay. What kind of cake do you want?

W: I want a heart-shaped chocolate cake.

M: Sorry, but they're all sold out. What about a round cake instead?

W: That will be fine.

M: What is your address?

W: 506 Riverside Street.

M: Okay. Also, we can write a message on the cake. Is this a birthday cake?

W: No, it's for my son's graduation. He'll become a high school student soon.

M: Okay.

(전화벨이 울린다.)

남: Happy Bakery입니다. 무엇을 도와드릴까요?

여: 안녕하세요. 케이크를 주문하고 싶어요.

남: 알겠습니다. 어떤 종류의 케이크를 원하시죠?

여: 하트 모양의 초콜릿 케이크요.

남: 죄송합니다만, 그것들은 품절이에요. 대신에 둥근 모양의 케이크는 어떨까요?

여: 그거 좋겠네요.

남: 주소가 어떻게 되시죠?

여: Riverside가 506번지요.

남: 알겠습니다. 그리고 케이크 위에 메시지를 쓸 수 있어요. 생일 케이크인가요?

여: 아니요, 아들 졸업을 위한 거예요. 곧 고등학생이 되거든요.

남: 알겠습니다.

어휘

bakery[béikəri] 명 빵집 heart-shaped[hɑ́rtʃèipt] 형 하트 모양의 be sold out 품절되다 instead[instéd] 부 대신에 address[ǽdres] 명 주소 message[mésidʒ] 명 메시지 graduation[grædʒuéiʃən] 명 졸업

문제 해설

Q: 여자가 주문한 케이크를 고르시오.

둥근 모양이고, 졸업 축하 메시지가 들어간 것이다.

5

W: How can I help you?

M: I have an account here, but I don't have a cash card. So I'd like to get one.

W: If you get a credit card, you can use it as a cash card, too. What do you think?

M: Well, I just need a cash card.

W: All right. Could you show me your ID card?

M: Here it is.
W: Could you please fill out this form?
M: Okay.
W: If you wait for a second, I'll go get the card.

여: 무엇을 도와드릴까요?
남: 여기에 계좌가 있는데요, 현금 카드가 없어요. 하나 발급하려고요.
여: 신용 카드를 발급하시면 현금 카드로도 쓸 수 있으세요. 어떠신가요?
남: 음, 전 그냥 현금 카드만 필요한데요.
여: 좋습니다. 신분증을 보여주시겠어요?
남: 여기 있어요.
여: 이 양식을 작성해 주시겠어요?
남: 알겠습니다.
여: 잠시만 기다리시면 카드를 가져다 드릴게요.

어휘
account[əkáunt] 명 계좌　cash card 현금 카드
credit card 신용 카드　ID card 신분증
(= identification card)　fill out 작성하다　form[fɔːrm]
명 양식, 서식　[문제] open an account 계좌를 개설하다

문제 해설
Q: 남자는 왜 은행에 갔나?
　　계좌의 돈을 입출금 할 수 있는 현금 카드를 발급하러 갔다.

6

W: Hi, I want to get my hair cut.
M: Okay. How short?
W: I want really short hair. Please cut off about 10 cm.
M: All right. Do you also want to get a perm?
W: I don't think so.
M: In my opinion, you would look better with curly hair.
W: I like my straight hair, but I want to change the color.
M: What color do you want?
W: Brown or blond. Which one would be better?
M: Blond would look better on you.
W: All right.

여: 안녕하세요. 머리를 자르고 싶어요.
남: 알겠어요. 얼마나 짧게요?
여: 아주 짧은 머리를 원해요. 10cm 정도 잘라내 주세요.
남: 좋습니다. 파마도 원하세요?

여: 아니요.
남: 제 생각에는 곱슬머리가 더 잘 어울리실 것 같아요.
여: 전 생머리가 좋아요. 그렇지만 색깔은 바꾸고 싶어요.
남: 어떤 색을 원하세요?
여: 갈색이나 블론드색이요. 어떤 게 더 나을까요?
남: 블론드색이 더 잘 어울릴 거예요.
여: 알겠어요.

어휘
get one's hair cut (미용실에서) 머리를 자르다　cut
off 잘라내다　perm[pəːrm] 명 파마　in my opinion
내 생각에　curly[kə́ːrli] 형 곱슬곱슬한　straight[streit]
형 곧은　blond[blɑnd] 명 블론드색

문제 해설
Q: 여자가 원하는 머리 스타일을 고르시오.
　　여자가 하려고 하는 머리는 블론드색의 짧은 생머리이다.

7

W: I always do my homework right after I get home from school. That way, I can relax afterwards without any worries. While I do my homework, my mom prepares dinner. Then I help her set the table. I used to watch TV after dinner, so my parents called me a couch potato. But last week I started to play badminton with my dad instead. It's really good exercise.

여: 저는 항상 학교에서 집으로 돌아오면 바로 숙제를 합니다. 그래야 그 이후에 아무 걱정 없이 쉴 수 있어요. 숙제를 하는 동안 엄마는 저녁을 준비해요. 그러면 제가 상 차리는 걸 돕죠. 저녁 식사 후에는 TV를 보곤 해서 부모님이 절 couch potato라고 불렀었죠. 하지만 지난 주부터 그 대신에 아빠와 배드민턴을 치기 시작했어요. 그건 정말 좋은 운동이에요.

어휘
that way 그래야, 그런 식으로　relax[rilǽks] 동 쉬다,
긴장을 풀다　afterwards[ǽftərwərdz] 부 나중에
worry[wə́ːri] 명 걱정　prepare[pripέər] 동 준비하다
set the table 상 차리다　used to-v ~하곤 했다
couch potato 소파에 앉아서 TV만 보는 사람, 게으르고
비활동적인 사람　badminton[bǽdmintn] 명 배드민턴

문제 해설
Q: 소녀가 방과 후에 하지 않는 것을 고르시오.
　　과거에는 TV를 봤지만 지난 주부터 배드민턴을 친다고 했다.

8

W: Can I help you?

M: Yes, please. I want to send this package to America.

W: What's in it?

M: Just some clothes and several books.

W: Could you put it on here? We need to know the weight.

M: All right. Here it is.

W: It's 850 grams. Which would you prefer, regular mail or express mail?

M: Is regular mail much cheaper?

W: It's about half the price. But it takes about six days longer.

M: Then I'll use express mail. How much will it cost?

W: It'll be $100.

여: 도와드릴까요?

남: 네. 미국으로 이 소포를 부치려고 해요.

여: 무엇이 들어 있어요?

남: 그냥 옷들과 책 몇 권이에요.

여: 여기에 놔 주시겠어요? 무게를 알아야 해요.

남: 알겠어요. 여기요.

여: 850그램이네요. 보통 우편과 빠른 우편 중에서 어떤 것이 더 좋으세요?

남: 보통 우편이 훨씬 싼가요?

여: 절반 정도의 가격이에요. 그렇지만 6일 정도 더 걸려요.

남: 그렇다면 빠른 우편으로 할게요. 얼마죠?

여: 100달러입니다.

어휘

package[pǽkidʒ] 명 소포 several[sévərəl] 형 몇몇의
weight[weit] 명 무게 prefer[prifə́:r] 통 선호하다
regular mail 보통 우편 express mail 빠른 우편
half[hæf] 형 절반의, ~의 반의 [문제] receipt[risí:t]
명 영수증 content[kántent] 명 내용물

문제 해설

Q: 틀린 정보를 고르시오.

보통 우편이 6일 더 걸린다는 말을 듣고 남자는 빠른 우편을 선택했다.

Listening ★ Challenge p. 36

A 1 ④ 2 ③, ④ B 1 ① 2 ③

A [1-2]

W: Steve, can you go get some fruit from the market for me?

M: Why me? Can't you ask Jack, instead?

W: Your brother has a test tomorrow. He's too busy.

M: But my favorite drama is on TV right now.

W: I'm sorry, but I need you to do this now. If you go, I'll make spaghetti — your favorite.

M: But I don't feel like eating that today.

W: Okay, then I'll buy you a comic book.

M: Thanks, Mom! So, what do you need?

W: Oranges, strawberries, and melons.

M: Got it.

W: Oh, there are some oranges left in the refrigerator. Just forget about oranges.

M: Okay.

여: Steve, 시장에 가서 과일 좀 사다 줄 수 있겠니?

남: 왜 저예요? Jack에게 대신 부탁하시면 안 돼요?

여: 네 남동생은 내일 시험이 있어. 너무 바쁘잖니.

남: 그렇지만 지금 TV에서 제가 제일 좋아하는 드라마가 하는 걸요.

여: 미안하지만 네가 지금 해 줬으면 해. 네가 가면 네가 제일 좋아하는 스파게티 해 줄게.

남: 하지만 오늘은 그거 별로 먹고 싶지 않아요.

여: 좋아, 그럼 만화책을 사 줄게.

남: 고마워요, 엄마! 그럼 뭐가 필요하신 거예요?

여: 오렌지랑 딸기, 멜론이야.

남: 알았어요.

여: 아, 냉장고에 오렌지가 좀 남아 있구나. 오렌지는 빼렴.

남: 알았어요.

어휘

fruit[fru:t] 명 과일 market[má:rkit] 명 시장
favorite[féivərit] 형 가장 좋아하는; 명 가장 좋아하는 것
feel like v-ing ~하고 싶다 comic book 만화책
strawberry[strɔ́:bèri] 명 딸기 melon[mélən] 명 멜론
refrigerator[rifrídʒərèitər] 명 냉장고 [문제] offer
[ɔ́(:)fər] 통 제안하다

문제 해설

Q1: 왜 소년은 시장에 가기로 결정했나?

① 과일을 먹고 싶었다.

② 엄마를 돕고 싶었다.

③ 엄마가 스파게티를 해 주겠다고 제안했다.

④ 엄마가 만화책을 사 주겠다고 제안했다.

엄마가 만화책을 사 주겠다고 해서 가기로 마음을 먹었다.

Q2: 소년이 살 과일 두 종류를 고르시오.

엄마가 부탁한 대로 딸기와 멜론을 살 것이다.

B [1-2]

(*Telephone rings.*)

M: Hello, Royal Chinese Restaurant.

W: Hi. I ordered some food five minutes ago, and I want to add two egg rolls.

M: Could you tell me your address?

W: My address is 135 New York Street.

M: And your phone number please?

W: It's 3142–0357.

M: Okay. So you ordered two boxes of fried rice, one seafood noodle, and two egg rolls, correct?

W: That's right. When can I get my food?

M: In about 30 minutes. It'll take some time today because of the rain.

W: Okay. Also, I didn't get chopsticks last time. So please don't forget to bring chopsticks.

M: Don't worry. You'll get them.

(전화벨이 울린다.)

남: 여보세요, Royal 중식당입니다.

여: 안녕하세요. 5분 전에 음식을 주문했는데요, 에그롤 두 개를 추가하고 싶어서요.

남: 주소를 말씀해 주시겠어요?

여: 주소는 뉴욕가 135번지예요.

남: 그리고 전화번호는요?

여: 3142–0357이요.

남: 알겠습니다. 볶음밥 두 상자와 해물면 하나, 에그롤 두 개를 주문하신 거 맞죠?

여: 맞아요. 언제 받게 되나요?

남: 30분쯤 후에요. 비 때문에 오늘 시간이 좀 걸려요.

여: 알겠어요. 그리고 지난번에 젓가락이 안 왔거든요. 그러니 젓가락 가져오는 거 잊지 마세요.

남: 걱정 마세요. 가져다 드릴게요.

어휘

add[æd] 동 추가하다   egg roll 에그롤, 스프링롤
fried rice 볶음밥   seafood[síːfùːd] 명 해산물
correct[kərékt] 형 옳은, 정확한   noodle[núːdl] 명 면,
국수   chopstick[tʃɑ́pstik] 명 젓가락   [문제] cancel
[kǽnsəl] 동 취소하다   make a reservation 예약하다

문제 해설

Q1: 여자는 무엇을 하고 있나?

음식을 추가로 주문하고 있다.

Q2: 틀린 정보를 고르시오.

볶음밥은 한 상자가 아니라 두 상자를 주문했다.

Critical ★ Thinking   p. 37

1 ① 2 ②, ④

M: Do you help your mother do housework?

W: Sure. Our family shares the work.

M: How do you share it?

W: Well, for example, when mom cooks, I set the table. Then after dinner, dad washes the dishes.

M: Really?

W: Yes. I also clean the bathroom and dad sometimes prepares lunch.

M: That's surprising. My mom takes care of all the housework.

W: Then your mother must have hard time! Housework is hard to do alone.

M: Is it? I've never thought about it.

W: Your mother will be very pleased if you help her.

M: You're right. I'm going to help her from now on.

남: 넌 엄마가 집안일 하시는 것을 도와드려?

여: 물론이지. 우리 가족은 일을 분담해.

남: 어떻게 분담해?

여: 음, 예를 들면, 엄마가 요리할 때 난 상을 차려. 저녁을 먹고 나면 아빠가 설거지를 하셔.

남: 정말?

여: 응. 난 욕실도 청소하고 아빠는 가끔 점심을 준비하셔.

남: 놀랍다. 우리 엄마는 모든 집안일을 맡아 하시는데.

여: 그럼 너네 어머니는 힘드실 거야! 집안일은 혼자 하기 힘들어.

남: 그래? 한 번도 그런 생각 해 본 적 없는데.

여: 네가 엄마를 도와드리면 아주 기뻐하실 거야.

남: 네 말이 맞아. 지금부터 엄마를 도와드려야겠다.

어휘

housework[háuswə̀rk] 명 집안일, 가사   share[ʃɛər]
동 나누다   bathroom[bǽθrù(ː)m] 명 욕실   take care

38

of ~을 돌보다; *책임을 맡다   alone[əlóun] ⑨ 혼자서
pleased[pliːzd] ⑩ 기뻐하는   try to-v ~하도록 노력하
다   [문제] various[vέ(ː)əriəs] ⑩ 여러 가지의   role
[roul] ⑬ 역할

문제 해설
Q1: 그들은 주로 무엇에 대해 이야기하고 있나?
　　① 집안일 분담
　　② 집안일의 여러 가지 종류
　　③ 집안일을 하는 어려움
　　④ 가정에서의 어머니의 역할
　　가족들이 집안일을 분담하는 것에 대한 내용이다.
Q2: 소녀가 하는 집안일의 종류 두 개를 고르시오.
　　상 차리기와 욕실 청소를 한다고 했다.

UNIT 06 Entertainment

Getting ★ Ready   p. 38

A 1 ⓑ   2 ⓓ   3 ⓖ   4 ⓐ   5 ⓕ
B 1 ⓕ   2 ⓒ   3 ⓔ

B 1 여: 어느 극장에서 그 연극을 상연하죠?
　　남: Gallery 극장이에요.
　2 여: 'Hamlet'을 예매하고 싶어요.
　　남: 죄송합니다. 표가 매진이에요.
　3 여: A구역 자리로 가능한가요?
　　남: 죄송합니다. C구역 좌석만 가능합니다.

Listening ★ Start   p. 39

1 ③ / going to a musical, can't forget, heard
a lot, sounds more interesting
2 ④ / so excited, seem satisfied, played the
part, my favorite

1

M: Laura, how about going to a musical this
weekend?
W: That's a wonderful idea. I still can't forget
The Lion King at Eastside Theater.
M: Yes, it was great. Now that theater is
showing *Cats*.

W: Right. I heard a lot about it.
M: Also, *Notre Dame de Paris* is playing at
Gallery Theater. Which one do you want
to see?
W: Well, *Cats* sounds more interesting than
Notre Dame de Paris.
M: Good. Let's see that, then.

남: Laura, 이번 주말에 뮤지컬을 보러 가는 게 어때?
여: 멋진 생각이야. Eastside 극장에서 본 'The Lion King'
　　은 아직도 잊혀지질 않아.
남: 그래, 훌륭했지. 그 극장에서 지금 'Cats'를 상연 중이야.
여: 맞아. 그 얘기 많이 들었어.
남: 또, 'Notre Dame de Paris'는 Gallery 극장에서 상연해.
　　어떤 것을 보고 싶니?
여: 음, 'Cats'가 'Notre Dame de Paris'보다 더 재미있을
　　것 같아.
남: 좋아. 그럼 그걸 보자.

어휘
musical[mjúːzikəl] ⑬ 뮤지컬   wonderful[wʌ́ndərfəl]
⑩ 멋진, 훌륭한   still[stil] ⑨ 아직   forget[fərgét] ⑧
잊다 (forget-forgot-forgotten)   theater[θíː(ː)ətər] ⑬
극장   show[ʃou] ⑧ 보여주다; *상연하다   sound
[saund] ⑧ 생각되다, ~하게 들리다

문제 해설
Q: 그들이 볼 뮤지컬은?
　　여자가 'Cats'가 더 재미있을 것 같다고 해서 그것을 보
　　기로 정했다.

2

W: Michael, how was the ice ballet? You
were so excited about it.
M: Well, the show was beautiful.
W: But you don't seem satisfied.
M: I went there to see my favorite skater,
Rachel Wake.
W: Yes, you're a big fan of hers.
M: But she didn't skate in the show
yesterday. Helen Bloom played the part
instead.
W: Helen Bloom is also famous.
M: Yes, but Rachel is my favorite. I really
wanted to see her.
W: I'm sorry to hear that.

★ ★

여: Michael, 아이스 발레 어땠니? 너 아주 신났었잖아.

남: 음, 쇼는 아름다웠어.

여: 하지만 만족스러워 보이지 않네.

남: 난 내가 제일 좋아하는 스케이터인 Rachel Wake를 보
러 간 거였거든.

여: 응, 넌 그녀의 열성 팬이잖아.

남: 그런데 그녀는 어제 쇼에서 스케이트를 타지 않았어.
Helen Bloom이 대신 그 역을 연기했어.

여: Helen Bloom 역시 유명하잖아.

남: 그래, 하지만 난 Rachel이 가장 좋아. 그녀를 정말 보고
싶었는데.

여: 유감이다.

어휘

ballet[bæléi] 몡 발레   excited[iksáitid] 혱 흥분한
satisfied[sǽtisfàid] 혱 만족한   part[pɑːrt] 몡 부분;
*(배우의) 역   [문제] relieved[rilíːvd] 혱 안심한

문제 해설

Q: 남자의 현재 기분은?
그는 보고 싶던 스케이터가 공연에 나오지 않아서 실망했다.

Listening ★ Practice   p. 40

1 ③ 2 ③ 3 ② 4 (1) Bad (2) Good
(3) Good (4) Bad 5 ③ 6 ② 7 ③ 8 ④

1

(Telephone rings.)

M: Eden Theater. How may I help you?

W: I bought a ticket for tomorrow, but I can't
go.

M: Okay. What's your name?

W: Edwards. Betty Edwards.

M: Do you want to cancel the reservation?

W: No. I just want to change the date to next
Saturday.

M: Do you mean July 23rd?

W: Yes. Can the seat still be in the section A?

M: Sorry. Only B section seats are available
then.

W: That's okay.

(전화벨이 울린다.)

남: Eden 극장입니다. 무엇을 도와드릴까요?

여: 내일 표를 샀는데, 갈 수가 없어서요.

남: 알겠습니다. 성함이 어떻게 되시죠?

여: Edwards예요. Betty Edwards요.

남: 예약하신 것을 취소하고 싶으세요?

여: 아니요. 그냥 날짜를 다음 주 토요일로 바꾸고 싶어요.

남: 7월 23일 말이죠?

여: 네. 여전히 A구역 좌석으로 가능한가요?

남: 죄송합니다. 그때는 B구역 자리만 가능한데요.

여: 괜찮아요.

어휘

cancel[kǽnsəl] 통 취소하다   reservation[rèzərvéiʃən]
몡 예약 section[sékʃən] 몡 구역 available[əvéiləbl]
혱 이용 가능한, 얻을 수 있는 [문제] make a
reservation 예약을 하다 another[ənʌ́ðər] 혱 다른

문제 해설

Q: 여자가 Eden 극장에 전화를 건 이유는?
여자는 예약한 날짜를 변경하기 위해 전화했다.

2

M: I'm John Wilson from Weekly Theater.
Nice to meet you.

W: Nice to meet you, too.

M: You've just finished the last show. How
do you feel?

W: I can't believe that it's over. I was happy
to play the part of Juliet.

M: You acted with Patrick Roberts in this
play. How was that?

W: Patrick is a great actor, so I really enjoyed
it.

M: What's your plan after this?

W: I'm going to take a break for a while.

M: I see. Well, I hope to see you in another
play soon.

남: 저는 〈Weekly Theater〉의 John Wilson입니다. 만나서
반갑습니다.

여: 저 역시 반갑습니다.

남: 마지막 공연을 막 끝내셨는데요. 소감이 어떠신가요?

여: 끝났다는 게 믿어지지 않아요. Juliet 역을 하게 되어 기
뻤어요.

남: 이 연극에서 Patrick Roberts 씨와 함께 연기하셨죠. 그
건 어땠나요?

여: Patrick은 훌륭한 배우여서 전 아주 즐겁게 했습니다.

남: 다음 계획은 어떤 것이죠?

여: 잠시 휴식을 취하려고 해요.

남: 알겠습니다. 음, 곧 다른 연극에서 뵙게 되길 바래요.

40

어휘

weekly[wíːkli] 형 주간의   over[óuvər] 부 끝나서
act[ækt] 동 연기하다   actor[ǽktər] 명 배우   take a
break 휴식을 취하다   for a while 잠시 동안   hope
[houp] 동 바라다   play[plei] 명 연극

문제 해설

Q: 상황을 가장 잘 묘사한 것은?

남자 기자가 연극 배우인 여자를 인터뷰하고 있는 상황
이다.

3

M: Do you know what a drawing show is? It
is usually held in a theater or a concert
hall. When you go to an art gallery, you
can see only the end result of a picture.
But at a drawing show, you can see how
a picture is drawn from beginning to
end. It really is like magic.

남: 드로잉 쇼가 뭔지 아세요? 그것은 주로 극장이나 콘서트
홀에서 열립니다. 미술관에 가면 그림의 최종 결과물만
을 볼 수 있습니다. 하지만 드로잉 쇼에서는 그림이 어떻
게 그려지는지를 처음부터 끝까지 볼 수 있습니다. 그것
은 정말 마술과 같습니다.

어휘

drawing show 드로잉 쇼   hold[hould] 동 개최하다
(hold−held−held)   concert hall 연주회장, 콘서트홀
art gallery 미술관   end[end] 명 마지막; 형 최종의
result[rizʌ́lt] 명 결과   beginning[bigíniŋ] 명 시작
magic[mǽdʒik] 명 마술   [문제] audience[ɔ́ːdiəns] 명
관객

문제 해설

Q: 드로잉 쇼에 관해 사실인 것은?

① 미술관에서 열린다.

② 그림이 어떻게 그려지는지 보여준다.

③ 유명한 화가들이 그린 그림을 보여준다.

④ 관중이 함께 그림을 그릴 수 있다.

그림을 그리는 과정을 처음부터 끝까지 보여주는 쇼이다.

4

W: How was the play yesterday?

M: I heard it was very funny. But I thought
the story was boring.

W: Really?

M: Yes. But the stage sets were fantastic. It
looked just like a real hospital.

W: How were the actors?

M: The actors weren't famous, but they acted
really well.

W: That's good.

M: But I was angry when some people took
pictures during the show.

W: Oh, I can't believe that! They have no
manners.

여: 어제 연극은 어땠니?

남: 아주 재미있다고 들었거든. 하지만 난 스토리가 지루했
던 것 같아.

여: 정말?

남: 응. 하지만 무대 장치는 환상적이었어. 실제 병원과 꼭
같아 보이더라고.

여: 배우들은 어땠는데?

남: 유명한 배우들은 아니었지만 연기를 아주 잘 했어.

여: 다행이네.

남: 하지만 몇몇 사람들이 공연 중에 사진을 찍어서 화가 났어.

여: 아, 믿을 수가 없군! 예절이라곤 없구나.

어휘

funny[fʌ́ni] 형 재미있는   boring[bɔ́ːriŋ] 형 지루한
stage set 무대 장치   real[ríəl] 형 진짜의, 실제의
manner[mǽnər] 명 태도; *(~s) 예절

문제 해설

Q: 남자가 연극에 대해서 어떻게 느꼈는지 ✓표 하시오.

스토리는 지루했고 무대 장치는 훌륭했으며, 배우들의 연
기는 좋았으나 관중들의 예절은 좋지 않았다고 했다.

5

W: Shall we go to see the play *Our Town*
this week?

M: Okay. At which theater is it showing?

W: The Richmond Arts Center. It closes at
the end of this month.

M: Oh, we have to hurry then. When do you
want to go?

W: How about the 8 p.m. show on the 14th
of May?

M: The 14th is this Friday, right? I already
have plans.

W: Then how about this Saturday? It is
showing at 4 p.m. and 7 p.m.

M: The 4 p.m. show is better for me.

W: Okay.

41

여: 이번 주에 연극 'Our Town'을 보러 갈래?

남: 좋아. 어떤 극장에서 하지?

여: Richmond Arts Center야. 이번 달 말에 폐막이야.

남: 아, 그럼 서둘러야겠다. 언제 가고 싶니?

여: 5월 14일 오후 8시 공연이 어떨까?

남: 14일은 이번 금요일이네, 맞지? 난 이미 약속이 있어.

여: 그럼 이번 토요일은 어때? 오후 4시와 7시에 상연해.

남: 4시 공연이 더 좋겠어.

여: 좋아.

어휘

hurry[hə́:ri] 동 서두르다   already[ɔːlrédi] 부 이미

문제 해설

Q: 그들은 연극을 언제 볼 것인가?

　토요일 4시 공연을 보기로 했다. 14일이 금요일이라고 했으므로 토요일은 15일이다.

6

(Telephone rings.)

W: Thank you for calling Toronto Grand Theater.

M: Hello. I want to make a reservation for *Hamlet*.

W: Okay. Which date?

M: May 5th. I'd like to see the 7 p.m. show.

W: I'm sorry. The tickets are sold out.

M: How about May 7th at the same time?

W: Yes, seats are available then. How many tickets do you need?

M: I need two adult tickets.

W: Okay. May I have your name?

M: My name is Peter Jackson.

W: Okay.

(전화벨이 울린다.)

여: Toronto Grand 극장에 전화 주셔서 감사합니다.

남: 안녕하세요. 'Hamlet'을 예약하고 싶어요.

여: 알겠습니다. 날짜는요?

남: 5월 5일이요. 오후 7시 공연을 보고 싶어요.

여: 죄송합니다. 표가 매진되었어요.

남: 같은 시간으로 5월 7일은 어때요?

여: 네, 그때는 좌석이 있어요. 몇 장이 필요하신가요?

남: 어른 2장이요.

여: 알겠습니다. 성함이 어떻게 되시죠?

남: 제 이름은 Peter Jackson이에요.

여: 알겠습니다.

어휘

be sold out 매진되다   adult[ədʌ́lt] 명 어른

문제 해설

Q: 틀린 정보를 고르시오.

　5월 5일 표는 매진이어서 5월 7일 공연을 선택했다.

7

W: These days, many teenagers want to be musical actors. But this is not easy, because musical actors need many talents. So, what talents are needed? First, it's very important to sing and dance well. As you know, musicals are mostly singing and dancing. Also, you should know the importance of teamwork. Musical actors have to work with many people. Lastly, to make people laugh, you should have showmanship.

여: 요즘, 많은 십대들이 뮤지컬 배우가 되고 싶어합니다. 하지만 뮤지컬 배우에게는 많은 재능이 필요하기 때문에 그건 쉽지 않아요. 그럼, 어떤 재능이 필요할까요? 우선, 노래를 잘 하고 춤을 잘 추는 것이 아주 중요합니다. 아시다시피, 뮤지컬은 대부분이 노래와 춤입니다. 또한, 팀워크의 중요성도 알아야 합니다. 뮤지컬 배우는 많은 사람들과 함께 일해야 하거든요. 마지막으로, 사람들을 웃게 만들기 위해서 쇼맨십이 있어야 합니다.

어휘

teenager[tíːnèidʒər] 명 십대, 청소년   talent[tǽlənt] 명 재능   mostly[móustli] 부 대부분   importance [impɔ́ːrtəns] 명 중요성   teamwork[tíːmwə̀ːrk] 명 팀워크, 협동 작업   lastly[lǽstli] 부 마지막으로   laugh[læf] 동 웃다   showmanship[ʃóumənʃip] 명 쇼맨십, 청중을 끄는 수완   [문제] quality[kwɑ́ləti] 명 자질

문제 해설

Q: 여자는 주로 무엇에 대해 이야기하고 있는가?

① 뮤지컬이 어떻게 만들어지는지

② 어떻게 뮤지컬 배우가 될 수 있는지

③ 뮤지컬 배우에게 필요한 자질

④ 뮤지컬 배우들이 겪는 어려움

뮤지컬 배우가 되기 위해 갖추어야 할 자질에 대한 내용이다.

42

8

M: What an interesting show!

W: Right. I've seen dance shows before, but this one was the best.

M: What did you like most about it?

W: Well, I liked the male dancers. They were so cool.

M: I agree. The beautiful dances by the ballerina were good, too.

W: That's true. It was exciting to see both ballet and hip-hop dance on the same stage.

M: But I liked the music best. I think the powerful music played a big role in the show.

남: 재미있는 쇼였어!

여: 맞아. 전에 댄스 공연을 본 적이 있었지만 이번 것이 최고였어.

남: 넌 뭐가 제일 좋았니?

여: 음, 남자 댄서들이 좋았어. 참 멋지더라.

남: 동감이야. 난 발레리나의 아름다운 무용도 좋았어.

여: 그러게. 같은 무대에서 발레와 힙합 댄스를 모두 보니 너무 재미있었어.

남: 하지만 난 음악이 제일 좋았어. 역동적인 음악이 그 쇼에서 큰 역할을 했다고 생각해.

어휘

male[meil] 형 남자의   cool[kuːl] 형 멋진   ballerina [bæ̀lərí:nə] 명 발레리나   hip-hop[híphàp] 형 힙합 powerful[páuərfəl] 형 강한, 강력한   play a big role 중요한 역할을 하다   [문제] performance[pərfɔ́ːrməns] 명 *공연; 연기

문제 해설

Q: 댄스 공연에서 남자가 가장 좋아한 것은?
   남자는 역동적인 음악이 가장 좋았다고 했다.

Listening ★ Challenge p. 42

A 1 ② 2 ②   B 1 ① 2 (1) T (2) F (3) T

A [1-2]

W: Have you ever seen the musical *Rent*?

M: No, not yet.

W: How about seeing it with me?

M: I'd love to!

W: Then when do you want to go? How about this Friday?

M: Isn't it better to see it on Saturday or Sunday?

W: Well... we can only see Daniel Parker on Fridays.

M: Oh, he's your favorite actor, isn't he? Let's see it on Friday, then.

W: Thank you. I'll buy the tickets tomorrow.

M: I heard there is a movie version of the musical. Have you ever seen it?

W: No, but I have the DVD at home. We can go there now and watch it.

M: Great.

여: 뮤지컬 'Rent'를 본 적 있어?

남: 아니, 아직.

여: 나랑 같이 그걸 보는 게 어때?

남: 좋아!

여: 그럼 언제 가고 싶어? 이번 금요일은 어때?

남: 토요일이나 일요일에 보는 게 더 낫지 않아?

여: 음… 금요일에만 Daniel Parker를 볼 수 있거든.

남: 아, 그 사람이 네가 제일 좋아하는 배우지, 그렇지 않니? 그럼 금요일에 보자.

여: 고마워. 내일 표를 살게.

남: 그 뮤지컬의 영화 버전이 있다고 들었어. 본 적 있니?

여: 아니, 하지만 집에 DVD가 있어. 지금 가서 봐도 돼.

남: 좋아.

어휘

I'd love to. 그러고 싶어. 좋아.   version[vɔ́ːrʒən] 명 ~판, 개작   [문제] rent[rent] 통 빌리다

문제 해설

Q1: 그들은 무슨 요일에 뮤지컬 'Rent'를 볼 것인가?
   여자가 좋아하는 배우가 나오는 금요일에 가기로 했다.

Q2: 그들이 다음에 할 일은?
   여자의 집에 가서 DVD를 보기로 했다.

B [1-2]

M: On April 2009, a very special orchestra gave its first performance in Carnegie Hall. Its members were selected by video audition. About 4,000 audition tapes from all over the world were received. Finally, 90 musicians were chosen to become members of the orchestra. They practiced online together for months. They gathered in New York just three days before the concert, so they had only two days to practice together. Many people expected the performance to be bad. But the concert was a big success.

남: 2009년 4월, 아주 특별한 오케스트라가 카네기홀에서 첫 공연을 했습니다. 단원들은 동영상 오디션을 통해 선발되었습니다. 전 세계로부터 약 4,000개의 오디션 테이프가 접수되었습니다. 최종적으로, 90명의 연주자들이 오케스트라의 단원으로 선발되었습니다. 그들은 몇 달 동안 온라인 상으로 함께 연습했습니다. 그들은 공연이 있기 겨우 3일 전에 뉴욕에 모였고, 함께 연습할 시간은 2일뿐이었습니다. 많은 사람들이 공연이 별로일 거라고 예상했습니다. 그러나 공연은 크게 성공했습니다.

어휘
orchestra[ɔ́ːrkəstrə] 몡 오케스트라 select[silékt] 통 고르다, 선발하다 video[vídiòu] 몡 비디오, 동영상 audition[ɔːdíʃən] 몡 오디션 receive[risíːv] 통 받다, 입수하다 musician[mjuː(:)zíʃən] 몡 음악가, 연주자 online[ɔ́nlàin] 뿐 온라인 상에서 gather[ɡǽðər] 통 모이다 expect[ikspékt] 통 예상하다 success[səksés] 몡 성공 [문제] international[ìntərnǽʃənəl] 몡 국제적인 take part in 참가하다

문제 해설
Q1: 뉴스의 제목은?
  ① 최초의 온라인 오케스트라
  ② 최초의 국제적인 오케스트라
  ③ 뉴욕 오케스트라의 역사
  ④ 최대의 오케스트라 오디션
온라인으로 단원을 선발하고, 온라인 상에서 함께 연습하여 공연을 한 최초의 온라인 오케스트라에 관한 내용이다.

Q2: 오케스트라에 관해 사실이면 T, 사실이 아니면 F에 ✓표 하시오.
  (1) 약 4,000명의 사람들이 동영상 오디션에 참가했다.
  (2) 단원들은 뉴욕에서 몇 달 동안 함께 연습했다.
  (3) 그들의 공연은 대단히 성공했다.

Critical ★ Thinking p. 43

1 ③ 2 ③, ④

W: Jeremy, what did you do last weekend?
M: I went to see a musical. Ricky Smith was the main actor.
W: Are you talking about Ricky Smith from the TV series *Vacation*? I didn't know he did musicals.
M: Actually it's his first musical.
W: I'm sure his performance was very good. How lucky you were to see him close up!
M: Um... it wasn't all that good.
W: Why not?
M: Well, so many of his teenage fans were there. They screamed every time he came on stage.
W: Wasn't it hard to focus on the musical?
M: Yes, it was. Also, the ticket price went up a lot. That's because Ricky gets a lot of money for his performances.

여: Jeremy, 지난 주말에 뭐 했어?
남: 뮤지컬을 보러 갔어. Ricky Smith가 주연 배우였어.
여: TV 시리즈인 'Vacation'에 나왔던 Ricky Smith를 말하는 거야? 그 사람이 뮤지컬을 하는지 몰랐네.
남: 사실 이게 그의 첫 뮤지컬이야.
여: 그의 연기가 아주 좋았을 거라 확신해. 그를 가까이서 보다니 너 운이 좋구나!
남: 음… 그렇게 좋지만은 않았어.
여: 왜?
남: 음, 그의 십대 팬들이 아주 많이 왔어. 그가 무대에 나올 때마다 애들이 소리를 질렀어.
여: 뮤지컬에 집중하기 어렵지 않았니?
남: 응, 그랬어. 또, 표 값이 많이 올랐어. 그건 Ricky가 공연으로 많은 돈을 받기 때문이야.

어휘
main actor 주연 배우 series[sí(:)əriːz] 몡 연속물, 시리즈 lucky[lʌ́ki] 몡 운 좋은 close up 가까이에서 teenage[tíːnèidʒ] 몡 십대의 scream[skriːm] 통 소리치다 focus on ~에 집중하다 go up (값이) 오르다

문제 해설
Q1: Ricky Smith에 관해 사실이 아닌 것은?
  ① 뮤지컬에서 주연을 맡았다.
  ② TV 시리즈에 나왔다.
  ③ 전에 뮤지컬에 출연한 적이 있다.
  ④ 십대들에게 인기가 있다.
뮤지컬 공연은 이번이 처음이라고 했다.

44

Q2: Jeremy가 뮤지컬에 만족하지 <u>못한</u> 두 가지 이유를 고르시오.

① 주연 배우가 노래를 잘하지 못했다.
② 배우들을 가까이에서 볼 수 없었다.
③ 공연 도중에 너무 시끄러웠다.
④ 표가 아주 비쌌다.

그는 뮤지컬이 만족스럽지 않았던 이유로 십대 팬들이 시끄러웠던 점과 표가 너무 비싸진 점을 들었다.

UNIT 07 Health

Getting ★ Ready p. 44

A 1 ⓑ 2 ⓓ 3 ⓔ 4 ⓒ
B 1 ⓑ 2 ⓒ 3 ⓔ

B 1 남: 너 감기 걸렸니?
   여: 응, 콧물이 나.
 2 남: 저에게 뭔가 문제가 있나요?
   여: 위에 문제가 있네요.
 3 남: 내 여동생은 지난 주에 다리가 부러졌어.
   여: 안됐구나! 곧 낫길 바래.

Listening ★ Start p. 45

1 ③ / make an appointment, come in, make it, see you then
2 ①, ② / What's the matter, can't sleep, What's wrong with him, some cough syrup

1

(*Telephone rings.*)
W: City Hospital. How may I help you?
M: My back really hurts. I want to make an appointment for today.
W: Okay. What time can you come in?
M: How about 4 p.m.?
W: Our 4 p.m. appointments are full. Could you come in at 5 p.m. instead?
M: Well, I guess I can make it.
W: Great. Could you tell me your name?
M: My name is Jake Brown.
W: Okay. We'll see you then.

(전화벨이 울린다.)
여: City 병원입니다. 무엇을 도와드릴까요?
남: 등이 너무 아파서요. 오늘 진료 예약을 하고 싶습니다.
여: 알겠습니다. 몇 시에 오실 수 있나요?
남: 오후 4시 어때요?
여: 오후 4시는 예약이 꽉 찼어요. 대신 오후 5시에 오실 수 있나요?
남: 음, 갈 수 있을 것 같아요.
여: 좋아요. 성함을 말씀해 주시겠어요?
남: 제 이름은 Jake Brown입니다.
여: 알겠습니다. 그때 뵙죠.

어휘
back[bæk] ⑲ *등; 뒤 hurt[hə:rt] ⑧ *아프다; 다치게 하다 appointment[əpɔ́intmənt] ⑲ 약속, 예약 full[ful] ⑲ 가득 찬 make it *제시간에 도착하다; 성공하다

문제 해설
Q: 남자는 언제 병원을 방문하려고 하는가?
   오후 4시에는 예약이 꽉 차서 5시에 가기로 했다.

2

M: What's the matter?
W: Doctor, my son has a fever, and it won't go away.
M: Does he cough?
W: Yes, a lot. He can't sleep.
M: Let me look at him. Does he have a runny nose?
W: No. What's wrong with him?
M: Don't worry too much. He just has a cold.
W: What should I do?
M: I'll give you some cough syrup for him. It should be taken twice a day.
W: Okay. Thanks.

남: 무슨 문제신가요?
여: 의사 선생님, 제 아들이 열이 나는데, 열이 없어지질 않아요.
남: 기침도 합니까?
여: 네, 많이 해요. 잠도 못 자요.
남: 제가 한번 볼게요. 콧물도 납니까?
여: 아니요. 뭐가 잘못된 거예요?
남: 너무 걱정하지 마세요. 그냥 감기에 걸린 거예요.
여: 제가 어떻게 해야 하나요?
남: 아드님이 먹을 기침 시럽을 좀 드릴게요. 하루에 두 번 복용해야 합니다.
여: 알겠습니다. 감사합니다.

어휘

fever[fíːvər] 몡 열   cough[kɔ(ː)f] 동 기침하다; 몡 기침
have a runny nose 콧물이 나다   cold[kould] 몡 감
기   syrup[sírəp] 몡 시럽

문제 해설

Q: 아들의 문제를 두 개 고르시오.
  아들이 열이 나고 기침을 많이 한다고 했으나 콧물은 나
  지 않는다고 했다.

Listening ★ Practice   p. 46

1 ②   2 ④   3 ②   4 ②   5 ②, ④   6 (1) ⓑ
(2) ⓒ   (3) ⓐ   7 ②   8 ①

1

W: What can I do for you?
M: I have a 3 o'clock appointment. My name
   is Ben Smith.
W: Is this your first visit to our hospital?
M: Yes, it is.
W: Could you please answer a few questions
   for your file?
M: Okay.
W: What's your age and blood type?
M: I'm 27, and my blood type is A.
W: Have you ever had a serious disease?
M: No. Never.
W: Do you have any allergies?
M: Yes. I'm allergic to fish.
W: Thank you. Please wait for a second.

여: 무엇을 도와드릴까요?
남: 3시에 예약이 되어 있는데요. 제 이름은 Ben Smith입니다.
여: 이번이 저희 병원에 처음 방문하시는 겁니까?
남: 네.
여: 기록을 위해서 몇 가지 질문에 대답을 해 주시겠어요?
남: 알겠어요.
여: 나이와 혈액형이 어떻게 됩니까?
남: 27살이고 혈액형은 A형입니다.
여: 심각한 질병을 앓았던 적이 있습니까?
남: 아니요. 전혀 없어요.
여: 알레르기가 있나요?
남: 네. 생선에 알레르기가 있어요.
여: 감사합니다. 잠시만 기다려 주세요.

어휘

file[fail] 몡 서류, 기록   age[eidʒ] 몡 나이   blood
type 혈액형   serious[sí(ː)əriəs] 혱 심각한   disease
[dizíːz] 몡 질병   allergy[ǽlərdʒi] 몡 알레르기
allergic[ələ́ːrdʒik] 혱 알레르기 반응을 보이는   for a
second 잠시 동안   [문제] medical[médikəl] 혱 의학의

문제 해설

Q: 차트에서 잘못된 정보를 고르시오.
  남자의 혈액형은 A형이라고 했다.

2

W: Doctor, what's the result of my tests? Is
   something wrong with me?
M: You have a problem with your stomach.
   You need to be tested again.
W: Gee. Can it be done today?
M: Well, your stomach should be empty
   when it's taken.
W: I had breakfast. So it can't be taken
   today?
M: That's right. Please make an appointment
   for tomorrow with the nurse.
W: Okay.
M: And don't eat anything before you come.
W: I'll remember.

여: 의사 선생님, 제 검사 결과가 어때요? 저에게 뭔가 문제
   가 있어요?
남: 위에 문제가 있네요. 검사를 다시 받으셔야겠어요.
여: 이런. 오늘 받을 수 있어요?
남: 글쎄요, 검사를 받으려면 위가 비어 있어야 하는데요.
여: 아침을 먹었어요. 그럼 오늘은 받을 수 없나요?
남: 그렇죠. 간호사랑 내일로 예약을 잡으세요.
여: 알겠습니다.
남: 그리고 오기 전에 아무것도 드시지 마세요.
여: 기억할게요.

어휘

result[rizʌ́lt] 몡 결과   stomach[stʌ́mək] 몡 위
test[test] 동 검사하다; 몡 검사   empty[émpti] 혱 빈

문제 해설

Q: 여자가 다음에 할 일은?
  의사가 여자에게 재검사를 위한 예약을 잡으라고 했다.

3

M: Hello, what can I do for you?
W: My eyes are really dry. I don't know why.

M: Do they hurt much?

W: A little. They're getting red.

M: Then put this in your eyes three times a day.

W: Great. Thank you.

M: Do you wear contact lenses?

W: Yes, I do. Why?

M: You shouldn't wear them for a while.

W: Okay. I won't. How much is it?

M: It's $4. If it doesn't get better soon, you should see your doctor.

W: Okay, thanks.

남: 안녕하세요, 무엇을 도와드릴까요?

여: 눈이 아주 건조해요. 왜 그런지 모르겠어요.

남: 많이 아픈가요?

여: 약간이요. 눈이 충혈되고 있어요.

남: 그럼 하루에 세 번 이걸 눈에 넣어 주세요.

여: 좋아요. 감사합니다.

남: 콘택트렌즈를 끼나요?

여: 네, 그런데요. 왜요?

남: 당분간 끼시면 안 돼요.

여: 알겠습니다. 안 낄게요. 얼마예요?

남: 4달러입니다. 곧 좋아지지 않으면, 의사의 진찰을 받으셔야 합니다.

여: 알겠습니다. 감사합니다.

어휘

dry[drai] ⑱ 건조한   contact lenses 콘택트렌즈
for a while 잠시   get better 병이 낫다

문제 해설

Q: 대화가 이루어지고 있는 곳은?

여자는 눈이 건조해서 안약을 구입하고 있으므로 약국에서 이루어지는 대화임을 알 수 있다.

4

M: How is your mother? I heard she's in the hospital.

W: Yes. Her leg is getting better, but she has a bad cold.

M: I'm sorry to hear that. Is it bad?

W: Yes. Yesterday, she had a sore throat and coughed a lot.

M: How is she now?

W: She still has a sore throat and isn't eating much. She lost some weight.

M: She must be having a hard time.

W: Yes, she is. I hope she gets better soon.

남: 어머니는 좀 어떠시니? 입원하셨다고 들었는데.

여: 응. 어머니 다리가 낫고 있긴 한데, 심한 감기에 걸리셨어.

남: 유감이구나. 많이 안 좋으시니?

여: 응. 어제는 목이 아프시고 기침을 많이 하셨어.

남: 지금은 어떠시니?

여: 아직도 목이 아프시고 음식도 많이 못 드셔. 살도 빠지셨어.

남: 힘드시겠구나.

여: 응, 그러셔. 얼른 나으셨으면 좋겠어.

어휘

sore throat 인후염, 아픈 목   [문제] bored[bɔːrd] ⑱ 지루한

문제 해설

Q: 여자의 현재 기분은?

어머니가 편찮으시므로 걱정스러운 심정일 것이다.

5

W: I can't get enough sleep at night lately.

M: Why? Are you worried about something?

W: Not really. How can I get a good night's sleep?

M: Drink warm milk before you go to bed.

W: I'm allergic to milk.

M: Then how about exercising in the evening? It'll make you tired.

W: Okay. I should try that.

M: Also, try not to eat too much before going to bed.

W: That'll be difficult, but I'll try that too. Thanks for your advice.

여: 요즘 밤에 잠을 충분히 못 자겠어.

남: 왜? 뭔가 걱정되는 게 있니?

여: 그렇진 않아. 어떻게 하면 밤에 잠을 푹 잘 수 있을까?

남: 잠자리에 들기 전에 따뜻한 우유를 마셔.

여: 난 우유에 알레르기가 있는데.

남: 그럼 저녁에 운동을 하는 게 어때? 그렇게 하면 피곤해질 거야.

여: 알았어. 그렇게 해 봐야겠어.

남: 또 자기 전에 너무 많이 먹지 않도록 해.

여: 그건 어렵겠지만 그것도 해 볼게. 조언해줘서 고마워.

어휘

lately[léitli] ⑨ 최근에, 요즘   good[gud] ⑱ 충분한, 흡

47

★　★

족한　advice[ədváis] 몧 충고, 조언　[문제] follow
[fálou] 동 따르다

문제 해설
Q: 여자가 따를 조언을 두 개 고르시오.
　① 따뜻한 우유를 마셔라.
　② 저녁에 운동을 해라.
　③ 일들에 대해 걱정하지 않으려고 애써라.
　④ 자기 전에 너무 많이 먹지 마라.
저녁에 운동을 하고, 자기 전에 너무 많이 먹지 않도록
해 보겠다고 했다.

6

M1: I'm Tom. I went snowboarding last
　　winter and broke my leg. So I had to use
　　a wheelchair for a month.
M2: I'm Brad. I had a terrible stomachache
　　because of stress. So I could only eat
　　corn soup for a week.
M3: I'm Ron. I had a bad cold last month. I
　　had to stay in bed for two days.

남1: 나는 Tom이야. 나는 지난 겨울에 스노보드를 타러 갔
　　다가 다리가 부러졌어. 그래서 한 달 동안 휠체어를 써야
　　했어.
남2: 나는 Brad야. 나는 스트레스 때문에 심한 복통을 앓았
　　어. 그래서 일주일 동안 옥수수 수프만 먹을 수 있었어.
남3: 나는 Ron이야. 나는 지난 달에 심한 감기에 걸렸어. 이
　　틀 동안 침대에 누워 있어야 했어.

어휘
snowboard[snóubɔ̀ːrd] 동 스노보드를 타다
wheelchair[hwíːltʃèər] 몧 휠체어　terrible[térəbl] 혱
심한　stomachache[stʌ́məkèik] 몧 복통　corn[kɔːrn]
몧 옥수수　stay[stei] 동 머무르다

문제 해설
Q: 각 인물에 맞는 그림을 고르시오.
　(1) Tom은 다리가 부러져서 휠체어를 썼다고 했다.
　(2) Brad는 복통 때문에 일주일 동안 옥수수 수프만 먹었
　　　다고 했다.
　(3) Ron은 심한 감기에 걸려서 이틀 동안 침대에 있었다고
　　　했다.

7

M: Nancy, you don't look good. What's
　　wrong?
W: I have a runny nose. It's killing me.
M: Did you catch a cold?

W: No. It's because of my allergy.
M: What kind of allergy?
W: I'm allergic to flowers. This happens to
　　me every spring.
M: Oh. Do you have an eye problem, too?
W: Not really. But I cough a lot.
M: I heard that there's no cure for allergies.
W: Right. I just try not to go out often.
M: I feel sorry for you.

남: Nancy, 너 몸이 안 좋아 보여. 무슨 문제 있니?
여: 콧물이 나서 죽을 지경이야.
남: 감기에 걸렸어?
여: 아니. 알레르기 때문이야.
남: 무슨 알레르기?
여: 나는 꽃에 알레르기가 있어. 봄마다 이래.
남: 아. 눈에도 문제가 있니?
여: 그렇진 않아. 근데 기침을 많이 해.
남: 알레르기에는 치료법이 없다고 들었는데.
여: 맞아. 난 그냥 밖에 자주 안 나가려고 해.
남: 안됐네.

어휘
catch a cold 감기에 걸리다　happen[hǽpən] 동 생
기다, 일어나다　cure[kjuər] 몧 치료법

문제 해설
Q: 여자의 문제는?
　　여자는 꽃 알레르기가 있어서 콧물이 나고 기침을 많이
　　한다고 했다.

8

M: When you take a pill, don't take it with
　　juice or milk. They can prevent pills from
　　working well. Drink a cup of water when
　　you take a pill. If you don't drink enough
　　water, pills can hurt your stomach. And
　　there are some pills that you should not
　　take together. When you're not sure, you
　　must ask a doctor about it.

남: 알약을 복용할 때 주스나 우유와 함께 복용하지 마세요.
　　알약이 잘 작용하지 못하게 할 수 있습니다. 알약을 복용
　　할 때는 물을 한 컵 마시세요. 물을 충분히 마시지 않으
　　면 알약이 위를 상하게 할 수 있습니다. 그리고 함께 복
　　용하지 말아야 할 알약들이 있습니다. 확실히 모르겠다
　　면 반드시 의사에게 물어봐야 합니다.

어휘

pill[pil] 명 알약   prevent A from v-ing A가 ~하는 것을 막다 [문제] correctly[kəréktli] 부 올바르게 danger[déindʒər] 명 위험   meal[miːl] 명 식사

문제 해설

Q: 남자는 주로 무엇에 대해 이야기하고 있는가?

① 알약을 올바르게 복용하는 방법

② 알약이 체내에서 작용하는 방법

③ 알약을 과다 복용하는 것의 위험성

④ 식후에 알약을 복용하는 이유

남자는 알약을 복용할 때 주의할 점에 대해 얘기하고 있다.

Listening ★ Challenge   p. 48

A 1 ② 2 ④   B 1 ③ 2 (1) T (2) T (3) F

A [1-2]

W: Good afternoon! How can I help you?

M: Doctor, my stomach really hurts.

W: Do you have a fever?

M: No. But I have a headache. And my hands and feet are really cold.

W: Did you eat anything this morning?

M: Yes. I drank milk and ate some toast. But the milk tasted a little different today.

W: Well, that isn't making you sick. Did you eat them in a hurry?

M: Yes. I was late for school. So I ate really fast.

W: I think that made you sick. Don't eat anything today and just drink some warm water.

M: Okay. Thank you, doctor.

여: 안녕하세요! 무엇을 도와드릴까요?

남: 의사 선생님, 배가 너무 아파요.

여: 열이 나나요?

남: 아니요. 근데 두통이 있어요. 그리고 손발이 너무 차가워요.

여: 오늘 아침에 뭐 드신 게 있나요?

남: 네. 우유를 마시고, 토스트를 좀 먹었어요. 그런데 오늘 우유 맛이 조금 다르긴 했어요.

여: 음, 그것 때문에 아프진 않을 거예요. 급하게 먹었나요?

남: 네. 학교에 늦었거든요. 그래서 아주 빠르게 먹었어요.

여: 그것 때문에 아픈 것 같네요. 오늘 아무것도 먹지 말고 따뜻한 물만 좀 마시세요.

남: 알았어요. 감사합니다, 선생님.

어휘

headache[hédèik] 명 두통   toast[toust] 명 토스트 taste[teist] 동 ~한 맛이 나다   in a hurry 급히

문제 해설

Q1: 남자의 문제가 아닌 것은?

남자는 열은 나지 않는다고 했다.

Q2: 의사에 따르면, 남자가 아픈 이유는?

의사는 남자가 아침을 너무 급하게 먹은 것 때문에 아픈 것 같다고 했다.

B [1-2]

W: Have a problem with your teeth? Come to "Smile Dental Clinic." Our dentists have a lot of experience. They'll provide you with the best service. And you don't need to miss work for dental appointments any more. We are open until 9 p.m. on weekdays. Also, if you visit our clinic, we offer you a free checkup every six months. Our clinic is across from the W Department Store. We're waiting for you with smiles. Please visit us and get the best dental service in town.

여: 치아에 문제가 있나요? 'Smile Dental Clinic'으로 오세요. 저희 병원의 치과 의사들은 풍부한 경험을 가지고 있습니다. 그들은 여러분에게 최상의 서비스를 제공할 것입니다. 그리고 더 이상 치과 예약 때문에 일에 지장을 받으시지 않아도 됩니다. 저희는 주중에 저녁 9시까지 엽니다. 또한, 저희 병원에 방문하면 6개월마다 무료 검진을 해드립니다. 저희 병원은 W 백화점 건너편에 있습니다. 저희는 여러분을 미소로 기다리고 있습니다. 부디 방문하셔서 시내 최고의 치과 서비스를 받으십시오.

어휘

tooth[tuːθ] 명 이 (복수 teeth)   dental[déntl] 형 이의; *치과의   clinic[klínik] 명 개인 병원, 진료소   dentist [déntist] 명 치과 의사   experience[ikspí(ː)əriəns] 명 경험   provide[prəváid] 동 공급하다, 제공하다 weekday[wíːkdèi] 명 평일   offer[ɔ́(ː)fər] 동 제공하다 checkup[tʃékʌ̀p] 명 검진   department store 백화점 [문제] announcement[ənáunsmənt] 명 발표; 짧게 알리는 말   advertisement[æ̀dvərtáizmənt] 명 광고 documentary[dɑ̀kjuméntəri] 명 다큐멘터리   be located in ~ ~에 위치하다

문제 해설

Q1: 이 담화의 종류는?

치과를 광고하는 내용이다.

Q2: 사실이면 T에, 사실이 아니면 F에 ✓표 하시오.

(1) 이 병원은 주중에 오후 9시에 문을 닫는다.

(2) 첫 방문 이후에 무료 검진을 받을 수 있다.

(3) 이 병원은 W 백화점 안에 위치해 있다.

Critical ★ Thinking p. 49

1 ③ 2 (1) ⓐ (2) ⓒ

> W1: Many students are smoking in school. If they start smoking early, they are more likely to get serious diseases later. So, schools should do something. What do you think, Mr. Robin?
>
> M: We should punish students. If a student is caught smoking three times, he or she must leave school. They should know that smoking is wrong. Do you agree with me, Ms. Claire?
>
> W2: Strong punishment is not the answer. We should teach them how bad smoking is and that they can die early because of it. If they know the facts, they won't smoke.

여1: 많은 학생들이 학교에서 담배를 피우고 있습니다. 담배를 일찍 피우기 시작하면 나중에 심각한 질병에 더 걸리기 쉽죠. 그래서 학교는 뭔가를 해야 합니다. Robin 씨는 어떻게 생각하십니까?

남: 우리는 학생들을 처벌해야 합니다. 만약 학생이 세 번 담배를 피우다가 적발되면, 학교를 떠나야 해요. 그들은 흡연이 나쁘다는 것을 알아야 합니다. Claire 씨도 저에게 동의하십니까?

여2: 강한 처벌이 답은 아닙니다. 우리는 그들에게 흡연이 얼마나 나쁜지, 그리고 그것 때문에 일찍 죽을 수도 있다는 것을 가르쳐야 합니다. 학생들이 그 사실들을 안다면 담배를 피우지 않을 겁니다.

어휘

smoke[smouk] 동 담배 피우다 be likely to-v ~하기 쉽다 punish[pʌ́niʃ] 동 처벌하다 catch[kætʃ] 동 붙잡다; *발견하다 punishment[pʌ́niʃmənt] 명 처벌 fact[fækt] 명 사실

문제 해설

Q1: 그들은 주로 무엇에 대해 이야기하고 있는가?

① 흡연이 학생들에게 왜 옳지 않은가

② 학생들은 왜 학교에서 흡연을 시작하는가

③ 학교는 학생들이 담배를 피우지 못하게 하기 위해 무엇을 해야 하는가

④ 학교는 학생들에게 흡연의 위험성에 대해 가르쳐야 하는가

학생들의 흡연을 막기 위해 학교가 취해야 할 조치가 무엇인지에 대해 이야기하고 있다.

Q2: Robin 씨와 Claire 씨의 의견을 고르시오.

ⓐ 담배를 피우는 학생들은 처벌받아야 한다.

ⓑ 담배 피우는 학생들이 학교를 떠나도록 하는 것은 너무 가혹하다.

ⓒ 학교는 학생들에게 흡연의 위험성에 대해 가르쳐야 한다.

(1) Robin 씨는 담배를 피우는 학생을 처벌해야 한다고 주장한다.

(2) Claire 씨는 강력한 처벌보다는 학생들에게 흡연의 위험성에 대해 가르쳐야 한다고 주장한다.

UNIT 08 Sports

Getting ★ Ready p. 50

A 1 ⓐ 2 ⓒ 3 ⓔ 4 ⓑ 5 ⓓ
B 1 ⓑ 2 ⓒ 3 ⓕ

B 1 여: 넌 어떤 운동을 할 거니?

남: 난 이어달리기를 할 거야.

2 여: 게임이 어떻게 끝났니?

남: 우리 팀이 1점 차로 졌어.

3 여: 넌 테니스 칠 줄 아니?

남: 응. 난 요즘 강습을 듣거든.

Listening ★ Start p. 51

1 ② / watch a baseball game, so close up, wasn't bored

2 ③ / sports day, play basketball, I've packed it, wear my cap

1

> W: Yesterday, I went to watch a baseball game between the New York Yankees

and the Boston Red Sox. It was my first time to go to a stadium. I couldn't believe that I could see the players so close up! The game lasted for about four hours. It was quite long, but I wasn't bored for a minute. I will never forget that amazing game.

여: 나는 어제 New York Yankees와 Boston Red Sox 간의 야구 경기를 보러 갔어. 경기장에 간 것은 이번이 처음이었지. 나는 선수들을 그렇게 가까이서 볼 수 있다는 게 믿기지 않았어! 경기는 약 4시간 동안 지속되었어. 꽤 길었지만 한순간도 지루하지 않았어. 나는 그 굉장한 경기를 결코 잊지 못할 거야.

어휘
baseball[béisbɔ̀:l] 圀 야구　stadium[stéidiəm] 圀 경기장　last[læst] 동 지속되다　bored[bɔ:rd] 휑 지루한　amazing[əméiziŋ] 휑 굉장한　[문제] nervous[nɔ́:rvəs] 휑 긴장되는　disappointed[dìsəpɔ́intid] 휑 실망한

문제 해설
Q: 여자의 현재 기분은?
여자는 야구 경기를 경기장에서 직접 보고 나서 신난 상황이다.

2

M: Mom, did I tell you that tomorrow is sports day?
W: No, you didn't. Which sports are you going to play?
M: I'm going to run in a relay race and play basketball.
W: Oh, you should take your running shoes, then.
M: Of course.
W: What about your uniform?
M: I've packed it already.
W: Good. And don't forget to wear sunblock on your face.
M: I don't need it. I'm going to wear my cap.

남: 엄마, 내일이 운동회 날이라고 말씀드렸어요?
여: 아니, 안 했는데. 넌 어떤 운동을 할 거니?
남: 전 이어달리기를 하고 농구를 할 거예요.
여: 아, 그럼 운동화를 가져가야겠구나.
남: 그럼요.

여: 네 유니폼은?
남: 이미 샀어요.
여: 잘했어. 그리고 얼굴에 자외선 차단제를 바르는 것도 잊지 말고.
남: 그건 필요 없어요. 전 모자를 쓸 거예요.

어휘
sports day 운동회　relay race 이어달리기, 계주
basketball[bǽskitbɔ̀:l] 圀 농구　running shoes 운동화　uniform[júːnəfɔ̀:rm] 圀 유니폼　pack[pæk] 동 (짐을) 꾸리다　already[ɔːlrédi] 뷔 이미　sunblock[sʌ́nblɑ̀k] 圀 자외선 차단제

문제 해설
Q: 소년에게 필요하지 않은 것은?
소년은 모자를 쓸 것이므로 자외선 차단제는 필요하지 않다고 했다.

Listening ★ Practice　p. 52

1 ④　2 ③　3 ② 　4 ①　5 ③　6 ①　7 ③　8 ④

1

W: Dad, are you busy this weekend?
M: No, I'm not. Why?
W: A new sports center with a tennis court opened in Lake City. I want to play tennis with you there.
M: Oh, do you know how to play tennis?
W: I'm taking lessons at school these days. It's so much fun.
M: Good. We need to make a reservation for the court, don't we?
W: Yes, I'll call the center now.
M: Okay. I'll go to find my racket.

여: 아빠, 이번 주말에 바쁘세요?
남: 아니. 왜?
여: 테니스 코트가 있는 새로운 스포츠 센터가 Lake City에 오픈했대요. 거기서 아빠랑 테니스를 치고 싶어요.
남: 아, 넌 테니스 칠 줄 아니?
여: 요즘 학교에서 강습을 듣고 있어요. 정말 재미있어요.
남: 좋아. 코트를 예약해야 하겠지?
여: 네, 제가 지금 센터에 전화할게요.
남: 알았어. 난 내 라켓을 찾아봐야겠다.

51

어휘

court[kɔːrt] 명 경기장, (테니스 등의) 코트   make a reservation 예약하다   racket[rǽkit] 명 라켓

문제 해설

Q: 소녀가 다음에 할 일은?

소녀는 전화로 테니스 코트를 예약할 거라고 했다.

2

W: Dave, what are you watching?
M: A baseball game.
W: The Figure Skating Championships are on TV soon. Let's watch them.
M: Weren't they on yesterday? You watched figure skating last night.
W: Well, it was the short program. In figure skating, skaters must do two programs—a short program and then a free skating program.
M: I see. So will they do the free skating today?
W: That's right.
M: Then I'll record the baseball game and watch it later.
W: Great. Thank you.

여: Dave, 너 뭘 보고 있니?
남: 야구 경기.
여: 피겨스케이팅 선수권 대회가 곧 TV에서 방송될 거야. 그거 보자.
남: 그거 어제 하지 않았어? 너 어젯밤에 피겨스케이팅 봤잖아.
여: 음, 그건 쇼트 프로그램이었어. 피겨스케이팅에서는 선수들이 두 개의 프로그램을 해야 하는데, 쇼트 프로그램을 하고 그 다음 프리 스케이팅 프로그램을 하는 거지.
남: 그렇구나. 그럼 오늘 프리 스케이팅을 하는 거야?
여: 맞아.
남: 그럼 야구 경기는 녹화해서 나중에 봐야겠다.
여: 좋아. 고마워.

어휘

figure skating 피겨스케이팅   championship [tʃǽmpiənʃip] 명 《~s》 선수권 대회   skater[skéitər] 명 스케이팅을 하는 사람   record[rikɔ́ːrd] 통 녹화하다, 녹음하다

문제 해설

Q: 그들은 어떤 프로그램을 볼 것인가?

그들은 피겨스케이팅 경기 중계를 보기로 했다.

3

M: I want to start exercising. Do you have any suggestions?
W: How about in-line skating? It's my favorite sport.
M: What do you like about it?
W: First of all, because I do it outside, I get fresh air and sunlight.
M: Okay.
W: Also, there's no need to go far away. I mean, I can skate right in front of my house.
M: That's really good.
W: And I can either skate alone or together with friends.
M: It sounds perfect. I'll start right away.

남: 나 운동을 시작하고 싶은데 제안해 줄 거 있니?
여: 인라인 스케이팅은 어때? 내가 가장 좋아하는 운동인데.
남: 어떤 점이 좋은데?
여: 우선, 밖에서 하기 때문에 신선한 공기도 마시고 햇볕을 쬘 수 있지.
남: 그렇구나.
여: 그리고 멀리 갈 필요가 없어. 내 말은, 바로 집 앞에서 스케이트를 탈 수 있다는 거야.
남: 그건 정말 좋네.
여: 그리고 스케이트는 혼자서 탈 수도 있고 친구들이랑 함께 탈 수도 있어.
남: 완벽한 것 같네. 바로 시작해야겠다.

어휘

suggestion[səgdʒéstʃən] 명 제안   in-line skating 인라인 스케이트   first of all 우선   outside[àutsáid] 부 밖에서   fresh[freʃ] 형 신선한   sunlight[sʌ́nlàit] 명 햇빛   either A or B A거나 B거나   alone[əlóun] 부 혼자서   right away 곧, 바로   [문제] outdoor [áutdɔ̀ːr] 형 야외의   possible[pásəbl] 형 가능한   neighborhood[néibərhùd] 명 이웃, 근처   matter [mǽtər] 통 중요하다, 문제가 되다

문제 해설

Q: 인라인 스케이팅의 장점으로 언급되지 않은 것은?

① 야외 운동이다.

② 모든 연령대의 사람들이 즐길 수 있다.

③ 집 근처에서 연습할 수 있다.

④ 사람 수는 중요하지 않다.

인라인 스케이트를 탈 수 있는 나이에 관해서는 언급하지 않았다.

52

4

W: Mike, your scores have been getting worse.

M: You're right, Mrs. Wilson.

W: I don't feel you practice hard enough. What's the problem?

M: Well... I'm not sure whether I can become a great golfer.

W: And why is that?

M: Well, I was very disappointed with my last game.

W: It's true you didn't do very well last time. But just forget about it and keep practicing.

M: Do you think I can do well?

W: Of course. I can see you have talent. I've trained many golfers, you know.

M: Thank you.

여: Mike, 네 기록이 점점 안 좋아지고 있어.

남: Wilson 코치님 말씀이 맞아요.

여: 네가 충분히 열심히 연습하고 있는 것 같지 않아. 문제가 뭐야?

남: 저… 전 제가 훌륭한 골프 선수가 될 수 있을지 모르겠어요.

여: 왜?

남: 음, 저의 지난 경기에 아주 실망했거든요.

여: 네가 지난번에 아주 잘 하지 못한 건 사실이야. 하지만 그건 그냥 잊고 계속 연습해야지.

남: 선생님은 제가 잘 할 수 있을 거라고 생각하세요?

여: 물론이지. 난 네가 재능이 있다는 걸 알아. 내가 수많은 골프 선수들을 훈련시킨 거 알잖아.

남: 감사합니다.

어휘

score[skɔːr] 몡 득점 기록   golfer[gálfər] 몡 골프치는 사람, 골퍼   talent[tǽlənt] 몡 재능   train[trein] 통 훈련시키다   [문제] coach[koutʃ] 몡 코치   reporter [ripɔ́ːrtər] 몡 기자

문제 해설

Q: 화자 간의 관계는?

남자는 자신이 훌륭한 골프 선수가 될 수 있을지 고민하고 있고, 여자는 수많은 골프 선수들을 훈련시켰다고 했으므로 두 사람은 선수와 코치 관계임을 알 수 있다.

5

M: Look, Jerry has just got another strike.

W: Wow. He knocked down all ten pins. It's a turkey!

M: A turkey? What do you mean by that?

W: We call three strikes in a row a turkey.

M: That's funny. Anyway, I think Jerry is going to win the game.

W: I agree with that. Tony doesn't seem to be playing well.

M: Yes. He knocked down only five pins this time.

남: 봐, Jerry가 또 스트라이크를 쳤어.

여: 우와. 핀 10개를 모두 넘어뜨렸어. 터키를 쳤어!

남: 터키? 그게 무슨 뜻이야?

여: 스트라이크 세 번이 연속되는 것을 터키라고 불러.

남: 재미있네. 어쨌든 Jerry가 경기에서 이길 것 같아.

여: 내 생각도 그래. Tony는 잘하고 있는 것 같지 않아.

남: 응. 그는 이번에 핀을 다섯 개만 넘어뜨렸잖아.

어휘

strike[straik] 몡 스트라이크   knock down 넘어뜨리다   pin[pin] 몡 핀   turkey[tə́ːrki] 몡 칠면조; *(볼링) 터키   in a row 연속적으로   [문제] match[mætʃ] 몡 경기, 시합   tournament[túərnəmənt] 몡 토너먼트, 선수권 쟁탈전

문제 해설

Q: 그들은 어떤 스포츠 경기를 보고 있는가?

pin, strike, turkey 등의 표현들로 미루어 보아 볼링 경기를 보고 있음을 짐작할 수 있다.

6

M: To run a marathon, you must have a comfortable pair of shoes. New shoes can hurt your feet. On the race day, finish your meal at least three hours before the race. And be sure to stretch enough just before your race. During a marathon, drink cold water every 15 minutes. If you don't drink enough water, you could have serious health problems.

남: 마라톤을 뛰려면 편안한 신발을 신어야 합니다. 새 신발을 신으면 발이 아플 수 있어요. 경기를 하는 날엔 최소한 경기 세 시간 전에 식사를 마치세요. 그리고 경기를

53

하기 바로 전에 반드시 스트레칭을 충분히 하세요. 마라톤 중에는 15분마다 차가운 물을 마시세요. 물을 충분히 마시지 않으면 심각한 건강상의 문제가 생길 수도 있습니다.

어휘
marathon[mǽrəθàn] 명 마라톤 comfortable [kʌ́mfərtəbl] 형 편안한 finish[fíniʃ] 동 마치다 at least 적어도 be sure to-v 반드시 ~하다 stretch [stretʃ] 동 쭉 펴다, 스트레칭 하다 serious[sí(ː)əriəs] 형 심각한 [문제] warm-up[wɔ́ːrmʌ̀p] 명 준비 운동

문제 해설
Q: 남자는 주로 무엇에 대해 이야기하고 있는가?
  ① 마라톤을 뛰는 것에 대한 조언
  ② 십대를 위한 최고의 운동
  ③ 마라톤 선수가 되는 방법
  ④ 준비 운동의 중요성
남자는 마라톤을 뛸 때 주의해야 할 점에 대해 이야기하고 있다.

7

W: Now we will do the last yoga position for today. First, look straight ahead.
M: Look straight...
W: Put your left hand forward. And hold your right ankle with your right hand.
M: Like this?
W: Good. Then pull it up.
M: Wow, it's hard. How long should I stay like this?
W: Around 20 to 30 seconds. Then do the same position on the opposite side.
M: Okay.

여: 이제 오늘의 마지막 요가 자세를 할 거예요. 먼저 앞을 똑바로 보세요.
남: 앞을 똑바로 보고…
여: 왼손을 앞으로 내미세요. 그리고 오른손으로 오른쪽 발목을 잡으세요.
남: 이렇게요?
여: 좋아요. 그리고 들어 올리세요.
남: 우와, 힘드네요. 얼마 동안 이렇게 있어야 돼요?
여: 20초에서 30초 정도요. 그리고 나서 반대편으로 같은 동작을 하세요.
남: 알겠어요.

어휘
yoga[jóuɡə] 명 요가 position[pəzíʃən] 명 자세 straight[streit] 부 똑바로 ahead[əhéd] 부 앞으로 forward[fɔ́ːrwərd] 부 앞으로 ankle[ǽŋkl] 명 발목 pull[pul] 동 당기다 second[sékənd] 명 초 opposite[ápəzit] 형 반대쪽의

문제 해설
Q: 여자가 설명하고 있는 자세를 고르시오.
  한쪽 팔은 앞으로 내밀고 다른 손은 발목을 잡아 위로 드는 동작이다.

8

W: Congratulations! You were the MVP of today's game.
M: Thank you.
W: But you don't look happy. Did you get hurt during the game?
M: No. I'm okay.
W: Then what's the matter?
M: There were only a small number of people in the stadium. I was a bit disappointed.
W: Oh, I see. I guess handball isn't popular.
M: We won the gold medal in the Olympics last year. But nothing changed.
W: Cheer up! Someday people will be interested in handball.
M: I hope so.

여: 축하해! 네가 오늘 경기의 MVP였어.
남: 고마워.
여: 근데 넌 행복해 보이지가 않네. 경기 중에 다쳤니?
남: 아니. 난 괜찮아.
여: 그럼 뭐가 문제야?
남: 경기장에 사람들이 조금밖에 없었잖아. 난 조금 실망했어.
여: 아, 알겠어. 핸드볼이 인기 있는 것 같지 않아.
남: 우린 지난해에 올림픽에서 금메달을 땄어. 그런데 아무 것도 변하지 않았어.
여: 힘내! 언젠가 사람들이 핸드볼에 흥미를 가질 거야.
남: 그랬으면 좋겠어.

어휘
congratulation[kəngrætʃuléiʃən] 명 축하 MVP 최우수 선수 (= most valuable player) handball[hǽndbɔ̀ːl] 명 핸드볼 gold medal 금메달 the Olympics 올림픽, 올림픽 경기 Cheer up! 힘내! someday[sʌ́mdèi]

㊁ 언젠가 [문제] fail[feil] ⑧ 실패하다 few[fjuː] ⑱ 거의 없는, 조금밖에 없는

문제 해설
Q: 남자가 기분이 나쁜 이유는?
그는 MVP가 되었지만 경기장에 관중들이 조금밖에 없어서 실망했다.

Listening ★ Challenge p. 54

A 1 ① 2 ② B 1 ③ 2 ②

A [1-2]

W: Are you interested in playing football? Then join the Junior Premier Camp with Chelsea FC in London. In this program, you can learn football skills from Chelsea Academy coaches. You can also watch and enjoy Premier League games. We even offer home stay services in London. This camp will be held from the 13th to the 30th of January. Any child from 10 to 13 years of age can join. You can sign up online before December 15th. Don't miss this great chance!

여: 축구 하는 데 관심이 있나요? 그럼 런던에서 첼시 FC와 함께 하는 주니어 프리미어 캠프에 참가하세요. 이 프로그램에서 여러분은 첼시 아카데미의 코치들에게 축구 기술을 배울 수 있습니다. 여러분은 프리미어리그 경기도 보며 즐길 수 있습니다. 저희는 런던에서 홈스테이 서비스도 제공합니다. 이 캠프는 1월 13일에서 30일까지 열릴 것입니다. 10세에서 13세 어린이라면 누구나 참여할 수 있습니다. 여러분은 12월 15일 전까지 온라인 상으로 등록할 수 있습니다. 이 좋은 기회를 놓치지 마세요!

어휘
skill[skil] ⑱ 기술 Premier League (잉글랜드 축구의)
1부 리그, 프리미어리그 offer[ɔ́(ː)fər] ⑧ 제공하다
home stay 홈스테이 sign up 등록하다

문제 해설
Q1: 무엇에 대한 광고인가?
첼시 FC와 함께하는 주니어 축구 캠프에 대한 광고이다.
Q2: 틀린 정보를 고르시오.
이 캠프는 1월 13일에서 30일까지 열린다고 했다.

B [1-2]

W: Today we're going to have an interview with a sports hero, Kobe Bryant.
M: Hello. This is Kobe Bryant of the LA Lakers.
W: The LA Lakers became the champions of the NBA. How do you feel?
M: I feel fantastic!
W: Just before the game ended, your team was losing by one point, 96–95.
M: Right, I thought we would lose the game.
W: But you made a three-point shot at the very last minute.
M: Right. Thanks to me, my team won the game 98–96.
W: It was really amazing! I couldn't believe my eyes.
M: Haha... me neither.
W: You proved that you really are the best basketball player.
M: Thank you.

여: 오늘은 스포츠 영웅인 Kobe Bryant와 인터뷰를 하겠습니다.
남: 안녕하세요. LA Lakers의 Kobe Bryant입니다.
여: LA Lakers가 NBA에서 챔피언이 됐는데요. 기분이 어떻습니까?
남: 엄청 좋죠!
여: 경기가 끝나기 직전에 당신의 팀이 96대 95로 1점 차로 지고 있었잖아요.
남: 맞아요, 우리가 경기에 질 거라고 생각했어요.
여: 하지만 당신이 마지막 순간에 3점 슛을 성공시켰죠.
남: 네. 제 덕분에 저희 팀은 98대 96으로 경기를 이겼어요.
여: 정말 멋졌어요! 제 눈을 믿을 수가 없었어요.
남: 하하… 저도요.
여: 당신이 정말 최고의 농구 선수라는 걸 증명했어요.
남: 감사합니다.

어휘
interview[íntərvjùː] ⑱ 인터뷰 hero[hí(ː)rou]
⑱ 영웅 champion[tʃǽmpiən] ⑱ 챔피언, 우승자
fantastic[fæntǽstik] ⑱ 환상적인, 굉장한 point[pɔint]
⑱ (경기의) 득점 shot[ʃɑt] ⑱ (농구의) 슛 prove[pruːv]
⑧ 증명하다

문제 해설
Q1: 화자 간의 관계는?
여자가 농구 선수인 남자를 인터뷰하고 있으므로 기자와

55

선수의 관계임을 알 수 있다.

Q2: 경기 결과를 고르시오.

　LA Lakers가 95대 96으로 지고 있다가 98대 96으로 역
전을 했다.

Critical ★ Thinking　p. 55

1 (1) Against (2) For (3) For
2 (1) ⓑ (2) ⓒ (3) ⓐ

M1: I'm Jack. Some sports players appear on TV too often. They seem to think that they are big movie stars or something. I don't understand why they waste their time. They should focus on improving their skills.

W: I'm Lisa. I heard sports players need a lot of money for training. By being on TV, they can earn money to pay for their training costs. Then they can do well in their sports.

M2: I'm Chad. Sports players appear on TV shows because many people want to see them. I don't think they're different from movie stars or singers. It is natural for popular players to appear on TV often.

남1: 난 Jack이야. 어떤 운동 선수들이 TV에 너무 자주 나와. 그들은 자신들이 대단한 영화 배우라도 된다고 생각하는 것 같아. 나는 그들이 왜 시간을 낭비하는지 이해가 안 돼. 그들은 자신들의 기술을 향상시키는 데 집중해야 해.

여: 난 Lisa야. 난 운동 선수들이 훈련을 하는 데 돈이 많이 필요하다고 들었어. TV에 나옴으로써 그들은 훈련 비용을 지불할 돈을 벌 수 있어. 그렇게 해서 그들은 자신의 종목에서 잘할 수 있어.

남2: 난 Chad야. 운동 선수들은 많은 사람들이 그들을 보고 싶어하기 때문에 TV 프로그램에 나오는 거야. 난 그들이 영화 배우나 가수들과 다르다고 생각하지 않아. 인기 있는 선수들이 TV에 자주 나오는 건 자연스러운 거야.

어휘
appear[əpíər] 동 나타나다; *출연하다 waste[weist] 동 낭비하다 focus on ~에 집중하다 improve [imprú:v] 동 향상시키다 earn[əːrn] 동 벌다 cost [kɔ(:)st] *명 비용; 동 비용이 들다 natural[nǽtʃərəl] 형 자연의; *당연한 [문제] popularity[pὰpjulǽrəti] 명 인기

문제 해설

Q1: 각 인물이 운동 선수들이 TV 프로그램에 나오는 것에 대해 찬성하는지 반대하는지 ✓표 하시오.

　Jack은 운동 선수의 TV 출연이 시간낭비라고 부정적으로 생각하는 반면 Lisa와 Chad는 긍정적으로 생각한다.

Q2: 각 인물과 그들의 의견을 연결하시오.

　ⓐ 선수들은 그들의 인기 때문에 TV에 나온다.

　ⓑ 선수들은 연습에만 집중해야 한다.

　ⓒ 선수들은 TV에 나옴으로써 훈련을 위한 돈을 벌 수 있다.

　(1) Jack은 운동 선수들이 자신들의 기술을 향상시키는 데 집중해야 한다고 했다.

　(2) Lisa는 선수들이 TV에 나오면 훈련에 드는 비용을 벌 수 있으므로 경기에서 더 잘할 수 있다고 했다.

　(3) Chad는 운동 선수들이 TV에 나오는 것은 대중이 원하기 때문이라고 했다.

UNIT 09 Travel

Getting ★ Ready　p. 56

A 1 ⓒ　2 ⓓ　3 ⓐ　4 ⓔ　5 ⓖ
B 1 ⓒ　2 ⓑ　3 ⓔ

B 1 남: 제가 체크아웃 하고 나서 저의 배낭 좀 보관해주시 겠어요?

　여: 물론이죠. 그냥 여기에 두고 가시면 됩니다.

2 남: 어떤 방을 원하세요?

　여: 트윈 룸으로 할게요.

3 남: 창가 좌석을 원하시나요, 아니면 통로 측 좌석을 원하시나요?

　여: 그건 상관 없지만 앞쪽 좌석으로 주세요.

Listening ★ Start　p. 57

1 ④ / made a flight reservation, Which date, all booked, I'll take that one
2 ④ / travel by plane, lots of water, keep you awake, walk around the aisles

1

(*Telephone rings.*)

M: USA Airlines. How may I help you?

W: I made a flight reservation yesterday, but I want to change the date.

M: Okay. What is your name?

W: Kelly Grant. It was for a flight to Toronto on September 6th, 10 a.m.

M: Okay. Which date do you want to change it to?

W: The same time on September 8th.

M: I'm sorry. That flight is all booked.

W: Really? What time is the next flight after that?

M: 1 p.m.

W: I'll take that one.

M: Okay.

(전화벨이 울린다.)

남: USA 항공사입니다. 무엇을 도와드릴까요?

여: 어제 항공편을 예약했는데요, 날짜를 바꾸고 싶어서요.

남: 알겠습니다. 성함이 어떻게 되세요?

여: Kelly Grant입니다. 9월 6일 오전 10시 토론토 행 비행기였어요.

남: 알겠습니다. 어느 날짜로 변경하시길 원하세요?

여: 9월 8일 같은 시간으로요.

남: 죄송합니다. 그 항공편은 모두 예약되었네요.

여: 정말이요? 그 다음 항공편은 몇 시죠?

남: 오후 1시예요.

여: 그걸로 할게요.

남: 알겠습니다.

어휘

airline[έərlàin] 명 항공 회사   flight[flait] 명 *항공편; 비행   book[buk] 동 예약하다

문제 해설

Q: 여자의 항공편은 언제인가?

여자는 9월 8일 오전 10시 항공편이 모두 예약된 상태여서 9월 8일 오후 1시 항공편을 예약했다.

2

M: Do you have any plans to travel by plane? Then let me give you some tips. First, the air inside a plane is dry, so drink lots of water or juice. But don't drink too much alcohol, coffee, or tea. Caffeine will keep you awake during the flight. Also, you may be in an uncomfortable position for a long time. So, it's good to stretch your body and walk around the aisles often.

남: 비행기로 여행할 계획이 있나요? 그러면 여러분께 몇 가지 조언을 해 드리겠습니다. 먼저 비행기 내부의 공기는 건조하므로 물이나 주스를 많이 드세요. 하지만 술이나 커피, 또는 차는 너무 많이 마시지 마세요. 카페인은 비행 내내 여러분을 깨어 있도록 할 것입니다. 또한 여러분은 오랜 시간 불편한 자세로 있게 될지도 모릅니다. 그러므로 자주 스트레칭을 하고 복도를 돌아다니는 것이 좋습니다.

어휘

tip[tip] 명 조언   alcohol[ǽlkəhɔ(ː)l] 명 술   caffeine [kǽfiːn] 명 카페인   awake[əwéik] 형 깨어 있는   uncomfortable[ʌnkʌ́mfərtəbl] 형 불편한   position [pəzíʃən] 명 자세   stretch[stretʃ] 동 쭉 펴다, 스트레칭하다   aisle[ail] 명 복도, 통로

문제 해설

Q: 남자는 주로 무엇에 대해 이야기하고 있는가?

① 비행기에서의 최고의 자리

② 당신이 받을 수 있는 비행기 서비스

③ 비행기에서 할 수 있는 운동

④ 비행기에서 편하게 있을 수 있는 방법

남자는 편안한 비행을 위한 방법들을 조언해 주고 있다.

Listening ★ Practice p. 58

1 ② 2 ① 3 ③ 4 ④ 5 ④ 6 (1) F (2) T (3) F 7 ③ 8 ④

1

W: Charles, I'm going to travel to London this summer.

M: Great!

W: But the hotels are really expensive.

M: How about staying at a youth hostel?

W: Aren't they mostly far from the city center?

M: Perhaps. Then why don't you look for a B&B? There are many B&Bs in the city center.

W: What's a B&B?

M: It provides private bedrooms and offers breakfast. So, it's called a "Bed and

57

Breakfast," or B&B.
W: Aren't they quite expensive?
M: They're more expensive than a youth hostel, but cheaper than a hotel.
W: I should search for one, then.

여: Charles, 난 이번 여름에 런던으로 여행 갈 거야.
남: 좋겠네!
여: 근데 호텔이 너무 비싸.
남: 유스호스텔에 머무는 게 어때?
여: 유스호스텔은 대부분 시내에서 멀리 떨어져 있지 않니?
남: 아마 그럴 거야. 그럼 B&B를 찾아보는 게 어때? 시내에 B&B가 많거든.
여: B&B가 뭐야?
남: 거기서는 개인 침실이랑 아침 식사를 제공해 줘. 그래서 'Bed and Breakfast', 또는 B&B라고 불리지.
여: 꽤 비싸지 않니?
남: 유스호스텔보다는 비싸지만 호텔보다는 싸.
여: 그럼 그걸 찾아봐야겠다.

어휘
youth hostel 유스호스텔 mostly[móustli] 🄫 대부분, 대개 perhaps[pərhǽps] 🄫 아마도 provide[prəváid] 🄭 제공하다 private[práivit] 🄮 개인의, 사적인 quite [kwait] 🄫 꽤 search[səːrtʃ] 🄭 찾다

문제 해설
Q: 여자는 런던에서 어디에 머무를 것인가?
　여자는 B&B를 찾아보겠다고 했다.

2

M: Hello. I want to know the check-out time.
W: Our check-out time is 11 o'clock in the morning.
M: 11 a.m.? My flight is at 4 p.m. Is it possible to check out at 1 p.m.?
W: Yes, it's possible. But there's an extra charge.
M: How much is it?
W: It's $15 per hour.
M: That's expensive. Instead, could you keep my backpack after I check out?
W: Of course. That's free.
M: Then I'll check out at 11 a.m. and leave my backpack at the front desk.
W: Okay.

남: 안녕하세요. 체크아웃 시간을 알고 싶은데요.
여: 저희 체크아웃 시간은 오전 11시예요.
남: 오전 11시요? 제 비행편이 오후 4시라서요. 오후 1시에 체크아웃을 할 수 있을까요?
여: 네, 가능합니다. 하지만 추가 요금이 있어요.
남: 얼마예요?
여: 시간당 15달러예요.
남: 비싸네요. 대신 체크아웃 후에 제 배낭을 보관해주실 수 있어요?
여: 물론이죠. 그건 무료예요.
남: 그럼 오전 11시에 체크아웃하고 제 배낭을 프런트에 놓고 갈게요.
여: 알겠습니다.

어휘
check-out[tʃékàut] 🄮 체크아웃, 방을 비울 시각 possible[pásəbl] 🄮 가능한 check out (계산을 하고) 호텔에서 나오다, 체크아웃하다 extra[ékstrə] 🄮 추가의, 여분의 charge[tʃɑːrdʒ] 🄮 요금 per[pər] 🄫 ~마다, ~당 backpack[bǽkpæk] 🄮 배낭 front desk (호텔 등의) 프런트

문제 해설
Q: 남자가 체크아웃을 할 시간은?
　남자는 오전 11시에 체크아웃을 하기로 했다.

3

W: How may I help you?
M: I want to know which bus goes to the British Museum.
W: I'm sorry, but there's no direct bus. You need to change buses.
M: Well, that won't be easy. This is my first time here.
W: Why don't you try the tube?
M: The tube? Are you talking about the subway?
W: Yes. The nearest station is only five minutes away on foot.
M: How about a taxi? How much will a taxi cost?
W: Taxis are expensive. It will cost about 15 pounds.
M: Well... I'll just take the tube.

여: 무엇을 도와드릴까요?
남: 어느 버스가 대영 박물관으로 가는지 알고 싶어요.

여: 죄송합니다만 직행 버스가 없어요. 버스를 갈아타셔야 해요.

남: 음, 쉽진 않겠네요. 여기 온 건 이번이 처음이거든요.

여: tube를 타시는 게 어때요?

남: tube요? 지하철을 말씀하시는 건가요?

여: 네. 가장 가까운 역이 걸어서 5분 거리에 있거든요.

남: 택시는 어때요? 택시 요금은 얼마나 나올까요?

여: 택시는 비싸요. 약 15파운드 나올 거예요.

남: 음… 그냥 tube를 타야겠네요.

어휘

direct[dirékt] 형 직접적인; *직행의 tube[tju:b] 명 《영》지하철 subway[sʌ́bwèi] 명 《미》지하철 on foot 걸어서, 도보로 cost[kɔ(:)st] 동 비용이 들다

문제 해설

Q: 남자는 대영 박물관에 어떻게 갈 것인가?

버스는 갈아타야 하고 택시는 요금이 비싸서 지하철을 타기로 했다.

4

(*Telephone rings.*)

W: Thank you for calling the Hilltop Hotel.

M: Yes. I want to make a reservation for two nights from July 15th.

W: Okay. So you'll be checking out on the 17th. What type of room do you want?

M: I'd like a twin room. How much is it?

W: It's $200 for two nights.

M: What? It was $180 last time.

W: That's because July is the busy season. Do you still want to make a reservation?

M: I guess so.

W: Could you please tell me your name?

M: My name is Steve Arnold.

(전화벨이 울린다.)

여: Hilltop 호텔에 전화 주셔서 감사합니다.

남: 네. 7월 15일부터 이틀간 예약을 하고 싶어요.

여: 알겠습니다. 그럼 17일에 체크아웃을 하시겠네요. 어떤 방을 원하세요?

남: 트윈룸으로 하고 싶어요. 얼마예요?

여: 이틀에 200달러예요.

남: 뭐라고요? 지난번엔 180달러였는데요.

여: 7월이 성수기라서요. 그래도 예약하길 원하시나요?

남: 그래야겠네요.

여: 성함을 말씀해 주시겠습니까?

남: 제 이름은 Steve Arnold입니다.

어휘

twin room 트윈룸(침대가 두 개 있는 방) busy season 성수기 [문제] check-in[tʃékin] 명 *체크인, 숙박 수속; 탑승 수속 total[tóutl] 형 총계의, 전체의 rate[reit] 명 비율; *요금

문제 해설

Q: 잘못된 정보를 고르시오.

7월은 성수기 요금이 적용되어 총 요금이 200달러라고 했다.

5

M: Excuse me.

W: Yes. What can I do for you?

M: I've been waiting a long time for my bag, but it hasn't come out.

W: Okay. Could you please tell me your flight number?

M: It's GT210.

W: Could you show me your baggage tag?

M: Yes. Here it is.

W: Wait for a second... oh, our airline made a mistake. Your bag was sent to Hong Kong airport.

M: What? What should I do, then?

W: I'm terribly sorry about this. I'll contact Hong Kong airport to get your bag.

남: 실례합니다.

여: 네. 무엇을 도와드릴까요?

남: 오랫동안 제 가방을 기다리고 있는데요, 나오질 않아요.

여: 알겠습니다. 항공편 번호를 말씀해 주시겠습니까?

남: GT210이에요.

여: 수하물 꼬리표 좀 보여주시겠어요?

남: 네. 여기요.

여: 잠시만요… 아, 저희 항공사에서 실수를 했네요. 고객님의 가방이 홍콩 공항으로 운송됐어요.

남: 뭐라고요? 그럼 어떻게 해야 하죠?

여: 정말 죄송합니다. 제가 홍콩 공항에 연락해서 고객님의 가방을 받을 수 있도록 하겠습니다.

어휘

baggage tag 수하물 꼬리표 make a mistake 실수하다 airport[ɛ́ərpɔ̀rt] 명 공항 terribly[térəbli] 부 매우 contact[kántækt] 동 교신하다, 연락을 취하다

59

문제 해설

Q: 남자의 문제는?

① 그는 자신의 항공편 번호를 모른다.

② 그는 가방을 잘못 집었다.

③ 그는 수하물 꼬리표를 잃어버렸다.

④ 그의 가방이 다른 공항으로 운송됐다.

항공사의 실수로 남자의 가방이 홍콩 공항으로 운송되었다.

6

M: DB Airlines is offering an online check-in service starting this month. With this service, you can choose your seat on the DB airlines homepage. Plus, you can use a special counter for service users at the airport. This means you can save time at the airport. This service is offered from 48 hours to 3 hours before the flight.

남: DB 항공은 이번 달부터 온라인 탑승 수속 서비스를 제공하고 있습니다. 이 서비스를 이용해 DB 항공 홈페이지에서 좌석을 선택하실 수 있습니다. 게다가 공항에서 서비스 이용자들을 위한 특별 카운터를 이용하실 수 있습니다. 이는 공항에서 시간을 절약하실 수 있다는 걸 의미합니다. 이 서비스는 비행 48시간에서 3시간 전까지 제공됩니다.

어휘

online[ɔ́nlàin] 형 온라인의   homepage[hóumpèidʒ] 명 홈페이지   counter[káuntər] 명 계산대, 카운터 [문제] available[əvéiləbl] 형 이용 가능한

문제 해설

Q: 온라인 탑승 수속 서비스에 관해 사실이면 T, 사실이 아니면 F를 쓰시오.

(1) 한 달 동안 제공되었다.

(2) 공항에서 탑승 수속을 더 빨리 할 수 있게 할 것이다.

(3) 비행 2시간 전에 이용 가능하다.

7

W: When you travel, packing your bags is as important as planning the trip. So, how should you pack? First, don't pack your bag tightly. Usually, bags become heavier with things you buy during the trip. And take old clothes. That way, you can wear them and then throw them away. It will make your bag lighter. Also, take some plastic bags to put wet or dirty clothes in. That way, you can keep your bag clean.

여: 여행할 때 가방을 꾸리는 것은 여행을 계획하는 것만큼 중요합니다. 그럼 짐을 어떻게 싸야 할까요? 먼저, 가방을 빽빽하게 채워서 꾸리지 마세요. 보통 가방은 여행 중에 사는 물건들로 더 무거워집니다. 그리고 오래된 옷들을 챙기세요. 그러면 그것들을 입고 나서 버릴 수 있으니까요. 그러면 가방이 더 가벼워지죠. 또한, 축축하거나 더러운 옷을 담을 비닐봉지를 몇 개 챙기세요. 그렇게 함으로써 가방을 깨끗하게 유지할 수 있습니다.

어휘

pack[pæk] 통 (짐을) 꾸리다   tightly[táitli] 부 빽빽하게, 꽉   throw away 버리다   light[lait] 형 가벼운 plastic bag 비닐봉지   [문제] empty[émpti] 형 비어 있는   space[speis] 명 공간

문제 해설

Q: 여자의 충고가 아닌 것은?

① 짐을 꾸릴 때 빈 공간을 남겨두어라.

② 오래된 옷들을 챙겨라.

③ 자주 사용하는 물건들을 위쪽에 넣어라.

④ 축축하거나 더러운 옷들을 넣을 비닐봉지를 가져가라.

물건을 넣는 위치에 대해서는 언급하지 않았다.

8

W: Do you want a window seat or an aisle seat?

M: Aisle, please. It's a long flight, so a window seat wouldn't be comfortable.

W: Okay. There are two aisle seats left.

M: Oh, in that case, can I get a seat near the front?

W: That seat is right in front of the screen. Is that okay?

M: Well, I don't want that one. It'll make my eyes feel tired.

W: Then, do you want the seat in the back?

M: Yes. It'll be better.

W: Okay. Here's your ticket. Your seat is 24C.

M: Thanks.

여: 창가 좌석을 원하시나요, 통로 좌석을 원하시나요?

남: 통로 측이요. 장거리 비행이라서 창가 좌석은 불편할 거예요.

여: 알겠습니다. 통로 측 좌석은 두 좌석 남았네요.

남: 아, 그럼 앞쪽 좌석에 앉을 수 있을까요?

여: 그 좌석은 스크린 바로 앞에 있어요. 괜찮으세요?

남: 음, 그 좌석은 별로네요. 눈이 피로할 거예요.

여: 그럼 뒤쪽에 있는 좌석을 원하세요?

남: 네. 그게 낫겠네요.

여: 알겠습니다. 표는 여기 있어요. 좌석은 24C예요.

남: 감사합니다.

어휘

in that case 그렇다면   screen[skríːn] 명 스크린, 화면

문제 해설

Q: 남자의 자리를 고르시오.

　뒤쪽에 있는 통로 측 좌석이다.

Listening ★ Challenge　p. 60

A 1 ②　2 ①　B 1 ④　2 ③

A [1-2]

M: Jessica, what are you doing?

W: I'm reading a travel guidebook.

M: Are you still planning your trip?

W: Yes. I haven't decided how to get from Paris to Barcelona.

M: Why don't you take Lion Airlines?

W: Lion Airlines? I've never heard of it.

M: It only flies in Europe. It's famous for low prices.

W: That's good!

M: But the ticket price goes up as more people book the flight.

W: So, if I buy a ticket early, it will be cheaper.

M: That's right.

W: Wow! I'll book a ticket on the website now.

M: But there are no extra services like drinks or meals.

W: That doesn't matter. Thanks for the tip.

남: Jessica, 뭐 하고 있니?

여: 여행 안내 책자를 읽고 있어.

남: 아직도 여행 계획을 세우고 있는 중이야?

여: 응. 파리에서 바르셀로나로 어떻게 갈지 결정을 못 했어.

남: Lion 항공을 타는 게 어때?

여: Lion 항공? 그건 한 번도 못 들어 봤는데.

남: 유럽에서만 운항해. 저가로 유명하지.

여: 좋구나!

남: 근데 더 많은 사람들이 항공편을 예약할수록 표값이 올라가.

여: 그러니까 표를 빨리 사면 더 저렴하겠구나.

남: 그렇지.

여: 우와! 지금 웹사이트에서 표를 예매해야겠어.

남: 근데 음료나 식사 같은 추가 서비스는 없어.

여: 그건 상관없어. 알려줘서 고마워.

어휘

guidebook[gáidbùk] 명 안내 책자   matter[mǽtər] 동 중요하다   [문제] cancel[kǽnsəl] 동 취소하다   information[ìnfərméiʃən] 명 정보

문제 해설

Q1: 여자가 다음에 할 일은?

　여자는 바로 비행기표를 예매하겠다고 했다.

Q2: Lion 항공에 관해 사실이 아닌 것은?

　Lion 항공은 유럽 내에서만 운항한다고 했다.

B [1-2]

W: Where should we travel this summer?

M: I want to go to Turkey.

W: Turkey is a beautiful country. But I visited Turkey and Greece last year.

M: Then where do you want to go?

W: How about Australia? There are many things we can do there.

M: I've been there, but it wasn't fun.

W: Did you ride a sandboard?

M: No. I just swam and went biking.

W: I heard riding a board on the sand is really fun. Also, we can go bungee-jumping.

M: I never want to try bungee-jumping. But riding a sandboard sounds fun.

W: There you go. Let's try it.

M: All right. Maybe I can go to Turkey next year.

여: 이번 여름에 어디로 여행을 가야 할까?

남: 난 터키에 가고 싶어.

여: 터키는 아름다운 나라지. 근데 작년에 터키랑 그리스에 다녀왔어.

남: 그럼 어디로 가고 싶은데?

여: 호주는 어때? 그곳엔 우리가 할 수 있는 것들이 많거든.

남: 거긴 가 봤는데 재미없었어.

여: 샌드보드는 탔니?

남: 아니. 그냥 수영하고 자전거를 탔어.

여: 모래 위에서 보드를 타는 게 정말 재미있다고 들었어. 그리고 번지 점프도 하러 갈 수 있고.

남: 번지 점프는 절대 시도하고 싶지 않아. 하지만 샌드보드

타는 건 재미있을 것 같다.

여: 그래. 한번 해 보자.

남: 좋아. 터키는 내년에 갈 수 있겠지.

어휘

sandboard[sǽndbɔ̀ːrd] 명 샌드보드 bike[baik] 동 자전거를 타다 sand[sænd] 명 모래 bungee-jump [bʌ́ndʒiːdʒʌ̀mp] 동 번지 점프를 하다

문제 해설

Q1: 그들이 가려고 하는 나라는?

두 사람은 올해 호주에 가기로 했다.

Q2: 두 사람이 하려는 활동을 고르시오.

샌드보드와 번지 점프 중에 남자가 번지 점프는 싫지만 샌드보드를 타고 싶다고 했다.

Critical ★ Thinking p. 61

1 (1) For (2) Against (3) For
2 (1) ⓑ (2) ⓓ (3) ⓒ

W1: I'm May. I always take package tours. Planning a trip takes time, and it's very stressful. But I don't need to worry about a thing when I take a package tour.
M: I'm Chris. When you travel on a package tour, you travel with the same people the whole time. But travel is about meeting local people and learning about new cultures.
W2: I'm Tina. I went to France last summer. I planned the tour all by myself, but I wasted time trying to find places. Having a tour guide can save time.

여1: 난 May야. 난 항상 패키지 여행을 해. 여행을 계획하는 것은 시간이 들고 아주 스트레스를 받거든. 하지만 패키지 여행을 하면 하나도 걱정할 필요가 없어.

남: 난 Chris야. 패키지 여행을 하면 모든 시간을 같은 사람들이랑 여행하잖아. 하지만 여행이란 건 현지 사람들을 만나고 새로운 문화를 배우는 거야.

여2: 난 Tina야. 난 지난 여름에 프랑스에 갔어. 여행을 모두 혼자서 계획했는데 장소들을 찾으려고 노력하다가 시간을 낭비했어. 여행 가이드가 있으면 시간을 절약할 수 있어.

어휘

package tour 패키지 여행 stressful[strésfəl] 형 스트레스가 많은 whole[houl] 형 모든, 전체의 local

[lóukəl] 형 지방의, 고장의 culture[kʌ́ltʃər] 명 문화 by oneself 혼자서 waste[weist] 동 낭비하다 [문제] mix with ~ ~와 어울리다

문제 해설

Q1: 각 인물이 패키지 여행에 대해 찬성하는지 반대하는지 ✓표 하시오.

(1) May는 여행을 계획하는 데에 시간도 많이 들고 스트레스도 받기 때문에 패키지 여행을 한다고 했다.

(2) Chris는 패키지 여행을 하면 계속 같은 사람들과 여행해야 하므로 현지 사람들을 만나고 새로운 문화를 배우기 힘들다고 생각한다.

(3) Tina는 여행을 할 때 여행 가이드가 있으면 여행지에서 시간을 낭비하지 않을 수 있다고 생각한다.

Q2: 각 인물의 의견을 고르시오.

ⓐ 난 내가 관심 있는 장소만 방문하고 싶어.

ⓑ 패키지 여행을 하면 여행을 계획하는 시간을 절약할 수 있어.

ⓒ 패키지 여행을 하면 시간을 낭비하지 않고 여행을 할 수 있어.

ⓓ 패키지 여행을 하는 동안에는 현지 사람들과 어울려 그들의 문화를 배우는 게 힘들어.

UNIT 10 IT

Getting ★ Ready p. 62

A 1 ⓑ 2 ⓐ 3 ⓒ B 1 ⓒ 2 ⓐ 3 ⓓ
C 1 ⓒ 2 ⓑ 3 ⓐ

C 1 남: 너는 하루에 인터넷 하는 데 시간을 얼마나 보내니?
여: 하루에 두 시간 정도.

2 남: 네 휴대 전화에 문제가 있니?
여: 응. 상대방의 소리를 들을 수가 없어.

3 남: 그녀에게 이메일로 연락해보는 게 어때?
여: 아마도 그렇게 해야 할 것 같아.

Listening ★ Start p. 63

1 ① / surfing the Internet, What's wrong, shut down, didn't save it, right away
2 ③ / bought this for me, download English files, record classes

62

1

M: Are you busy right now?
W: No, I'm surfing the Internet. Why?
M: I'm in big trouble. I don't know what to do.
W: What's wrong?
M: I was doing my Chinese homework when my computer shut down again.
W: I don't know much about computers. Do you need to do homework all over again?
M: I think so. I didn't save it.
W: Why don't you ask Paul about it? He knows a lot about computers.
M: Good idea. I'll call him right away.

남: 너 지금 바쁘니?
여: 아니, 인터넷을 검색하고 있어. 왜?
남: 큰 문제가 생겼어. 어떻게 해야 할지 모르겠어.
여: 뭐가 문젠데?
남: 중국어 숙제를 하고 있었는데 내 컴퓨터가 또 다운돼 버렸어.
여: 난 컴퓨터에 대해서 잘 모르는데. 숙제를 전부 다시 해야 해?
남: 그래야 할 것 같아. 저장을 안 했거든.
여: Paul한테 물어보는 게 어때? 그 애가 컴퓨터에 대해서 많이 알잖아.
남: 좋은 생각이야. 바로 그에게 전화해야겠어.

어휘
surf the Internet 인터넷을 검색하다   Chinese
[tʃàiníːz] 명 중국어   shut down 작동이 중단되다
right away 즉시

문제 해설
Q: 소년이 다음에 할 일은?
　소년은 Paul에게 전화해서 컴퓨터 문제에 대해 물어보기로 했다.

2

W: Last year, my dad bought this for me on my 12th birthday. Because of its small size, it's easy to carry around. It's very useful when studying English. I can download English files from computers and listen to them over and over. Plus, I can download my favorite songs whenever I want to. Sometimes, I record classes with it. It helps me review my classes later on.

여: 작년에, 우리 아빠가 내 12번째 생일에 이것을 사주셨어. 그것은 크기가 작아서 가지고 다니기 쉬워. 영어 공부를 할 때 아주 유용하지. 컴퓨터에서 영어 파일을 다운로드해서 반복해서 들을 수 있어. 게다가 내가 원할 때마다 가장 좋아하는 노래들을 다운로드할 수 있어. 때로는 그것으로 수업을 녹음하기도 해. 나중에 내가 수업을 복습하는 데 도움이 돼.

어휘
carry [kǽri] 동 지니고 다니다   useful [júːsfəl] 형 유용한
download [dáunlòud] 동 다운로드하다   over and
over 반복해서, 계속   record [rikɔ́ːrd] 동 기록하다; *녹음하다   review [rivjúː] 동 복습하다

문제 해설
Q: 소녀는 무엇에 대해 이야기하고 있는가?
　작은 크기로, 영어 파일이나 음악 파일을 다운로드해서 들을 수 있고, 녹음기로도 사용 가능한 것은 MP3이다.

Listening ★ Practice   p. 64

1 ①　2 (1) Good　(2) Good　(3) Bad　3 ④
4 ①　5 ①　6 ③　7 ④　8 ④

1

M: Hello?
W: Hey, Chris. I can see you now.
M: Wow. It's exciting to see you on a computer screen.
W: I agree. You look different today.
M: I changed my glasses. How do I look?
W: You look good. It doesn't feel like you're in Canada.
M: I know. I like looking at your face while we talk.
W: So do I. And it costs nothing.
M: Why don't we set a regular time to talk online?
W: Okay. Fridays are good for me.
M: Let's talk every Friday afternoon, then.

남: 안녕?
여: 안녕, Chris. 이제 네가 보여.
남: 우와. 컴퓨터 화면에서 너를 보니 신난다.
여: 나도 그래. 너 오늘 달라 보여.
남: 안경을 바꿨거든. 어때?
여: 근사한데. 네가 캐나다에 있는 것처럼 느껴지지가 않아.
남: 맞아. 얘기하면서 네 얼굴을 볼 수 있어서 좋다.

63

여: 나도 그래. 그리고 비용도 안 들잖아.

남: 우리 일정한 시간을 정해놓고 온라인에서 이야기하면 어떨까?

여: 좋아. 난 금요일이 괜찮아.

남: 그럼 매주 금요일 오후에 얘기하자.

어휘

set[set] 통 정하다, 지정하다 (set-set-set)　regular [régjulər] 형 규칙적인　online[ɔ́nlàin] *부 온라인 상에서; 형 온라인의

문제 해설

Q: 그들은 무엇을 하고 있는가?

컴퓨터 화면을 통해 서로의 얼굴을 보면서 대화를 하는 상황이므로 인터넷으로 화상전화를 하고 있음을 알 수 있다.

2

M: In my free time, I play a computer game called *Aliens*. It has so many cute characters in it. It's fun to change their clothes and weapons. Best of all, the storyline of saving the earth from aliens is exciting. But my friend Jenny thinks it's boring. For me, the problem with this game is the sound. The same melody is repeated over and over, so I sometimes turn the volume off.

남: 나는 여가 시간에 'Aliens'라는 컴퓨터 게임을 해. 이 게임에는 귀여운 캐릭터들이 정말 많아. 그들의 옷과 무기를 바꾸는 게 재미있어. 무엇보다도, 외계인들로부터 지구를 구한다는 줄거리가 흥미로워. 하지만 내 친구인 Jenny는 이게 지루하다고 생각해. 내게 있어 이 게임의 문제점은 음향이야. 같은 멜로디가 계속 반복돼서 때로는 소리를 꺼버려.

어휘

alien[éiljən] 명 외계인　character[kǽriktər] 명 등장인물, (만화 등의) 캐릭터　weapon[wépən] 명 무기 best of all 무엇보다도, 첫째로　storyline[stɔ́:rilàin] 명 줄거리　earth[əːrθ] 명 지구　melody[mélədi] 명 멜로디　repeat[ripí:t] 통 반복하다　turn off 끄다 volume[válju:m] 명 음량

문제 해설

Q: 남자가 'Aliens'에 대해서 어떻게 느끼는지 √표 하시오.

남자는 이 게임에 귀여운 캐릭터가 많이 나오고 줄거리도 흥미롭다고 생각하지만 음향에는 불만족스러워 한다.

3

W: I sent you the photos of us by email. Did you get the file?

M: No. When did you send it?

W: I sent it around 1 p.m.

M: I just checked my mail, but there was no new mail. Did you send it to the correct address?

W: Isn't it micky@kkmail.com?

M: That's right. How strange.

W: Did you check your spam mailbox?

M: I did, but it wasn't there. Oh, I know what happened.

W: What?

M: I don't have enough storage space in my mailbox.

여: 너한테 이메일로 우리 사진을 보냈어. 파일 받았니?

남: 아니. 언제 보냈어?

여: 오후 1시쯤에 보냈어.

남: 방금 메일 확인했는데 새로 온 메일이 하나도 없었어. 올바른 주소로 보냈어?

여: micky@kkmail.com 아니야?

남: 맞아. 정말 이상하네.

여: 네 스팸 메일함 확인했어?

남: 확인했는데, 거기에 없었어. 아, 무슨 일이 생긴 건지 알겠어.

여: 뭔데?

남: 내 메일함에 충분한 저장 공간이 없네.

어휘

email[í:mèil] 명 전자 우편, 이메일　correct[kərékt] 형 올바른　spam[spæm] 명 스팸 메일　mailbox [méilbàks] 명 메일함　happen[hǽpən] 통 일어나다 storage[stɔ́:ridʒ] 명 저장　space[speis] 명 공간

문제 해설

Q: 남자가 사진을 받지 못한 이유는?

남자의 메일함에 충분한 저장 공간이 없다고 했다.

4

M: I'm angry that so many people don't follow netiquette.

W: What happened?

M: I was chatting with some guy a couple of days ago.

W: And?

M: He just left in the middle of chatting.
W: Without saying goodbye?
M: Right. And that wasn't the first time.
W: Really?
M: I was playing an online game with some girl recently and she said really bad words when she lost.
W: That's not nice.
M: I think people should behave well online.
W: Right. Too many people think they can do anything online.

남: 너무 많은 사람들이 네티켓을 따르지 않아서 화가 나.
여: 무슨 일 있었어?
남: 며칠 전에 어떤 애랑 채팅을 하고 있었거든.
여: 그런데?
남: 채팅 하던 중에 그냥 나가버리더라.
여: 인사말도 없이?
남: 응. 근데 그게 처음이 아니었어.
여: 정말?
남: 최근에 어떤 여자애랑 온라인 게임을 하고 있었는데 그 애가 지니까 욕을 하더라고.
여: 그러면 안 되는데.
남: 나는 사람들이 온라인 상에서 예의 바르게 행동해야 한다고 생각해.
여: 맞아. 온라인 상에서는 뭐든 할 수 있다고 생각하는 사람들이 너무 많아.

문제 해설
Q: 그들은 주로 무엇에 대해 이야기하고 있는가?
두 사람은 온라인 상에서도 예절을 지켜야 한다고 얘기하고 있다.

5

W: I found something interesting on YouTube recently. An Italian man was teaching people how to cook Korean bulgogi. I was surprised to see a foreigner making it. He also said that he loves singing Korean songs. He even said he's good at taekwondo. Thousands of people watched this video. It was ranked the top video of the week. I was so proud to be Korean.

여: 최근에 유튜브에서 흥미로운 것을 발견했어. 한 이탈리아 남자가 사람들에게 한국의 불고기를 요리하는 방법을 가르쳐주고 있었지. 나는 외국인이 그것을 만드는 것을 보고 놀랐어. 그는 또 한국 노래를 부르는 것을 좋아한다고 말했어. 그는 심지어 태권도도 잘한대. 수천 명의 사람들이 이 비디오를 봤어. 그것은 그 주 최고의 동영상으로 랭크되었어. 나는 한국인이라는 게 너무나 자랑스러웠어.

문제 해설
Q: 여자가 본 비디오를 고르시오.
외국인이 불고기를 요리하는 방법을 가르쳐주는 동영상을 봤다고 했다.

6

M: The days of paper books are coming to an end. That's because of e-books. Now you don't need to carry heavy books. You can read e-books on laptops, PMPs, MP3 players, and even cellphones. You can easily download e-books from online bookstores. They're cheaper than paper books. And if you need to know something while reading an e-book, you can use the search program to look for more information in the e-book.

남: 종이책의 시대는 끝나가고 있습니다. 그 이유는 전자책 때문입니다. 이제 무거운 책을 가지고 다닐 필요가 없습니다. 노트북 컴퓨터, PMP, MP3 플레이어, 그리고 심지어 휴대전화를 통해서 전자책을 읽을 수 있습니다. 전자책은 온라인 서점에서 쉽게 다운로드할 수 있습니다. 그것들은 종이책보다 쌉니다. 그리고 전자책을 읽다가 뭔가를 알아야 할 필요가 있으면 전자책에 있는 검색 프로그램을 사용해서 더 많은 정보를 찾을 수 있습니다.

명 전자책   laptop[læptὰp] 명 노트북 컴퓨터, 휴대용 컴퓨터   bookstore[búkstɔ̀ːr] 명 서점   search[sǝːrtʃ] 명 검색, 조사   [문제] device[diváis] 명 장치, 기기   letter[létǝr] 명 글자

문제 해설
Q: 전자책의 좋은 점으로 언급되지 <u>않은</u> 것은?
   전자책을 이용할 수 있는 많은 기기, 저렴한 가격, 검색 프로그램에 관해서는 언급했으나 다양한 글자 크기에 대해서는 언급하지 않았다.

7

M: Have you talked to Jennifer recently?
W: No, I haven't. Why?
M: I called her, but she didn't answer the phone.
W: Really? Maybe she's busy.
M: Well, I also sent her an email, but I didn't get any reply.
W: Jennifer doesn't check her email very often. But I saw she was logged into messenger today.
M: Really?
W: Yes. She was on around lunchtime. Why don't you contact her through messenger?
M: I guess I should do that.

남: 최근에 Jennifer랑 얘기한 적 있니?
여: 아니, 없는데. 왜?
남: 전화했는데 전화를 받지 않아서.
여: 정말? 바쁜가 보네.
남: 음, 그 애한테 이메일도 보냈는데 아무런 답이 없었어.
여: Jennifer는 이메일을 자주 확인하지 않거든. 하지만 오늘 그 애가 메신저에 접속해 있는 걸 봤는데.
남: 정말?
여: 응. 점심시간 쯤에 접속했어. 메신저로 연락해 보는 게 어때?
남: 그래야겠어.

어휘
reply[riplái] 명 응답, 회답   log into 접속하다   messenger[mésǝndʒǝr] 명 메신저   contact[kántækt] 동 연락을 취하다   [문제] blog[blɑːg] 명 블로그

문제 해설
Q: 남자는 Jennifer에게 어떻게 연락할 것인가?
   여자가 메신저로 연락해 보라고 하자 남자가 그래야겠다고 했다.

8

W: Alex, what's the most valuable thing you own?
M: It's this.
W: Wow. It has a really nice design.
M: It does. I never get bored with it.
W: Do you talk on the phone a lot?
M: Yes. I also watch TV on the subway.
W: Can you surf the Internet with it?
M: Sure. I send emails and chat online with it.
W: Great. Does the camera work well, too?
M: Yes. I don't even need to carry a digital camera when I go out.
W: Wow. I should get one like that, too.

여: Alex, 네가 가지고 있는 가장 소중한 물건은 뭐니?
남: 이거야.
여: 우와. 디자인이 정말 예쁘다.
남: 그렇지. 이건 전혀 질리지가 않아.
여: 통화 많이 하니?
남: 응. 지하철에서 TV도 봐.
여: 그걸로 인터넷 검색도 할 수 있어?
남: 물론이지. 이메일도 보내고 온라인 채팅도 해.
여: 대단하네. 카메라도 잘 돼?
남: 응. 외출할 때 디지털 카메라를 가지고 다닐 필요가 없어.
여: 우와. 나도 그런 걸 하나 사야겠어.

어휘
valuable[vǽljuǝbl] 형 가치 있는, 소중한   own[oun] 동 소유하다   get bored with 싫증을 느끼다   digital camera 디지털 카메라

문제 해설
Q: 그들은 무엇에 대해 이야기하고 있는가?
   통화, 인터넷 검색, 이메일 보내기, 온라인 채팅, 카메라 기능이 모두 있는 최신 휴대전화에 대해 이야기하고 있다.

Listening ★ Challenge   p. 66

A 1 ①, ③   2 ③   B 1 (1) ⓑ (2) ⓓ (3) ⓐ   2 ③

A [1-2]

M: How may I help you?
W: My cellphone doesn't work well. I often can't hear the other person.
M: Anything else?

W: Yes. There's a lot of noise when I'm on the phone.

M: Have you dropped it before?

W: Yes, once.

M: That could be the reason. Can you see the letters on the screen?

W: Yes. Do you think you can fix it?

M: I think I can.

W: Great. When can I pick it up?

M: It'll take about two days. Today is Tuesday, so come back on Thursday.

W: But I really need to use my phone every day. Could you fix it by tomorrow, please?

M: Okay, I will.

남: 무엇을 도와드릴까요?

여: 제 휴대전화가 잘 작동되질 않아요. 상대방 소리가 자주 안 들려요.

남: 다른 문제도 있나요?

여: 네. 통화를 할 때 잡음이 너무 많이 나요.

남: 전에 떨어뜨린 적이 있나요?

여: 네, 한 번이요.

남: 그게 이유일 수도 있겠네요. 화면 상에 글자는 보여요?

여: 네. 고칠 수 있을 것 같나요?

남: 할 수 있을 것 같네요.

여: 다행이네요. 언제 가지러 오면 돼요?

남: 이틀 정도 걸릴 거예요. 오늘이 화요일이니까 목요일에 다시 오세요.

여: 근데 저는 휴대전화를 정말 매일 써야 하거든요. 내일까지 고쳐주실 수 없나요?

남: 알았어요. 그렇게 하죠.

어휘

work[wəːrk] 통 일하다; *작동하다 noise[nɔiz] 명 소음, 잡음 drop[drɑp] 통 떨어뜨리다 fix[fiks] 통 고치다

문제 해설

Q1: 여자의 휴대전화의 문제점을 두 개 고르시오.

① 상대방의 소리를 들을 수가 없다.

② 다른 사람이 그녀의 소리를 들을 수 없다.

③ 통화 중에 잡음이 많이 난다.

④ 화면이 깨졌다.

상대방 소리가 잘 안 들리고 통화 시 잡음이 많다고 했다.

Q2: 여자는 전화기를 언제 가지러 갈 것인가?

오늘은 화요일인데, 그 다음 날에 찾기로 했으므로 수요일에 가지러 갈 것이다.

B [1-2]

W: How much time do you spend on the Internet each day?

M: About an hour. Why?

W: According to a study, Canadians use the Internet the most per month.

M: Really? How long do they spend on it?

W: They spend around 40 hours on it.

M: Wow. How about the United States?

W: The USA was ranked fourth. Israel was second and Korea was third.

M: I didn't think that Canada would be first.

W: Me, neither. Do you know which website has the most visitors?

M: Maybe Google or Yahoo?

W: You're wrong. It was the Microsoft homepage.

M: Really? I've never visited it before, but maybe I should.

여: 넌 하루에 인터넷을 하는 데 시간을 얼마나 보내니?

남: 한 시간 정도. 왜?

여: 연구에 따르면 캐나다인들이 한 달에 인터넷을 가장 많이 사용한대.

남: 정말? 시간을 얼마나 쓰는데?

여: 40시간 정도 쓴대.

남: 우와. 미국은 어때?

여: 미국은 4위를 차지했어. 이스라엘이 2위였고, 한국은 3위였어.

남: 캐나다가 1위를 할 줄은 몰랐어.

여: 나도. 어느 웹사이트에 방문객이 가장 많은지 아니?

남: 아마 Google이나 Yahoo?

여: 틀렸어. Microsoft사의 홈페이지였어.

남: 정말? 난 거기 한 번도 방문한 적이 없는데, 방문해봐야겠네.

어휘

according to ~에 따르면 study[stʌ́di] 명 공부; *연구 Canadian[kənéidiən] 명 캐나다인 Israel[ízriəl] 명 이스라엘 website[wébsàit] 명 웹사이트 visitor[vízitər] 명 방문객

문제 해설

Q1: 각 빈칸에 알맞은 나라를 고르시오.

한 달 인터넷 사용 시간을 나타낸 표이다. 가장 인터넷 사용 시간이 많은 나라는 캐나다이고, 이스라엘이 2위,

미국이 4위라고 했다.

Q2: 사람들이 가장 많이 방문하는 웹사이트는?

　　Microsoft사의 홈페이지 방문객이 가장 많다고 했다.

Critical ★ Thinking　p. 67

1 (1) Against (2) For (3) For
2 (1) ⓒ (2) ⓑ (3) ⓓ

M1: I'm Mike. I believe that students should not carry cellphones. Do they really need to have them? I don't think so. They just exchange text messages in class. It means they can't focus on studying.

W: I'm Judy. I think cellphones are great tools for studying. Many cellphones have dictionaries and can connect to the Internet. They are useful during class and also for homework.

M2: I'm Alex. These days, students communicate with each other by exchanging text messages. They need cellphones to connect with friends.

남1: 나는 Mike야. 나는 학생들이 휴대전화를 가지고 다니지 말아야 한다고 생각해. 그들에게 그것들이 정말 필요할까? 난 그렇게 생각하지 않아. 그들은 그저 교실에서 문자 메시지를 주고받을 뿐이야. 그건 그들이 공부하는 데 집중할 수 없다는 뜻이야.

여: 난 Judy야. 내 생각에 휴대전화는 공부하는 데 훌륭한 도구인 것 같아. 많은 휴대전화에 사전이 있고 인터넷에 접속할 수도 있어. 그것들은 수업 중에, 그리고 숙제할 때도 유용해.

남2: 난 Alex야. 요즘에 학생들은 문자 메시지를 주고 받으면서 서로 연락해. 친구들과 연락하려면 휴대전화가 필요하지.

어휘
exchange[ikstʃéindʒ] ⑧ 교환하다; *주고받다　text message 문자 메시지　tool [tu:l] ⑲ 도구　dictionary[díkʃənèri] ⑲ 사전　connect[kənékt] ⑧ 접속되다; 연락하다　communicate[kəmjú:nəkèit] ⑧ 연락하다

문제 해설
Q1: 각 인물이 학생들의 휴대폰 사용에 찬성하는지 반대하는지 ✓표 하시오.

Mike는 휴대전화 사용의 좋지 않은 점에 대해, Judy와 Alex는 좋은 점에 대해 얘기했다.

Q2: 각 인물의 의견을 고르시오.

　ⓐ 휴대전화는 건강에 좋지 않다.
　ⓑ 휴대전화는 공부하는 데 유용하다.
　ⓒ 학생들은 휴대전화 때문에 공부에 집중할 수 없다.
　ⓓ 문자 메시지는 학생들이 친구들과 연락하는 방식이다.
　(1) Mike는 학생들이 교실에서 문자 메시지를 주고받느라 공부에 집중할 수 없다고 했다.
　(2) Judy는 휴대전화에 사전이 있고 인터넷에 접속할 수도 있어서 공부하는 데 유용하다고 했다.
　(3) Alex는 학생들이 친구들과 연락하는 데 휴대전화가 필요하다고 했다.

UNIT 11 Superstitions

Getting ★ Ready　p. 68

A 1 ⓑ　2 ⓓ　3 ⓒ　4 ⓐ　5 ⓔ
B 1 ⓑ　2 ⓔ　3 ⓐ

B 1 남: 난 오늘 Amy와 놀이 공원에 갈 거야.
　　여: 드디어 데이트 신청했구나? 데이트에 행운을 빌게!
　2 남: 어제 나 돼지꿈을 꿨어.
　　여: 그건 행운의 징조야.
　3 남: 너 걱정거리가 있어 보여. 무슨 일이야?
　　여: 내 올해 운세를 봤는데 안 좋았어.

Listening ★ Start　p. 69

1 ② / as a lucky color, decorate the wedding hall, wrapped in red, wear red uniforms
2 ③ / a black cat, find a penny, see a spider, an unlucky sign

1

M: In China, people think of red as a lucky color. They think that red brings money and keeps ghosts away. So, on someone's wedding day, Chinese people decorate the wedding hall in red and the bride wears a red dress. On New Year's Day,

★　★

many items in stores are wrapped in red and people celebrate with red fireworks. Also, many servers in Chinese restaurants wear red uniforms.

남: 중국 사람들은 빨강을 행운의 색이라고 생각해요. 빨간색이 돈을 벌게 해 주고 귀신을 쫓아준다고 여기죠. 그래서 결혼식 날에 중국인들은 예식장을 빨간색으로 꾸미고 신부는 빨간 드레스를 입어요. 새해 첫날에는 상점의 많은 물건들이 빨간색으로 포장되고 사람들은 빨간색 폭죽으로 축하를 하죠. 또한 중국 식당의 많은 종업원들이 빨간색 유니폼을 입어요.

어휘

lucky[lʌ́ki] 휑 행운의　ghost[goust] 명 유령, 귀신　decorate[dékərèit] 동 장식하다　bride[braid] 명 신부　New Year's Day 새해 첫날　item[áitəm] 명 상품, 품목　wrap[ræp] 동 싸다　celebrate[séləbrèit] 동 축하하다　firework[fáiərwə̀ːrk] 명 불꽃, 폭죽　server[sə́ːrvər] 명 시중드는 사람, 식당 종업원　uniform[júːnəfɔ̀ːrm] 명 유니폼

문제 해설

Q: 남자는 주로 무엇에 대해 이야기하고 있나?
　① 빨간색이 행운을 의미하는 나라들
　② 빨간색에 대한 중국인들의 사랑
　③ 전 세계에서 빨간색이 가지는 다양한 의미
　④ 새해를 축하하는 중국의 방식
중국에서 빨간색이 행운의 색으로 여겨져 곳곳에 활용되고 있음을 예를 들어 설명하고 있다.

2

W1: In the US, if a black cat walks in front of you, it's bad luck.
M: In England, if you find a penny on the ground, you'll have good luck all day.
W2: In Japan, if you see a spider in the morning, it's a sign of good luck. But if you see one in the evening, it's an unlucky sign.

여1: 미국에서는 검은 고양이가 네 앞에 지나가면 운이 나쁜 거야.
남: 영국에서는 길에서 1페니를 발견하면 하루 종일 운이 좋을 거야.
여2: 일본에서는 아침에 거미를 보면 행운의 징조야. 하지만 저녁에 보면 불행의 징조야.

어휘

luck[lʌk] 명 행운　penny[péni] 명 페니 《영국의 화폐 단위》　ground[graund] 명 땅　spider[spáidər] 명 거미　sign[sain] 명 신호; *징조　unlucky[ʌnlʌ́ki] 휑 불행의

문제 해설

Q: 운이 좋을 사람은?
　길에서 1페니를 발견하는 것은 행운을 나타낸다고 했다.

Listening ★ Practice　p. 70

1 ③　2 ①　3 ④　4 ③　5 ③　6 ②　7 ④　8 ②

1

M: Did you study a lot for the exam?
W: Not much, so I'm nervous.
M: Oh, when did you last wash your hair? It smells.
W: Four days ago.
M: Why?
W: I can't help it. If I wash my hair, I'll do badly on my exam.
M: What?
W: It's true. I washed my hair before the last exam and got a low grade.
M: I want to change my seat!
W: Come on, it's not that bad.
M: Oh, no. The teacher is coming. It's time to sit down.
W: Let's talk again after the exam.

남: 시험 공부 많이 했니?
여: 많이 못해서 떨려.
남: 아, 너 머리를 언제 마지막으로 감았어? 냄새 나.
여: 4일 전이야.
남: 왜 안 감았어?
여: 어쩔 수 없어. 머리를 감으면 시험을 망칠 거라고.
남: 뭐라고?
여: 사실이야. 지난번 시험을 치기 전에 머리를 감았는데 점수가 낮게 나왔어.
남: 나 자리 바꾸고 싶어!
여: 야, 그렇게 심하진 않아.
남: 이런. 선생님 오신다. 자리에 앉을 시간이야.
여: 시험 치고 나서 다시 얘기하자.

어휘

smell[smel] 동 고약한 냄새가 나다　I can't help it.

69

어쩔 수 없다.　badly [bǽdli] ⑨ *나쁘게; 몹시　grade [greid] ⑨ 등급; *점수　[문제] beauty shop 미용실

문제 해설

Q: 이 대화가 이루어지고 있는 곳은?

　　교실에서 시험 치기 직전의 상황이다.

2

W: Murphy's Law means that bad things keep happening. Today was my Murphy's Law day. I took a taxi because I was late for school. But the taxi driver got lost! I was so late! Then, I got a bad score on a test. Most of the questions were from the only part I didn't study. Plus, on my way home, I left my cellphone on the bus and I couldn't find it. What a terrible day!

여: 머피의 법칙은 나쁜 일들이 계속해서 일어나는 것을 의미해. 오늘은 내게 머피의 법칙이 일어난 날이었어. 나는 학교에 늦어서 택시를 탔어. 그런데 택시 기사가 길을 잃은 거야! 나는 아주 늦고 말았어! 그 다음엔 시험에서 나쁜 점수를 받았어. 대부분의 문항들이 내가 공부하지 않은 유일한 부분에서만 나왔어. 게다가 집에 오는 길에 버스에 휴대전화를 두고 내렸는데, 찾을 수가 없었어. 정말 끔찍한 날이야!

어휘

Murphy's Law 머피의 법칙　keep v-ing 계속해서 ~하다　get lost 길을 잃다　score [skɔːr] ⑨ 점수　on one's way home 집으로 가는 길에

문제 해설

Q: 소녀에게 일어나지 않은 일은?

　　소녀가 택시 기사와 싸웠다는 말은 하지 않았다.

3

W: Steven, I can't find a wedding dress I like.

M: But you're a fashion designer. Why don't you make one yourself?

W: I want to. But if the bride makes her own dress, the marriage will be unhappy.

M: Do you believe that superstition?

W: Of course.

M: Then how about asking Jane Williams to make it for you?

W: Jane Williams, our high school classmate?

M: Yes. I heard she became a famous wedding dress designer.

W: Really? I didn't know that.

M: Just tell her what kind of dress you want.

W: That's a good idea.

여: Steven, 마음에 드는 웨딩드레스를 못 찾겠어.

남: 근데 넌 패션 디자이너잖아. 네가 직접 하나 만드는 게 어때?

여: 그러고 싶어. 하지만 신부가 자신의 드레스를 만들면 결혼이 불행할 거야.

남: 그 미신을 믿어?

여: 물론이지.

남: 그럼 Jane Williams에게 널 위해 드레스를 만들어 달라고 부탁하는 게 어때?

여: 우리 고등학교 동창인 Jane Williams 말이야?

남: 응. 걔가 유명한 웨딩드레스 디자이너가 됐다고 들었거든.

여: 정말? 난 몰랐는데.

남: 그 애한테 네가 어떤 종류의 드레스를 원하는지 말해 봐.

여: 그거 좋은 생각이야.

어휘

fashion designer 패션 디자이너　marriage [mǽridʒ] ⑨ 결혼　superstition [sùːpərstíʃən] ⑨ 미신　classmate [klǽsmèit] ⑨ 학우, 동급생　[문제] borrow [bárou] ⑧ 빌리다

문제 해설

Q: 여자는 자신의 문제를 어떻게 해결할 것인가?

　　여자는 고등학교 동창에게 드레스 제작을 부탁하기로 했다.

4

W: David, look at this necklace. Isn't it pretty?

M: Wow, it is pretty. I like the red stone.

W: Yes, it's a ruby. It's my birthstone.

M: What's a birthstone?

W: Each month has a birthstone. Good things will come to you if you wear your birthstone.

M: I was born in May. Do you know the birthstone of May?

W: It's emerald.

M: You mean the green stone?

W: Yes. Why don't you wear one? You might find a girlfriend.

M: Really? I should wear one!

여: David, 이 목걸이 좀 봐. 예쁘지 않니?

남: 우와, 예쁘네. 빨간색 보석이 마음에 들어.

여: 응, 그건 루비야. 내 탄생석이지.

남: 탄생석이 뭐야?

여: 각 달에는 탄생석이 있어. 자신의 탄생석을 착용하고 다니면 좋은 일이 생길 거야.

남: 난 5월에 태어났어. 5월의 탄생석이 뭔지 아니?

여: 에메랄드야.

남: 녹색 보석 말이니?

여: 응. 하나 착용하는 게 어때? 여자 친구를 찾게 될 수도 있잖아.

남: 정말? 하나 해야겠다!

어휘

necklace[néklis] 명 목걸이　stone[stoun] 명 돌; *보석
ruby[rú:bi] 명 루비　birthstone[bə́:rθstòun] 명 탄생석
be born 태어나다　emerald[émərəld] 명 에메랄드

문제 해설

Q: 남자의 탄생석은 어느 것인가?

남자의 탄생석은 에메랄드로 녹색 보석이라고 했다.

5

W: Ted, could you pass me the salt?

M: Here. Oops! Sorry.

W: Oh, you spilled it. Spilling salt is bad luck.

M: Oh, no! I have a blind date today.

W: Don't worry. If you throw some salt over your left shoulder, you will be fine.

M: Then give me the salt again.

W: Do you want a girlfriend that badly?

M: Of course! I'm tired of going to the movies with my friends.

W: (laughs) Here's the salt. Good luck on your date!

여: Ted, 나한테 소금 좀 건네 줄래?

남: 여기. 앗! 미안.

여: 이런, 엎질렀잖아. 소금을 엎지르는 건 운이 나쁜 건데.

남: 아, 안돼! 나 오늘 소개팅이 있단 말이야.

여: 걱정 마. 왼쪽 어깨 너머로 약간의 소금을 던지면 괜찮아질 거야.

남: 그럼 소금 좀 다시 줘.

여: 그렇게 절실히 여자 친구를 갖고 싶니?

남: 당연하지! 친구들이랑 영화 보러 가는 거 지겨워.

여: [웃으며] 소금 여기 있어. 데이트에 행운을 빌게!

어휘

pass[pæs] 통 지나가다; *건네주다　salt[sɔːlt] 명 소금
spill[spil] 통 엎지르다　blind date 소개팅　throw
[θrou] 통 던지다 (throw–threw–thrown)　shoulder
[ʃóuldər] 명 어깨　be tired of 싫증나다

문제 해설

Q: 남자가 다음에 할 일은?

불운을 막기 위해 왼쪽 어깨 너머로 소금을 던질 것이다.

6

M: When some British people wake up on the first morning of the month, they say "white rabbits" three times. They believe it brings good luck for the month. They also think that putting money in the pocket of new clothes brings good luck. However, British people never open an umbrella inside the house. They think it's bad luck. And when a bird flies into a house, it's a sign that someone will die.

남: 어떤 영국 사람들은 달의 첫날 아침에 잠에서 깨면 "흰색 토끼"라고 세 번 말해. 그들은 그것이 그 달에 행운을 가져다 줄 것이라고 믿어. 그들은 또한 새 옷 주머니에 돈을 넣어 두면 행운이 올 것이라고 믿어. 그러나 영국 사람들은 집 안에서 절대로 우산을 펴지 않아. 그들은 그것이 불운을 가져온다고 생각해. 그리고 새가 집 안으로 날아들면 누군가가 죽을 징조야.

71

어휘

British[brítiʃ] 형 영국의　wake up 깨다, 일어나다
pocket[pákit] 명 주머니　however[hauévər] 부 그러나　umbrella[ʌmbrélə] 명 우산　inside[ínsàid] 전
~의 내부에　[문제] raise[reiz] 통 올리다; *기르다

문제 해설

Q: 몇몇 영국 사람들이 행운을 가져오기 위해 하는 것은?

행운을 가져오는 행동에는 달의 첫날 아침에 "흰색 토끼"를 세 번 말하기, 새 옷의 주머니에 돈 넣기가 있다고 했다.

7

W: What are you doing?

M: I'm shopping online to buy a present for my girlfriend.

W: Is it her birthday?

M: No. She's taking an important exam.

W: Why don't you get her a necklace with four-leaf clovers on it?

M: I want to give her something more special.

W: How about a ring with a message on it?

M: Well...

W: Oh, how about a keychain with a rabbit foot on it?

M: A rabbit foot?

W: In England, people believe that a rabbit foot brings good luck.

M: Interesting! I think I'll get one.

여: 뭐 하고 있어?

남: 여자 친구에게 줄 선물을 사려고 온라인으로 쇼핑을 하고 있어.

여: 그녀의 생일이니?

남: 아니. 중요한 시험을 치거든.

여: 네잎 클로버가 있는 목걸이를 주는 게 어때?

남: 난 그녀에게 더 특별한 걸 주고 싶어.

여: 메시지가 쓰여 있는 반지는 어때?

남: 글쎄…

여: 아, 토끼 발이 달린 열쇠고리는 어때?

남: 토끼 발?

여: 영국에서는 토끼 발이 행운을 가져다 준다고 믿거든.

남: 재미있네! 그걸 사야겠어.

어휘

four-leaf clover 네잎 클로버   message[mésidʒ] 명 메시지   keychain[kíːtʃèin] 명 열쇠고리

문제 해설

Q: 소년이 여자 친구에게 사 줄 것은?
   토끼 발이 달린 열쇠고리를 사주기로 했다.

8

M: I read my fortune for this year, but it was bad.

W: What did it say?

M: I'm going to get bad grades and break up with my girlfriend.

W: Why do you believe that? You will get good scores if you study hard!

M: I don't know…

W: And if you're nice to your girlfriend, you'll stay together.

M: Maybe. But I'm still worried.

W: Look, if something bad happens, it's not because of your fortune. It's because of you.

남: 나의 올해 운세를 읽었는데, 안 좋았어.

여: 뭐래?

남: 내가 성적이 나쁠 거고 여자 친구와 헤어질 거래.

여: 그걸 왜 믿니? 네가 열심히 공부하면 좋은 점수를 받을 거야!

남: 모르겠어…

여: 그리고 네가 여자 친구에게 잘해 주면 너희들은 계속 함께 할 거야.

남: 아마도 그렇겠지. 하지만 난 아직도 걱정돼.

여: 이봐, 나쁜 일이 생긴다면 그건 너의 운 때문이 아니야. 그건 너 때문인 거지.

어휘

fortune[fɔ́ːrtʃən] 명 운세, 운명; 운   break up with ~와 헤어지다   stay[stei] 통 머무르다, 그대로 있다

문제 해설

Q: 소녀의 의견을 가장 잘 묘사하는 것은?
   ① 인생의 모든 것은 운이다.
   ② 자신의 운명은 자신이 만든다.
   ③ 불행은 결코 혼자서 오지 않는다.
   ④ 불행은 종종 행운을 가져온다.
   소녀는 자신이 하기에 따라서 결과는 달라질 것이라고 얘기하고 있으므로, 자신의 운명은 자신이 만들어 가는 것이라고 생각하는 것이다.

Listening ★ Challenge   p. 72

A 1 ① 2 ②   B 1 ④ 2 (1) T (2) T (3) F

A [1-2]

M: You look worried. What's up?

W: I lost my ring. Have you seen a ring around here?

M: I saw a gold ring on the desk. Is it a heart-shaped ring?

W: No, it's just a plain silver ring.

M: I guess that one isn't yours, then.

W: Oh, no. It's very important to me. I must find it.

M: Did your boyfriend give it to you?

W: No. But I need it to win the hockey game tomorrow.

M: How can a ring help you win a hockey game?

W: You might not believe it, but each time I didn't wear it, I lost the game.

M: Well, cheer up. I'll help you find it.

남: 너 걱정이 있어 보여. 무슨 일이야?

여: 내 반지를 잃어버렸어. 이 주위에서 반지 봤니?

남: 책상에서 금반지를 봤는데. 그거 하트 모양의 반지니?

여: 아니, 아무 장식이 없는 은반지야.

남: 그럼 그건 네 것이 아닌가 보네.

여: 아, 이런. 그거 나한테 정말 중요한 건데. 꼭 찾아야 해.

남: 네 남자 친구가 너한테 준 거니?

여: 아니. 하지만 내일 하키 경기에서 이기려면 그게 필요해.

남: 반지가 하키 경기에서 이기는 것과 무슨 상관이 있니?

여: 넌 안 믿을지도 모르지만 내가 그걸 안 낄 때마다 경기를 졌거든.

남: 음. 기운 내. 내가 찾는 걸 도와 줄게.

어휘

gold[gould] 형 금으로 된, 금의　heart-shaped
[háːrtʃèipt] 형 하트 모양의　plain[plein] 형 평범한; *장
식이 없는　silver[sílvər] 형 은의, 은으로 된　hockey
[háki] 명 하키 [문제] victory[víktəri] 명 승리
prevent[privént] 통 막다

문제 해설

Q1: 여자의 반지는 어느 것인가?

　　장식이 없는 은반지라고 했다.

Q2: 그 반지가 여자에게 왜 중요한가?

　　① 그녀의 남자 친구가 그녀에게 주었다.

　　② 그녀는 그것이 승리를 가져다 준다고 생각한다.

　　③ 그녀는 그것을 사는 데 돈을 많이 지불했다.

　　④ 그녀는 그것이 그녀가 다치는 것을 막아준다고 생각
　　　한다.

　　여자는 그 반지를 껴야 하키 경기에서 이길 수 있다고 믿
　　는다.

B [1-2]

W: What do you want to know?

M: I want to know whether I'll get a job this year.

W: All right. When is your birthday?

M: It's December 15th, 1982.

W: Yes, you'll have good luck getting a job this year. You'll soon be hired by a large company.

M: Wow, that's great!

W: Yes. However, you'll have some problems with your health.

M: Oh, no! Which part of my body?

W: Your stomach. So be careful about what kind of food you eat.

M: Okay. Also, I have a girlfriend. Will I get married to her?

W: Actually, I see you breaking up with her.

M: Oh, no!

여: 뭘 알고 싶으신가요?

남: 제가 올해 직장을 구할지 알고 싶어요.

여: 알았어요. 생일이 언제죠?

남: 1982년 12월 15일이에요.

여: 네, 올해 일자리를 얻는 데에는 운이 좋을 거예요. 곧 대
　기업에 취직하겠네요.

남: 우와, 잘됐네요!

여: 네. 하지만 건강상에 좀 문제가 있을 거예요.

남: 아, 이런! 몸 어느 부위요?

여: 위요. 그러니 먹는 음식의 종류에 주의하세요.

남: 알겠어요. 그리고 저에게 여자 친구가 있는데요. 제가 그
　녀와 결혼을 하게 될까요?

여: 사실 당신은 그녀와 헤어진다고 나오네요.

남: 아, 안돼요!

어휘

hire[haiər] 통 고용하다　company[kámpəni] 명 회사
stomach[stámək] 명 위　careful[kέərfəl] 형 주의하는
get married to ~와 결혼하다　[문제] patient
[péiʃənt] 명 환자　counselor[káunsələr] 명 상담사
fortune teller 점쟁이

문제 해설

Q1: 화자 간의 관계는?

　　여자가 남자에게 올해의 운세에 대해 이야기해 주고 있
　　으므로 두 사람은 점쟁이와 손님의 관계임을 알 수 있다.

Q2: 여자의 말에 따라, 사실이면 T를, 사실이 아니면 F를 쓰
　시오.

　　(1) 남자는 올해 대기업에 취직할 것이다.

　　(2) 남자의 위에 어떤 문제가 있을 것이다.

　　(3) 남자는 자신의 여자 친구와 결혼할 것이다.

Critical ★ Thinking　p. 73

1 ④　2 ②

M: How's your practice going?

W: I'm trying my best. But I'm worried about having the sophomore jinx.

M: The sophomore jinx? What's that?

W: It's when your first effort is successful, but your second effort isn't.

M: For example?

W: When a writer publishes a first book successfully but fails with the second one, that's the sophomore jinx.

M: I see. But your new song is really good.

It'll be a big hit.

W: Do you really think so?

M: Yes, I do. Cheer up!

W: Okay. If this becomes a big hit, I'll buy you a wonderful dinner!

남: 연습은 어떻게 되어 가고 있니?

여: 최선을 다하고 있어. 하지만 2년차 징크스가 있을까 봐 걱정돼.

남: 2년차 징크스? 그게 뭔데?

여: 처음의 노력이 성공적인데 두 번째 노력이 성공적이지 않을 때를 말하는 거야.

남: 예를 들면?

여: 작가가 첫 번째 책은 성공적으로 출판했는데 두 번째 책은 실패하는 게 2년차 징크스야.

남: 그렇구나. 하지만 너의 새 노래는 정말 좋아. 크게 성공할 거야.

여: 정말 그렇게 생각해?

남: 응. 힘내!

여: 알았어. 이번에 크게 성공하면 너한테 근사한 저녁 사줄게.

어휘

try one's best 최선을 다하다 **sophomore**[sάfəmɔ̀ːr] 명 2학년생 **jinx**[dʒiŋks] 명 징크스, 불운 **effort**[éfərt] 명 노력 **successful**[səksésfəl] 형 성공적인 **writer** [ráitər] 명 작가 **publish**[pʌ́bliʃ] 동 출판하다 **hit**[hit] 명 *성공; 타격 **wonderful**[wʌ́ndərfəl] 형 훌륭한, 멋진 [문제] **author**[ɔ́ːθər] 명 저자 **actress**[ǽktris] 명 여배우

문제 해설

Q1: 여자의 직업은?

　남자가 여자의 새 노래가 좋다고 하면서 격려해주는 것으로 보아 여자의 직업은 가수임을 짐작할 수 있다.

Q2: 2년차 징크스를 겪은 사람은?

　① Eva: 난 학교에서 1학년 때보다 2학년 때 더 높은 성적을 받았어.

　② Dan: 나의 첫 번째 영화는 크게 성공했는데 두 번째 영화는 실패했어.

　③ Emma: 나의 첫 번째 책이랑 두 번째 책 모두 실패했어.

　첫 번째에는 성공하고 두 번째에 실패하는 경우가 2년차 징크스이다.

UNIT 12 Lifestyle

Getting ★ Ready p. 74

A 1 ⓓ 2 ⓒ 3 ⓑ 4 ⓔ 5 ⓐ

B 1 ⓐ 2 ⓑ 3 ⓕ

B 1 여: 넌 결혼하고 싶니?

　　남: 아니, 난 혼자 살고 싶어.

　2 여: 너 왜 고기를 먹지 않게 됐어?

　　남: 난 동물을 사랑해서 채식주의자가 됐어.

　3 여: 넌 왜 도시에 살고 싶어 하니?

　　남: 언제든지 갈 수 있는 쇼핑몰이 많으니까.

Listening ★ Start p. 75

1 ①, ④ / with two jobs, Her main job, a lot of money, saving enough money

2 ④ / work part-time, rather than, Why not, work hard, care about

1

M: I heard there are many people with two jobs these days.

W: My sister is one of them.

M: Really? What does she do?

W: Her main job is as a nurse. But she's working as a waitress on weekends.

M: Wow, then she must earn a lot of money.

W: I think so. She wants to open a bakery after saving enough money.

M: That's nice.

남: 요즘엔 직업이 두 개인 사람들이 많대.

여: 우리 언니도 그런 사람들 중의 하나야.

남: 정말? 직업이 뭔데?

여: 원래 직업은 간호사야. 하지만 주말엔 식당 종업원으로 일하지.

남: 우와, 그럼 분명 돈을 많이 벌겠구나.

여: 그런 것 같아. 언니는 돈을 충분히 모은 후에 빵집을 열고 싶어 해.

남: 좋지.

어휘

main[mein] 형 주된, 주요한　nurse[nə:rs] 명 간호사
waitress[wéitris] 명 (호텔·음식점의) 여자 종업원
earn[ə:rn] 동 벌다　bakery[béikəri] 명 빵집　save
[seiv] 동 저축하다

문제 해설

Q: 여자의 언니가 현재 가지고 있는 직업을 두 개 고르시오.
　주된 직업은 간호사이지만, 주말에는 식당 종업원으로 일
　한다고 했다.

2

M: What do you do these days?
W: I work part-time for a game company. I'm
　a web designer.
M: Oh, so you work part-time rather than
　full-time?
W: Yes. I don't want to work full-time.
M: Why not?
W: I want to work only when I want to. I
　don't want to work hard every day.
M: I see. But you can't earn much money.
W: I don't care about money.

남: 너 요즘에 무슨 일 하니?
여: 게임 회사에서 시간제로 일하고 있어. 난 웹 디자이너야.
남: 아, 그러니까 전일제가 아니라 시간제로 일한다고?
여: 응. 전일제로 일하고 싶진 않아.
남: 왜?
여: 난 내가 일하고 싶을 때만 일하고 싶어. 매일 열심히 일
　하고 싶진 않아.
남: 그렇구나. 하지만 돈을 많이 못 벌잖아.
여: 난 돈은 신경 안 써.

어휘

part-time[pá:rtàim] *부 시간제 근무로; 형 시간제 근무의
web designer 웹 디자이너　rather than ～보다는
오히려　full-time[fúltàim] 부 전일제 근무로; 형 전일제
근무의　care about ～에 대해서 신경 쓰다

문제 해설

Q: 여자가 시간제로 일하는 이유는?
　① 전일제 직장을 못 구해서
　② 너무 피곤해서 전일제로 일할 수 없어서
　③ 오후에 공부를 해야 해서
　④ 일하고 싶을 때만 일할 수 있어서
　여자는 일하고 싶을 때만 일하기를 원해서 시간제로 일
　한다고 했다.

1 ①　2 ②　3 ③　4 ②　5 ③　6 ④　7 ②　8 ③

1

W: What are you doing this weekend?
M: I'm going to Japan.
W: Really? Are you going sightseeing?
M: No. I'm going to buy a new video game.
　It's only sold in Japan.
W: Only for that? But airplane tickets are
　expensive. Also, you need to find a place
　to stay.
M: I'll stay at my friend's house. And many
　people visit other countries to shop
　these days.
W: Really?
M: My friend goes to Hong Kong to buy
　clothes every year.
W: Oh, that's surprising.

여: 너 이번 주말에 뭐해?
남: 일본에 갈 거야.
여: 정말? 관광하러 가는 거니?
남: 아니. 새로 나온 비디오 게임을 사려고. 그건 일본에서만
　팔거든.
여: 단지 그것 때문에? 하지만 비행기표가 비싸잖아. 게다가
　머물 곳도 찾아야 하고.
남: 난 내 친구 집에 머물 거야. 그리고 요즘엔 다른 나라에
　쇼핑하러 가는 사람들이 많아.
여: 정말?
남: 내 친구는 매년 옷을 사러 홍콩에 가.
여: 아, 놀라운 걸.

어휘

go sightseeing 관광하러 가다　surprising
[sərpráiziŋ] 형 놀라운　[문제] trend[trend] 명 유행

문제 해설

Q: 남자가 일본에 가는 이유는?
　남자는 일본에 새 비디오 게임을 사러 간다고 했다.

2

W: A new cosmetic brand called "Skin
　Doctor" has just come into stores. Skin
　Doctor products are made from natural
　materials, so they're good for people with

sensitive skin. When you visit our stores, you can choose the color and fragrance of your cosmetics. And Skin Doctor cares about our environment. If you bring back your empty cosmetic bottles, we'll give you free samples. It's also possible to order products online.

여: 'Skin Doctor'라는 새로운 화장품 브랜드가 막 입점했습니다. Skin Doctor의 상품은 천연 재료로 만들어져서 민감성 피부를 가진 분들에게 좋습니다. 저희 매장을 방문하시면 화장품 색상과 향을 선택할 수 있습니다. 그리고 Skin Doctor는 환경을 염려합니다. 빈 화장품 용기를 가져오시면 무료 샘플을 드립니다. 온라인으로 상품을 주문하실 수도 있습니다.

어휘

cosmetic[kɑzmétik] 명 화장품; 형 화장의 brand [brænd] 명 상표, 브랜드 product[prɑ́dəkt] 명 상품 natural[nǽtʃərəl] 형 자연의, 천연의 material [mətí(:)əriəl] 명 재료, 원료 sensitive[sénsətiv] 형 민감한 fragrance[fréigrəns] 명 향 environment [inváiərənmənt] 명 환경 empty[émpti] 형 빈 bottle [bátl] 명 병 sample[sǽmpl] 명 견본 [문제] exchange[ikstʃéindʒ] 동 교환하다

문제 해설

Q: 잘못된 정보를 고르시오.

> **당신의 피부를 위해 Skin Doctor를 쓰세요.**
> ① Skin Doctor 제품은 천연 재료로 만들어졌습니다.
> ② 화장품 용기 색상을 고를 수 있습니다.
> ③ 빈 용기를 샘플과 교환할 수 있습니다.
> ④ 상품을 오프라인과 온라인으로 구매할 수 있습니다.

3

W: What are you doing?
M: I'm writing a product review about my new camera.
W: Do you often write product reviews?
M: I always write them after buying a product.
W: So do I. I like to share information about products with other people.
M: That's right. That helps people buy good products.
W: Do you write reviews for that reason?
M: Yes. But I also believe that product

reviews help companies make better products.
W: I agree. They won't want any bad reviews, so they'll try to make good products.

여: 뭐 하고 있니?
남: 새로 산 카메라에 대한 상품평을 쓰고 있어.
여: 넌 상품평을 자주 쓰니?
남: 상품을 구매하고 나서 항상 써.
여: 나도 그래. 다른 사람들이랑 상품에 대한 정보를 공유하는 게 좋아.
남: 맞아. 그러면 사람들이 좋은 상품을 사는 데 도움이 돼.
여: 넌 그 이유 때문에 상품평을 쓰는 거니?
남: 응. 하지만 상품평은 기업이 더 좋은 상품을 만드는 데에도 도움이 될 거라고 생각해.
여: 맞아. 그들은 나쁜 상품평은 원하지 않으니까 좋은 상품을 만들려고 노력할 거야.

어휘

review[rivjúː] 명 복습; *논평, 비평 share[ʃɛər] 동 공유하다 reason[ríːzən] 명 이유

문제 해설

Q: 그들은 주로 무엇에 대해 이야기하고 있는가?
① 그들이 온라인으로 쇼핑을 하는 이유
② 좋은 카메라를 사는 방법
③ 그들이 상품평을 쓰는 이유
④ 상품에 대한 정보를 얻는 방법

4

W: Jerry, I heard you saved a lot of money. You must be well paid.
M: Not really. You probably earn more than me. But I just try not to spend money.
W: How?
M: Well, I carry a lunch box instead of eating at restaurants.
W: Oh, really?
M: And I don't drink expensive coffee. I usually drink instant coffee.
W: But you sometimes go to expensive restaurants.
M: That's only when I have discount coupons. Then I can enjoy good food for less money.

여: Jerry, 너 돈 많이 모았다며. 너 벌이가 좋은가 보구나.

남: 꼭 그렇진 않아. 네가 나보다 더 많이 벌 거야. 하지만 난 그저 돈을 안 쓰려고 노력할 뿐이야.

여: 어떻게?

남: 음, 식당에서 먹는 대신 도시락을 가지고 다녀.

여: 아, 정말?

남: 그리고 비싼 커피는 안 마셔. 주로 인스턴트 커피를 마셔.

여: 하지만 넌 때때로 비싼 음식점에 가잖아.

남: 그건 내가 할인 쿠폰을 가지고 있을 때뿐이야. 그러면 적은 돈으로 좋은 음식을 즐길 수 있거든.

어휘

probably[prάbəbli] ⑨ 아마   instant coffee 인스턴트 커피   discount coupon 할인 쿠폰

문제 해설

Q: 남자가 돈을 절약하는 방법이 <u>아닌</u> 것은?

남자는 도시락을 싸서 다니고 비싼 커피 대신 인스턴트 커피를 마신다고 했다. 또한, 할인 쿠폰이 있을 때에만 비싼 음식점에 간다고 했다.

5

M: What kind of man do you want to marry?

W: Well, I haven't thought about it. I don't want to get married.

M: Really? Why not?

W: If I get married, I won't be able to live freely because of my new family.

M: But don't you think you'll be lonely?

W: No. I can enjoy various hobbies with many friends.

M: What about kids? Don't you want any?

W: Yes, I do. But my freedom is more important than having children.

M: That's interesting. But I still want to get married someday.

남: 넌 어떤 남자랑 결혼하고 싶어?

여: 음, 그것에 대해선 생각을 안 해 봤어. 난 결혼을 하고 싶지 않아.

남: 정말? 왜?

여: 결혼을 하면 새로운 가족 때문에 자유롭게 살 수 없게 되니까.

남: 하지만 네가 외로울 거라고는 생각하지 않니?

여: 아니. 많은 친구들이랑 다양한 취미를 즐길 수 있잖아.

남: 아이는? 전혀 원하지 않는 거야?

여: 원해. 하지만 아이를 갖는 것보다 자유가 더 중요해.

남: 재밌네. 하지만 난 여전히 언젠가 결혼하고 싶어.

어휘

marry[mǽri] ⑧ 결혼하다   be able to-v ~할 수 있다
freely[frí:li] ⑨ 자유롭게   lonely[lóunli] ⑩ 외로운
various[vέ(:)əriəs] ⑩ 다양한   freedom[frí:dəm] ⑨
자유   someday[sʌ́mdèi] ⑨ 언젠가

문제 해설

Q: 여자와 같은 의견을 가지고 있는 사람은?

① Neville: 난 외롭지 않도록 결혼을 하고 싶어.

② Sandra: 아이를 갖는 게 인생에서 가장 중요한 일이야.

③ Mark: 난 결혼하지 않고 내 삶을 즐기고 싶어.

여자는 아이보다는 자유가 더 중요하기 때문에 결혼을 하고 싶어하지 않는다.

6

W: These days, some people spend most of their free time at home. They don't feel any need to go out because they can enjoy various kinds of entertainment at home. Digital devices like computers and DVD players allow this. These people play games, listen to music, chat and shop online using their computers. They may also watch various movies on home theater systems. This kind of lifestyle is called "digital cocooning."

여: 요즘에 어떤 사람들은 여가 시간의 대부분을 집에서 보냅니다. 그들은 집에서 다양한 종류의 오락을 즐길 수 있기 때문에 밖으로 나갈 필요를 못 느낍니다. 컴퓨터나 DVD 플레이어와 같은 디지털 기기가 이걸 가능하게 하죠. 이러한 사람들은 컴퓨터를 이용해서 온라인으로 게임을 하고 음악을 듣고 채팅과 쇼핑을 합니다. 또한 홈 씨어터로 다양한 영화를 볼 것입니다. 이러한 생활 방식은 '디지털 코쿠닝'이라고 불립니다.

어휘

need[ni:d] ⑨ 필요   entertainment[èntərtéinmənt]
⑨ 오락, 여흥   digital[dídʒitəl] ⑩ 디지털의   device
[diváis] ⑨ 기기   allow[əláu] ⑧ 허락하다   chat[tʃæt]
⑧ 잡담하다; *채팅하다   cocooning[kəkú:niŋ] ⑨ 집에
틀어박힌 생활

문제 해설

Q: '디지털 코쿠닝'의 한 예는?

디지털 코쿠닝은 집에서 디지털 기기를 이용해 온갖 오락 활동을 즐기는 사람을 일컫는 말이다.

7

M: The YBC Channel is introducing a new program for men called *Your Style*. It shows the newest styles of men's clothing and accessories. Also, you can get information about wonderful restaurants for romantic dates. It'll even give you tips for choosing cosmetics according to your skin type. If you want to become a cool, fashionable guy, don't miss *Your Style*. This program is on Friday nights at 10 p.m.

남: YBC 채널에서 남성을 위한 새 프로그램인 'Your Style'을 시작합니다. 그것은 최신 스타일의 남성 의류와 장신구를 보여줍니다. 그리고 낭만적인 데이트를 위한 근사한 음식점에 대한 정보도 얻을 수 있습니다. 당신의 피부 타입에 따라 화장품을 선택하는 방법도 알려줄 것입니다. 멋지고 패셔너블한 남성이 되고 싶으시다면 'Your Style'을 놓치지 마세요. 이 프로그램은 금요일 밤 10시에 방영됩니다.

어휘
channel[tʃǽnəl] 몡 채널 introduce[ìntrədjúːs] 통 소개하다; *시작하다, (신제품을) 발표하다 romantic [roumǽntik] 혱 낭만적인 according to ~에 따라 fashionable[fǽʃənəbl] 혱 최신 유행의 miss[mis] 통 *놓치다; 그리워하다 [문제] best-selling[béstséliŋ] 혱 베스트셀러의

문제 해설
Q: 'Your Style'에서 얻을 수 있는 정보가 <u>아닌</u> 것은?
의류, 장신구, 데이트 장소, 화장품을 선택하는 방법에 관한 정보를 알려준다고 했다.

8

M: Mom, I have a big problem.
W: What is it?
M: Yesterday, I didn't take my cellphone to school, and I couldn't focus on anything.
W: Do you feel nervous when you don't have your cellphone?
M: Yes. I can't do anything without it.
W: How often do you use it during a day?
M: I think I use my cellphone all day long, listening to music, sending text messages, and talking.
W: I didn't know your problem was so serious.

남: 엄마, 저한테 큰 문제가 있어요.
여: 그게 뭔데?
남: 어제 학교에 휴대전화를 가져가질 않았는데 아무것에도 집중할 수가 없었어요.
여: 휴대전화를 가지고 있지 않으면 초조하니?
남: 네. 그게 없으면 아무것도 못하겠어요.
여: 하루에 얼마나 자주 사용하니?
남: 제 생각에 음악을 듣고 문자 메시지를 보내고 통화하느라 휴대전화를 하루 종일 쓰는 것 같아요.
여: 난 네 문제가 그렇게 심각한 줄 몰랐어.

어휘
nervous[nə́ːrvəs] 혱 초조한, 불안한 serious[sí(:)əriəs] 혱 심각한 [문제] treat[triːt] 통 다루다 limit[límit] 몡 제한, 한도 be sure to-v 반드시 ~하다

문제 해설
Q: 여자가 소년에게 해 줄 조언은?
① 중고 휴대전화를 사라.
② 휴대전화를 조심해서 다루어라.
③ 휴대전화를 사용하는 데 시간 제한을 두어라.
④ 나갈 때에 휴대전화를 꼭 들고 가라.
소년은 휴대전화를 지나치게 사용하는 것이 문제이므로 휴대전화를 사용하는 시간을 제한하는 것이 적절하다.

Listening ★ Challenge p. 78

A 1 ⓐ, ⓑ, ⓓ, ⓔ 2 ② B 1 ④ 2 ③

A [1-2]

W: Jason, are you eating seafood now?
M: Yes. What's the matter?
W: You're a vegetarian. Don't vegetarians only eat vegetables?
M: Well, actually, there are a few types of vegetarians.
W: Really? My sister is a vegetarian, and she only eats vegetables.
M: I'm a different kind of vegetarian. I don't eat meat, but I eat seafood.
W: What about eggs or milk?
M: I eat eggs and drink milk.
W: I see. By the way, why did you stop eating meat?
M: I became a vegetarian for my health.
W: Did you? My sister became a vegetarian because she loves animals so much.

여: Jason, 너 지금 해산물 먹고 있니?

남: 응. 무슨 문제 있어?

여: 넌 채식주의자잖아. 채식주의자들은 야채만 먹지 않니?

남: 음, 사실 채식주의에는 몇 가지 종류가 있어.

여: 정말? 내 여동생은 채식주의자인데 야채만 먹어.

남: 난 다른 종류의 채식주의자야. 난 고기는 안 먹지만 해산물은 먹어.

여: 달걀이나 우유는?

남: 난 달걀도 먹고 우유도 마셔.

여: 그렇구나. 그런데 고기는 왜 먹지 않게 되었어?

남: 난 건강을 위해서 채식주의자가 됐어.

여: 그랬니? 내 여동생은 동물을 너무 사랑해서 채식주의자가 됐어.

어휘

seafood[síːfùːd] 명 해산물   vegetarian
[vèdʒətɛ́(ː)əriən] 명 채식주의자   vegetable[védʒətəbl]
명 채소   actually[ǽktʃuəli] 부 사실

문제 해설

Q1: 남자가 먹는 음식을 모두 고르시오.
   남자는 해산물, 야채, 달걀, 우유를 먹는다고 했다.

Q2: 남자가 채식주의자가 된 이유는?
   남자는 건강을 위해서 채식주의자가 됐다고 했다.

B [1-2]

W: Do you want to try some of my "fair trade" chocolate?

M: What's that?

W: Well, do you know chocolate is made from cacao?

M: Yes, I do.

W: Many farmers work hard to produce cacao. But they receive a very small amount of money.

M: That's not fair.

W: But this chocolate is made after paying enough money to the farmers.

M: I see. How did you know that?

W: I read a book about chocolate for homework.

M: Please lend me the book later. I want to read it.

W: Okay.

M: And where did you buy this chocolate? I want to buy some too.

W: The shop is near here. Let's go together.

여: 너 '공정무역' 초콜릿 좀 먹어 볼래?

남: 그게 뭔데?

여: 음, 초콜릿이 카카오로 만들어진다는 거 아니?

남: 응, 알아.

여: 많은 농부들이 카카오를 생산하기 위해서 힘들게 일하는데 돈은 아주 적게 받거든.

남: 불공평하네.

여: 하지만 이 초콜릿은 그 농부들에게 돈을 충분히 지불하고서 만들어진 거야.

남: 그렇구나. 넌 그걸 어떻게 알았니?

여: 난 숙제로 초콜릿에 대한 책을 읽었어.

남: 나중에 그 책 좀 빌려줘. 나도 읽고 싶어.

여: 알았어.

남: 그리고 이 초콜릿을 어디서 샀어? 나도 좀 사고 싶은데.

여: 가게가 여기서 가까워. 같이 가자.

어휘

fair[fɛər] 형 공정한   trade[treid] 명 무역, 통상   cacao
[kəkáːou] 명 카카오 열매   farmer[fáːrmər] 명 농부
produce[prədjúːs] 동 생산하다   receive[risíːv] 동 받다   amount[əmáunt] 명 양   lend[lend] 동 빌려주다
(lend-lent-lent)   [문제] consider[kənsídər] 동 고려하다

문제 해설

Q1: 여자가 초콜릿을 살 때 고려한 것은?
   여자가 구매한 공정무역 초콜릿은 농부들에게 돈을 충분히 지불하고 만든 초콜릿이다.

Q2: 그들이 다음에 할 일은?
   남자가 공정무역 초콜릿을 사고 싶어하자 여자가 초콜릿 가게에 함께 가자고 했다.

Critical ★ Thinking   p. 79

1 (1) City (2) City (3) Countryside
2 (1) ⓑ (2) ⓐ (3) ⓒ

M1: I'm Ricky. The countryside doesn't have much public transportation, so it's hard to get around without a car. But in the city, I can go everywhere easily. It's better to live in the city than in the countryside.

W: I'm Mary. In the city, there are many shopping malls and theaters to visit any time. But these aren't available in the countryside, so life there would be really boring.

M2: I'm Jim. I really love country life because

79

> I can live in a clean environment. I was often sick in the city. But since I moved to the country, I feel much healthier.

남1: 난 Ricky야. 시골에는 대중 교통이 많지 않아서 차가 없으면 돌아다니기 힘들어. 하지만 도시에서는 어디든 쉽게 갈 수 있어. 시골보다는 도시에 사는 게 더 나아.

여: 난 Mary야. 도시에는 언제든 갈 수 있는 쇼핑몰과 극장이 많아. 하지만 이런 것들을 시골에서는 이용할 수 없어서 거기에서의 생활은 정말 지루할 거야.

남2: 난 Jim이야. 난 깨끗한 환경 속에서 살 수 있어서 시골 생활이 정말 좋아. 난 도시에서 자주 아팠어. 하지만 시골로 이사 온 이후로는 훨씬 건강해진 기분이야.

어휘

countryside[kʌ́ntrisàid] 몡 시골 public transportation 대중 교통 get around 돌아다니다 everywhere[évrihwὲər] 튄 어디에나 available [əvéiləbl] 혱 이용할 수 있는 boring[bɔ́ːriŋ] 혱 지루한 country[kʌ́ntri] 몡 시골; 혱 시골의, 전원 생활의 [문제] system[sístəm] 몡 체계, 시스템

문제 해설

Q1: 각 인물이 도시에서 살기를 선호하는지 시골에서 살기를 선호하는지 ✓표 하시오.

Ricky와 Mary는 도시에 살기를 선호하는 반면, Jim은 시골에 사는 것을 선호한다.

Q2: 각 인물과 그들의 의견을 연결하시오.

ⓐ 도시에는 흥미로운 장소가 많아.

ⓑ 도시에는 좋은 대중 교통 시스템이 있어.

ⓒ 난 깨끗한 환경 때문에 시골에 사는 게 즐거워.

(1) Ricky는 도시에는 대중 교통이 시골보다 더 잘 발달해 있어 어디든 쉽게 갈 수 있다고 했다.

(2) Mary는 도시에는 언제든 갈 수 있는 쇼핑몰과 극장이 많다고 했다.

(3) Jim은 깨끗한 환경 속에서 살 수 있어서 시골 생활이 좋다고 했다.

JUNIOR
LISTENING EXPERT

Level 2